ENDORSEMENTS

"For 10 years Wales Arts Review has challenged, provoked, encouraged enraged and inspired the arts in Wales. Perhaps most importantly it has helped us see where we are as a culture and the possibilities of what lies ahead."
–Michael Sheen

"Ten years is a short time in an ancient country like Wales, but Wales Arts Review has achieved a huge amount in its decade of existence. It has kept the arts in conversation not just with their audiences but with each other. Wales Arts Review was, from the start, tired of the old straw targets and the false oppositions. Curious and open-minded, alert to the present, it never suffered from fashionable amnesia or curated our nostalgias. Its ethos is to celebrate, but also to scrutinise, and this anthology is a fitting marker of its ambition, its range and its dynamism."
–Patrick McGuinness

"Wales Arts Review is a vital feature of our country's cultural life, and I can't imagine a Wales without it."
–Lleucu Siencyn, Chief Executive Literature Wales

"For a decade, Wales Arts Review has fulfilled the utterly vital task suggested by its name; that is, it has reviewed (with wit, insight, skill and sensitivity) the arts (the exploration of the human soul at one particular moment in history through all and myriad forms of creative endeavour) in Wales (a wet and wild little country on the western edge of the European continent which has produced, continues to produce, and will produce endlessly fascinating and variant modes of artistic expression). In short: what WAR does is essential to the life of an emergent nation. Long may it thrive."
–Niall Griffiths

Production Board

Craig Austin
Cerith Mathias
Dana Morris

With Special thanks to

Amgueddfa Cymru – National Museum Wales
Eleri Lloyd-Cresci,
Cyngor Llyfrau – Cymru, Books Council of Wales
Richard Davies, Parthian Books
Michael Freeman
Neil Holland of the Aberystwyth School of Art
Virginia Jones
Kids in Birmingham 1963
Dai Smith
Dale Stinchcomb, Houghton Library, Harvard University
Adrian Woodhouse

HOME TO YOU

10 YEARS OF
WALES ARTS review

EDITED BY
P.J. MORRIS

WITH A FOREWORD BY
GARY RAYMOND

All enquiries regarding contributors, as well as any requests for permission to make copies of any part of the work, should be sent to the publisher:

Wales Arts Review
4a, Brecon Court
William Brown Close
Cwmbran
NP44 3AB
United Kingdom
www.walesartsreview.org

British Library Cataloguing in Publication Data.
A catalogue record for this book is available from the British Library.

ISBN 978-1-7398517-0-5

10 9 8 7 6 5 4 3 2 1

Text design by Elaine Sharples
Text set in Crimson and Helvetica

Printed and bound in Great Britain by 4 Edge Limited

First edition

Dedicated to the memory of our friend, P. J. Morris,
for whom the publication of this anthology meant so much.

And to his son Orson, his greatest joy.

"Wales is a singular noun
but a plural experience"
Dai Smith

CONTENTS

SOME DARK PHILOSOPHERS:
Ten Years as Editor of Wales Arts Review

Gary Raymond

What does it mean to be editor of something like Wales Arts Review for ten years? For its first ten years? You may as well ask what is it like to live a life, with all its ups and downs, its stresses and joys, the minutiae that conglomerates to create some grand meaning? How do you reflect on a publication that has put out five thousand pieces – articles, reviews, interviews, features, news etc., etc., etc.? How can you look back across all that and be of one view on what Wales Arts Review has achieved? It's not even all that easy to say what it is we have become? We began as an online magazine, a journal, but those labels seem less and less relevant as the years have passed. "Media hub" sounds too Nathan Barley. "Platform" has always sat uneasily with me. It suggests a level of editorial distance I don't recognise. How have I come to think of it? Wales Arts Review is a living, breathing document of the art and culture of a country.

But we certainly began as a magazine, at least in the minds of us who founded it. And we began delivering our content in a weekly, and then fortnightly, newsletter (the newsletter that still exists today, back as a weekly), as if (I used to be fond of saying) it was being pushed through your letterbox every Saturday morning. And our inspirations were magazines and journals. A bit of *the Guardian*'s G2 here, a sprinkle of *the Paris*

Review there. We had no hesitation in talking and writing about our lofty ambitions. Pretensions. We didn't know any better. If we did, we might not have tried any of it. I'm proud of the ideological origins of *Wales Arts Review*, the shameless embracing of the highbrow, the revelling in the lowbrow. *Wales Arts Review* has been a journal of many brows.

I'm sure we put some noses out of joint in the early days. I know we did. I'm sure we still do. Back then we must have looked like upstarts. There was much good will for us out there, but also plenty looking forward to the day we fell flat on our faces. Exactly where a thing like *Wales Arts Review* should be, in that fault line, feeding off the tensions, looked at with a mixture of affection, admiration, suspicion, scorn, and plenty of other feelings along the spectrum. We ruffled feathers and we championed some of the unheard. As Michael Sheen has said of our first decade, "*Wales Arts Review* has challenged, provoked, encouraged, enraged and inspired the arts in Wales." Enraged, no doubt. Sorry about all that. But I believe unequivocally that we have never published a word that was not honest, even when we've been wrong. Just as it should be. We've been true to ourselves, and true to our roots, and true to the ideas of what a review should do when they first emerged in the eighteenth century.

We started as outsiders, rabble rousers from the town the rest of Wales, nevermind the keyholders of the middle classes who dominate(d) the creative industries in Wales, would have preferred to see slip off into the Severn Estuary and out to sea. But Newport breeds sterner folk. For the last seven of our ten years, *Wales Arts Review* has existed on the sustenance supplied by the Books Council of Wales' revenue funding, and regular injections of project funding by the Arts Council as and when we've made a convincing case that we needed it. The monies we have drawn down from those purses over the years I believe is testament to the essential value of what we have produced, because we certainly haven't been going around making friends or giving out massages or bags of sweets. We have worked hard for the funding that has meant we have been able to do our work. But the dominating narrative for *Wales Arts Review*, even when given the oxygen of funding, has been that the work has demanded we go way beyond what the money available would have otherwise produced. Writers have rarely been remunerated to the tune of their true value, and editors have regularly given at least double the volume of blood, sweat, and tears than they are contractually obliged to do. I'm not complaining. This is by way of highlighting what an extraordinary achievement *Wales Arts Review* is. The enthusiasm for it, the collaborations and contributions, over the years, tell a double-edged story; one of a nation desperate for thoughtful and thorough coverage and discussion around its art and culture, and simultaneously of a country uninterested in funding it properly.

What most people probably don't understand, or remember, is that *Wales Arts Review* was and is a working-class venture. Perhaps the intellectual ambitions of the *Review* have clouded that in the minds of people who think publishing the things we have written about cannot be a working-class preoccupation. Art, literature, music, theatre, film, opera, sculpture, dance. One thing we have never given a shit about is who this stuff is *supposed* to be for. We have written about it all, and I hope for the most part, we have done so with wit and compassion, and with an understanding that our readers could and should include the people we were as kids – curious passionate working-class oiks with dreams of being writers. "Libraries Give Us Power" was an early part of our mission statement, a mantra almost, and it's why we have always been free of a paywall, partially publicly subsidised, available to anyone with access to the internet. We should not forget that Wales has a powerful story when it comes to working class intellectualism. To doubt that claim of *Wales Arts Review*'s character is to misunderstand just *how* Welsh the *Review* is. I have frequently questioned whether we could have done this anywhere else, in any other country. I doubt it.

And it's easy to forget what a success *Wales Arts Review* is. The very fact it is easy to forget is testament in itself. We are part of the furniture nowadays. But let's just quantify it. In our ninth year, we were read in two hundred countries around the world. Two hundred countries engaging on some level or other with the art and culture of Wales. The theatre, the literature, the cinema, the television, the politics, the music, the sculpture, the painting, the thoughts and ideas of our little country, a place constantly vying for some shards of the international spotlight that being part of the UK should, but doesn't, promise. I regard that as a success. I'm not sure how to measure anything else. But I know good writing when I see it, and *Wales Arts Review* is packed with good writing. I regard that as a success. I feel *Wales Arts Review* is a force for good, that we have high standards, and those standards mean that the ideas expressed within our pages boast a country of mature, intelligent, and entertaining thinkers. The *Review*'s foundation is the idea that critical writing is an artform, and that it's worth reading for its own sake, regardless of what the subject matter is. A quarter of a million readers seem to agree. I regard that as a success.

But still, it's difficult to really be sure, as editor, that I've been right more times than I've been wrong, but we've published a lot of stuff over the last decade and I've always thought my primary skill has been packing the *Review* with people much more talented than I am. The truth is, it hasn't been my job to enjoy the successes of *Wales Arts Review*. My job has been to make sure it doesn't fail. And it hasn't failed.

Every venture needs a core ambition. What was ours and has it changed? I have to admit that the core ambitions of *Wales Arts Review*, from the moment it was conceived, were not the same ones we still talk about in-house. *Wales Arts Review* exists to give excellent writers the opportunity to cast a spotlight on the creative cultures of Wales, and that spotlight is available to the world for free. But that tenet came perhaps hours after the original idea for the *Review* was conceived. I remember the moment well. The entire concept decided on at half time during a Liverpool-Chelsea League Cup game watched at the Halfway pub on Cathedral Road in Cardiff. We wanted to create a publication that bypassed the prohibitive costs of running a print magazine (Dylan Moore and I had edited and published *The Raconteur* for a few years before this), and cast out the spectre of our experiences of Wales' dire magazine distribution mechanisms of the time. Amazing to think Welsh cultural life had next to no presence on the internet in 2012, but when we identified this as a niche in the market... well, I don't want to use the word radical, but...

The reason we wanted to be in publishing in the first place? We wanted a place to write. *Wales Arts Review* was about bringing the conversations of the pub, conversations about art and books and music and movies, to a place where anybody could pop their heads in. We felt very keenly that the world of periodicals in Wales was a closed shop to us. Perhaps it was because we weren't in the right clique, perhaps it was because we were from Newport, perhaps it was because we were crap. All of these were very possible and articulated to us by a variety of people at various points. So, we decided the only way to do what it was we wanted to do was to do it ourselves. And if we were crap, the best way to improve was to give ourselves the space in which to grow as writers, and to do so out there in the public eye where we could fall and rise in real time. Nobody else was going to do this for us. What underpinned the impetus of *Wales Arts Review* was the idea that in Wales, if you want to see anything done, you need to do it yourself. (I don't think much has changed).

In 2014, *Wales Arts Review* held a live event at the Riverfront in Newport to celebrate what we were and where we wanted to go. I gave a short speech, a bit of agitprop theatre, in which I said just this. (Not sure who I thought I was trying to be, but there was a lot of piss 'n' vinegar in it). If you want to get anything done in Wales, you'll have to do it yourself, and do it *in spite* of the moneymen and the politicians. There were a few of the literary old guard there that evening, and I think they appreciated the echoing of their own youthful calls to arms of a different era. Afterwards, at the bar, a Tory councillor came up and had a go at me, frothing at the mouth, indignant at my lack of respect as she listed off all the impressive things she'd done for her wealthy Caerleon constituents. She didn't offer us any money though.

Within a fortnight of that Liverpool-Chelsea game, the conversation had broadened, and two became six, the six holding note pads and vague ideas of what our roles would be in a new magazine. We gathered at Dylan Moore's flat (again in Cardiff). The night the thing was really born. But apart from those two foundational happenings, *Wales Arts Review* was for years a Newport endeavour; more accurately, we convened in the Murenger House, often at the top end of the bar on a Friday teatime where the editorial team would drink beer and hatch plans and allow the organic stuff to happen, the stuff that might be called *strategy* in another setting. Observers began to call the Murenger our office. If you had an idea, or a pitch, or a complaint, you could bring it to the bar. If you know the pub, you'll know the vibe, the ethos, you'll know of it as a watering hole, you'll know of its Dark Philosophers. It wasn't anything so staid and formal as an office. It was our forum.

For the first few years, *Wales Arts Review* operated with a budget of zero pounds and zero pence. We had a choice to either exist in the world as it was or not exist at all, lamenting the world for not being as we would have liked. It couldn't have prospered and made its mark without the borderline obsessive focus of the people who wrote and edited for the *Review* in those early years. Some brilliant, established figures encouraged us and wrote for us. But it boggles the mind now that so many worked so hard to ensure *Wales Arts Review* existed at all. And we did it for years. I remember well, our original design editor, Dean Lewis, an ex-welder with an animation degree, pulling an all-nighter to build our website using little more than his considerable intuitive talent and the manual that came with the software. I believe it was ready by dawn, a few hours before we'd announced we were going to launch. All those people excitedly waiting to see us fall flat on our faces over the years have no idea how close they have come to seeing it happen on day minus one.

Dean was perhaps the most obsessive perfectionist among us, but it's really a story of brilliant people doing whatever it takes to get things done. I am nervous of listing names, in the likelihood I miss one out, but it wouldn't be right to not mention the major contributors to *Wales Arts Review* over the years, the names that have appeared on the masthead at some point or another. The *Review* would not be what it is, and would not sit where it now sits, without every one of them. Ben Glover, Steph Power, Phil (P.J.) Morris, Dean Lewis, John Lavin, Emma Schofield, Cerith Mathias, Craig Austin, Durre Shahwar, Dylan Moore, Jafar Iqbal and the hundreds of writers who have written for us. In the last two years, a new breed of editors has helped push us up to the current heights and it's important too that I put the names of Caragh Medlicott, Bethan Hall, Rosie Couch, Josie Cray and Holly McElroy in this list of thanks. The talent that has moved through the virtual doors of the virtual office is significant not just because of what it has meant to the *Review*, but because many of these figures have gone on to shape various areas of Welsh cultural life in their own way. Many have gone on to work elsewhere, Moore and Lavin work as editors now at other publications, Steph Power has served as Chair of Tŷ Cerdd, Craig Austin serves on the board of Literature Wales, Cerith Mathias is a director of the Cardiff Book Festival, the Pontypridd Children's Book Festival, and is a bookshop owner; there are so many other examples of how *Wales Arts Review* is enduring through its alumni in many areas of cultural life in Wales. Each of those I've named have numerous other accomplishments to their names, and many other people besides have done things just as impressive. It's testament to the *Review*'s influence and draw that there is too much to mention even in an attempt to scratch the surface of what we've all done.

Perhaps it's both a strength and a weakness of the *Review* that our continual poor financial state means we have a high turnover of personnel. It means we are agile, always fresh in the perspectives we publish, but it also means everything, always, is like pushing a boulder up a steep hill. We stood ten years ago to argue for the professionalisation of arts writing in Wales, and we stand in no different spot today. There is a disconnect in the way Wales talks about itself, and the way it literally values the things it's talking about. With our commitment to the cause, we have compelled those who allocate the public funds to give us money, but it was always far short of what we needed. My god, what we could be achieving now for the arts and culture of Wales with proper funding to value the enormous talent we have in our ranks and at hand in our contacts list.

Most of those good people I name above moved on as time went by. I wouldn't like to say it was uniformly to do with money, but energy levels get strained, work becomes work and should be valued correctly; and, importantly, other opportunities begin to come up because of the profile the *Review*'s success gave us. By the time Phil Morris, who was the *Review*'s managing editor from 2012 to 2016 (and is editor of this brilliant anthology), guided the *Review* through its first block of core funding from the Books Council of Wales, the backbone of the *Review*'s team needed recognition, appreciation for the work we had done. For all of Phil's hard work, we were not given what we needed. It was the *Review*'s first and only existential crisis moment. The team, that founding body who had given so much, was about to walk. I wrote an open letter, saying something absurdly dramatic that I undoubtedly believed, something like "the decision to underfund us was a decision to close us down", and I published it on our website late on the Friday afternoon, knowing we would have control of the narrative and the public temperature on this over a weekend when the offices of the Books Council would be closed. Upstarts indeed. Maybe so, but I have to be honest: writing about that still makes me angry, still makes me resentful, that *Wales Arts Review* has never been properly funded by the organisations who have the power and the money to do so. I don't regret writing that open letter. Not all of the *Wales Arts Review* team agreed with the decision to go with this way, and that's important to note. But it worked. Phil and I had a phone call from the Chair of the Arts Council of Wales asking us what we needed, short of a U-turn from the Books Council, to continue operating. We decided the best course of action was to ask for the funds to build a new website that would incorporate space for advertising, so we could show our editorial team that we had commercial ambitions, and also that "the establishment" *did* have faith in us, even if the independent panel who handed out funding grants at the Books Council didn't have enough of it.

The public funding model of *Wales Arts Review* was never a crutch, it was never supposed to be the easy option, filling out applications rather than testing our mettle in the commercial marketplace. It is, rather, a central building block of the *Review*'s mission statement; that conversations and great writing about art and culture should be accessible to anybody, anywhere in the world, regardless of their economic background. The democratising power of the internet must not be eroded in favour of isolating these discussions behind paywalls or subscription models. We believed Wales could be the envy of the rest of the world having something like *Wales Arts Review* there to shine an entertaining critical light on the creative cultural movements of the country, funded by the public purse, in the spirit of the working class miners' libraries that educated so many generations. And when I have been in India or Japan or America or wherever, and I introduce the *Review* to people I meet there, we *are* envied for precisely this model. The public funding of *Wales Arts Review* has enabled us to be read in every country in the world at some point in our history (hats off to whoever was reading us in the icy wildernesses of Greenland in 2016), and, keeping in mind the (ever-decreasing) hurdles of internet connectivity, by people of all backgrounds.

Money has always been a hot topic of conversation throughout the *Review*, and if I seem to be banging on about it here a little too long, it's only because of how important the subject has been to the life of *Wales Arts Review*. It's frustrating that *Wales Arts*

Review has operated on a semi-professional level for so long, and before that as an amateur venture. But we should be open about that, because pretending otherwise is to give the systems of cultural motion in Wales a stature it does not yet deserve. That the *Review* is not in receipt of all the money we need is a damning indictment of how Wales views and values its culture. But, of course, I would think that, wouldn't I?

Which brings us to the question of value. What has *Wales Arts Review* been worth in its first ten years? It's difficult to be Welsh and immodest, but I'll give it a go. A cursory glance at what the *Review* has done will see writers that have come through our ranks, the other publications that have risen in our wake, the culture of debate in Wales that was once the purview of academic elites talking to one another in periodicals with tiny circulations and is now an open and vibrant public forum... you won't convince me we did not play a part in these developments. Yes, they may have happened anyway – we didn't invent the internet, we didn't invent social media, we didn't invent the issues. But they didn't happen *without* us. They happened in this version of reality where *Wales Arts Review* blazed the trails and kicked open doors.

There is too much to list if we're talking about the items we have published, the relationships we have forged, that have made me proud of the work we do. But when I think back over ten years I think of our scope and our reach and our depth. James Lloyd's Gezi Park protest features were an early example of our international ambitions. Our dedication to the literature of Wales has been important to me personally. We have sponsored the People's Choice Award at the Wales Book of the Year Awards for six years now. Our feature of twenty-four essays searching for the Greatest Welsh Novel did exactly what I hoped it would do; that is, not anoint a winner, but open a public conversation about the richness, excellence, and wonders of Welsh fiction. Our partnerships around Wales have been vital to our sense of worth, from the Wicked Film Festival in Rhyl which works to give access to the film industry to kids from disadvantaged backgrounds, to our relationship with Welsh Women's Aid. More recently, during Covid, we worked to raise money for artists who were facing financial hardship due to lockdown, and we raised close to seven grand, handing out sixteen essential hardship bursaries. Not long after we worked with Holly McElroy, who had come through an internship with us via Cardiff University, to set up our Environment section where we could publish work directly related to the climate crisis. Sometimes it feels like barely a week goes by when we haven't had the opportunity to work on something exciting. At the end of 2021, we decided to publish a list of the hundred greatest albums ever to come out of Wales, with a similar goal of being less interested in crowning a number one album, but more with giving those hundreds of thousands of people around the world who read us some Welsh music they might have previously not known about.

The real value of *Wales Arts Review* has always been in the editorial team's dedication to good writing. This may seem idealistic, in an age of fast eyes and dopamine hits, but what has evolved over the decade is an ideology that has become a successful business model. At the outset, when selling the idea of the *Review*, talking on panels and going to pitch meetings, I was forever talking about how our philosophy put the quality of the writing *way up here* as a priority, and everything else, whatever was number two on that list, as *way down here*. What that means now is that our archive is a rich and hardworking area of revenue for us. *Quality* is our business model. Even if back when I (at least) was a naïve kid, and was piss 'n' vinegar, pissing off local councillors, I was just trying to walk like Ben Bradlee and write like Gore Vidal. But we all knew somehow – *I knew* – that this wasn't worth doing if it was for any other reason than publishing good writing. Not for chasing hits, likes, retweets, not for luring celebrity endorsements or glitzy invites to red carpet events. It had to be about good writing. Way up here.

And so, in 2021, when we decided to end our presence on Facebook after the U.S. Congress compared their operational business strategy to that of Big Tobacco (i.e. getting children addicted to their product), it was not an existential question for our business like it might be for so many other organisations our size. The reason being, *Wales Arts Review* is not dependent on social media for its traffic. Our "naïve ideals" in 2012, of prioritising good writing way above any other consideration, was a business plan by 2021 that meant the *Review* was not built on the shifting sands of social media morality but was founded on the age-old semi-ruins of a belief in good stuff serving us well. Amidst all that precarity, and my cynical belief that we could be closed down at any moment, we were building a business that had longevity as one of its columns. Every day that *Wales Arts Review* survives, it's been getting stronger.

That's not to say we've always known what we're doing, and I have spent ten years learning on the job. I have had good friends and advisers. And we have Ben Glover, too, who has been managing editor since 2016. Ben is the unsung hero of *Wales Arts Review*; he is its backbone, its steady hand, and the quiet visionary away from the spotlight. Without his ideas, and his implementation of those ideas, the business model and the infrastructure of *Wales Arts Review* would be fragile and even more financially asthmatic. And aside from that, Ben is the perfect foil for me as editor because he's a dear friend, has an excellent intuitive mind for expansionist ideas, and he works bloody hard to make sure the *Review* keeps going, keeps growing, keeps improving.

But this has largely been instinct, and it is sheer luck I seem to have decent instincts. They are writers' instincts first and foremost, but they have strengthened into those of an editor, I think. An example. In 2018, a new BBC Wales drama was on the horizon. A friend of mine, an arts journalist and editor in London, had recently advised that the *Review* needed to do more writing on television. My editorial instinct told me that there simply wasn't much to write about when it came to Welsh TV, and we did a bit anyway. But I watched the first episode of this new drama and the whole while I was watching it, I couldn't shake the feeling the title made no sense to me. I was wrestling with what exactly the title was trying to get across. This spurred me on to write a short piece about it. Most of the review was dedicated to this question. I knew at the time it was flippant (I hoped it was witty), but it was TV and that wasn't what our readers were really coming to us for. The programme was *Keeping Faith*, and it soon became the most watched drama in the history of BBC iPlayer. Fifty thousand people read that review and I've regretted the flippant tone of it every day since. But my writerly instincts informed my editorial instincts on that occasion. We now write about TV regularly, and our reviews of Welsh language drama in particular frequently rate in our most read pages of any given month.

That's just a small insight into how organic the life of *Wales Arts Review* has been. Following instincts, having fun, not taking ourselves too seriously while at the same time taking the central tenets of our responsibilities as a critical journal very seriously indeed.What it comes down to is this: did anyone, at any point, think *Wales Arts Review* would last ten years? Definitely not. For my part, I always felt (and still do) that next week could be our last. I always feel like someone is waiting to pull the plug, eager to call time on this uppity Newport project. We're not the right type of Welsh, not Welsh enough, not Welsh language enough, not Welsh indy enough, not Welsh Labour enough, not Team Wales enough. As an editor of a thing like *Wales Arts Review*, you're always made to feel you're not enough of something or other. But I believe in the pages of *Wales Arts Review* you will find the definition of the country. It's better than any political movement or nationalistic prevailing wind. National identity is complex, and *Wales Arts Review* continues to compile it. The living, breathing document. Probably my belief in our precarity is no longer founded (although, I still need the "probably"), and it's just a hangover from the days of our youth when every day felt like your last. But reaching a milestone like ten years gives you pause, and in a moment of stillness, we might be allowed to think of what the next ten years could look like. What can the *Review* achieve, where will it go, and what will the editor's introduction look like to the twentieth anniversary anthology, and who will write it?

I was thirty-two when we decided to start *Wales Arts Review*. I was living above a charity shop storage room in Newport and signing on the dole. Since then, I've written five books, written three radio documentaries, I have my own BBC Radio show, got married and had a kid, and have been around the world working on various projects, from Tokyo to Mumbai, and the whole time *Wales Arts Review* has been the central reservation – the meridian strip, if you like – of all I have done and tried to do. *Wales Arts Review* has given me everything I haven't had to take for myself. Its first ten years has proved what can be achieved with little money and a lot of drive, and that spirit and guile is captured beautifully in the contents of this anthology, a collection that has been commissioned and compiled to speak not just of where Wales is now, but where *Wales Arts Review* has been these last ten years. I hope in the next ten years the *Review* will finally get the full support that it needs and deserves, and future editors will take it to an even higher plane.

Back when it became apparent *Wales Arts Review* had a readership, and that that readership was growing, something began to be heard when we all managed to get together and sit across a pub table from one another. It made me realise we did after all seem to know what success would look like, how we could measure it. We began to talk about the *Review* as if it was its own entity, an independent body; not the collective energy output of us mad starters, but something that would live beyond us. Maybe at the time it was fanciful. Say it enough times and it might just come true. But now it *is* true. And I for one look forward to watching the future of *Wales Arts Review*.

CHRONIC

Gwyneth Lewis

1

> 30. Saturn (*Saturnus*) is designated by the pagans as the origin of the gods and of all their posterity. Latin speakers declare that he is named from sowing (*satus*), as though the sowing of all things pertains to him, or from the length of time, because he is filled (*saturare*) with years. 31. Whence the Greeks say he has the name Cronos, that is, 'time'...because he is said to have devoured his sons: that is, he rolls back into himself the years that time has brought forth[1].

2

The day begins with the sound of Leighton, my husband, winding up the grandfather clock that I've inherited from my grandmother's family. Made in Llandysul in the eighteenth century, before the French Revolution, the mechanism is crude, like a bicycle chain and gears. The clock came from the family farm to my great-aunt's house on the back of a tractor, so it's a robust piece of furniture. Each morning, Leighton pulls up the foot-long weight so that the clock can 'walk', as the Welsh has it. The raised energy falls throughout the day and, if not lifted at the end of twenty-four hours, the mechanism stops. It's a crude working, and the hourly chimes sound like the

'Seconds out!' bell in a boxing match. The minute hand has gouged tracks in the enamel face. Time-keeping can be violent.

After he's wound the Crug-eryr clock for the day, Leighton brings me a large mug of black coffee in bed, resurrection juice, strong enough to raise the dead. Then my body lets me know if I can get up or not.

3

> The hour is the boundary of time, just as the word *ora* means a boundary like the shore of the sea, or the bank of a river, or the border of a garment.[2]

I was well. The strings that connected my will to my body were delicate but strong. The pulleys and levers were efficient and translated my least wish into an act. Sometimes I managed to lift above my weight, with minimal effort.

I've suffered from migraines since I was a teenager and had grown to expect attacks as part of my menstrual cycle. These blinding headaches could only be addressed by hiding from the light in a darkened room. But, from time to time, the wheels came off. Occasionally, the gears on my energy contraption slipped and I found myself moving as though under hundreds of atmospheres, in deep water.

I kept a record in my diary, marking each migraine with a cross. These stigmata began to colonise an ever-increasing number of days during each month. Clearly, this was no longer a hormonal matter, but I was too busy trying to make a living as a freelance writer to see the bigger picture. Days without a mark became rare.

Under the care of my GP, I tried and failed all the standard prophylactic treatments that stop migraine in most people.

4

I was quite unwell. Nobody likes to acknowledge that they're ill, even episodically. I refused to give in to chronic migraine for decades after it was already taking a significant toll on my life.

I used to be a person who was well, who had enough energy to meet the challenges of life. I worked hard and loved it. I socialised, could exercise, had a laugh. I could be relied on to do what I said would.

Increasingly, I found that I was unable to carry out anything I chose to do. The cord between my desire and my body had frayed and broken, leaving me unable to respond to my own will.

For example, I really want to go to hear the Takacs Quartet play Bela Bartok's music alongside Hungarian folk music he collected but, after buying expensive tickets, I just didn't have enough energy to go. I continued to meet my work obligations but did nothing else but recuperate.

5

Time moves at a different pace for distinct parts of the self, as a tidal current moves at various speeds, according to the depth.

My physique moves at a generational rate. I have my mother's hands, my father's gait. The brain moves quickly, the mind less so.

We poets are the time-sink of the word, like bogs that soak up carbon, eccentric in themselves but keeping the whole time economy stable. Poetry uses up time, because excess duration is a disease. The art is so labour-intensive that poets are those who plough chronicity, which is fatal, like nuclear waste, into safe bedrock of form. Time unleashed on the patient is violent. To be a patient is to be forced to undergo the double discomfort of illness and being unable to act in time.

6

There are no neurologists in Wales who specialise in migraine and the waiting list for the Headache Clinic at the University of Wales Hospital at the Heath was, at the time I was desperate, a year.

I worked, but because my brain is misfiring, by the end of the day, I was exhausted. I discovered that I have Irlen Syndrome, which means that print and walls are constantly moving. All this has to be compensated for in the brain, which works twice as hard to anchor the world in the visual cortex. Glasses with pink lenses helped but, like an infant, I tire and have to go to bed before it's dark.

7

I endure. I turn sixty, the family arranges to take me out for a meal. A week before, I realise that I can't even face the light in our bedroom, so going to a party is out of the question. The kids understand. I want to go to the ninetieth birthday lunch for an aunt in Aberaeron but know that driving or even getting dressed is beyond me.

8

A migraine is like having a nail driven through your skull, it's a crucifixion.

I open my eyes to see if the light makes me flinch or not. It's dazzling. I close my eyes, put a mask over them, then my hands. The blinds are down, and I put my head under the duvet and, even then, the room is too bright for my brain to bear.

9

I'm desperately unwell. There are no respites between an episode of being ill and the next. Like a megalopolis, illness has swallowed the villages of wellbeing that used to be distinct and become an undifferentiated conurbation of malaise. I'm never well. I am an invalid.

I wake up to the twenty-sixth day of migraine in one month. There's a sound of wailing in the room with me, which takes me aback because I'm alone. I can no longer raise the weight required to drive the basics of looking after myself. There's no more time in me to allow me to live my life. I'm unable to work or function at all.

> Night (nox) is so called from 'harming' (nocere), because it impairs.[3] This is the start of three years of being severely disabled by migraine.

10

I tell the neurologist that my life is over.

I've found my way to a migraine specialist in London. Arriving early for my appointment in a private hospital near the Tower of London, I walk around the area, killing time. In a nearby park a monument marks the site of the ancient scaffold at Tower Hill. This is the spot where Sir Thomas More was executed in 1535, by having his head chopped off. The pain of migraine can be so acute that migraineurs often entertain fantasies of being decapitated.

The consultant asks what form my attacks take. Sometimes an aura, sometimes not. A headache like a red-hot knife stabbed through my left eyeball, down the side of my nose and exiting at the base of my skull. Sometimes, my brain is unable to make sense of the words I hear or to interpret what my eyes are seeing, a bit like having a transient stroke. I experience the smell of burning, as some epileptics do before a fit. There's nausea and hyper-sensitivity to light, noise and smells. Something electrical has gone awry in my brain. I can't think, can't write. The pain is bad enough but, even more distressing to me is the mental fog that makes me clumsy with words, monosyllabic, dull. The creative disciplines which have taken me a lifetime to establish have been decimated by migraine.

I ask if I've brought this condition on myself by overwork. No, the consultant tells me, chronic migraine isn't the result of my inability to maintain a healthy work/life balance, it's a genetic brain disorder and not my fault. I cry with relief.

The next treatment to try is Botox injections in my forehead and scalp. I try this for nine months and it reduces the pain of the migraines by 30% but not the frequency. I'm rigorously disciplined about not overusing painkillers because that can cause further headaches. I'm allowed eight medication days per month. So, if I'm suffering twenty-six headache days, what do I do with myself for the rest of the time? I have two ice packs on the go, a tens machine for the trigeminal nerve which makes me look like Wonder Woman. One day, out of medication days, I decide just to walk through the city, hoping to manufacture endorphins to reduce the pain level. It doesn't work but I carry on, find myself miles from home, just to distract myself from the knife in my head. I can see myself packing up and taking to the road full time – anything not to have to spend another wretched day in bed. This is an attempt to translate the time of pain into space.

The following summer, I endure a migraine that lasts six weeks and which leaves me suicidal.

I apply for a Personal Independence Payment from the DWP, Department of Work and Pensions.

I was turned down, I learned on appeal, because I didn't cry during the interview. The Department of Work and Pensions don't register stoicism. There are rigid guidelines about how the long-term ill must present their pain. I failed. You must blub as though you were on a reality show. I wasn't convincing as a person disabled by a genetic brain disorder, even though I was suicidal. I should have studied my part more carefully, have had a method.

> 9. The 'dead of night' (intempestum) is the middle and inactive is the middle and inactive time (tempus) of night, when nothing can be done and all things are at rest in sleep, for time is not perceived on its own account, but by way of human activities, and the middle of the night lacks activity. 10. Therefore intempestus means 'inactive', as if it were 'without time; (sine tempore), that is, without the activity by which time is perceived... Hence the dead of night is so called because it lacks time, that is, activity.[4]

Without my husband, I don't know how I would have fed myself. During an attack, I'm too debilitated and confused to make food for myself, so I learn to keep baked beans in the house and, if there's nothing in the fridge, so that I can open the tin and eat them cold.

I start cooking a meal and have to lie down in the middle. I walk the dog. I cancel a lunch with an understanding friend. I can't even bear to talk on the phone.

I am in-valid. I no longer count.

11

The ill belong to different guilds, according to their conditions. There are the ME/Chronic Fatigue patients, who have been medically gaslit for decades. We migraineurs are the intellectuals of the chronic world and can claim kinship with Oliver Sacks and Hildegaard of Bingen, whose visions are thought to have been extensive migraine auras.

In our separate sections, the chronics find our specialist groups and websites, where we can read research-based strategies to maximise daily functioning. Some, understandably, will have fallen into the hands of the wellness industry, with its seductive talk of recovery (it's so often to run a marathon), its bogus blood tests and expensive nutritional supplements. Forget the marathon, I'd be grateful for a day without pain and confusion.

All will be wondering: has it come to this? What is this half-life? How do I keep living without giving in to despair?

The chronically ill know that there's no divide between body and mind. Lie in bed of an afternoon and hear your neighbours coming home from work, leaping out of their cars to ply lawn mowers, hold barbeques and socialise. Lack of action has turned toxic and time is eating you alive. Migraine leaves you being eaten alive by time.

There is an environmental aspect to this. I see ecosystem degradation and chronic ill health as the same issue, the one on the outside, the other felt in the nerves. Pollution is a chronic condition and how it helps Long Covid and other pathogens spread is now becoming clear.

> Energos is frequently used for land which is cultivated and therefore productive... Energos is used to describe a mine which produces minerals and which is not worked out. It is used of money, capital, which is not lying idle but which is put out to produce interest. In the papyri energos is used to describe a mill which is in working order. The Septuagint uses energos for a working day as opposed to the Sabbath when work was forbidden... these words have the meaning of vitality as opposed to uselessness, effective activity as opposed to ineffectiveness.[5]

12

Then comes the miracle.

A new class of drugs, the first designed specifically for migraineurs, is licensed in the US and, then, the UK. Researchers had noticed that, during a migraine, the brain has a higher level of a substance called Calcitonin Gene-Related Peptide (CGRP). Drugs are designed that reduce the level in various ways. I start on one called Aivomig, which I administer at home with a monthly injection. Within half an hour of the first dose, I can see better. For the first two weeks, I sleep almost full time. Something has changed the pattern of electrical activity in my brain. It turns down the pain volume and reveals deep exhaustion. To my delight, over months and years, the number of headache days decreases.

But, as with all miracles, it leaves me with another problem. As the pain clears, I'm regularly sleeping for thirty-six hours at a stretch. I ask the neurologist if this is part of the migraine. It may be but, he speculates that my brain has had such a battering in the last decade that it's worn out and is taking advantage of the respite from constant concussion to recover. On these days, no willpower in the world can get me out of bed. Even the dog knows that I can't get up and she comes back to her bed beside mine, to keep me company. I trust her assessment of my capabilities more than I do my own.

13

I meet with fellow migraineurs in cafes that have been selected for soft lighting and low background noise. We make dates to meet but tell each other that the 'usual restrictions apply'. This means that if one of us is too ill to drive or turn up, we understand that it's not that we don't want to come, we physically can't. We turn up in sunglasses, carry pouches of emergency medication for acute attacks. We're giddy with joy when we're just able to turn up.

We share characteristics with the guild of ME/Chronic Fatigue sufferers, but our physical constraints are different. One of us begins a campaign to get migraine services for patients in Wales. She mobilises us to attend a meeting for patients to contribute to the Welsh government's strategic review of neurology services in the NHS. We discover that migraine isn't even on the list of conditions that need attention, even though it's one of the most common and devastating chronic neurological disorders.

In Wales alone, it's estimated that there are four hundred thousand people who suffer from chronic migraine (defined as experiencing at least fifteen headache days a month, with eight of those having migraine features) and the same number who suffer from episodic migraine. Currently, medical students receive four hours of training about headache which, along with migraine, has not been seen as a sexy specialty because it's so difficult to treat. This means that research in the field has been woefully underfunded, considering its disease burden. According to the Migraine Trust, 25 million days are lost a year to it in the UK.

'Chronic' is often used as a generalised adjective for something bad, and has largely lost its precise meaning in relation to time, much as 'incredible' is used as a synonym for 'very'. 'My back is chronic' can mean little more than my back really hurts. A chronic condition, though, is one which is experienced specifically over time. Its effects never disappear. There's no interval between one episode and the next. Like Chronos eating his own children, the body consumes its own capacity for healing.

The health service that's the only hope for people with chronic conditions is, likewise, suffering from a chronic underfunding and concomitant inefficiency. So migraineurs – and others suffering from ongoing conditions – in Wales are ill, not only with a brain disorder, but with the National Health Service's long history of gaslighting women about their serious neurological and autoimmune illnesses.

You ask far more of medical, nursing or support staff than they can realistically deliver. Because they have a vocation, rather than what David Graeber calls a Bullshit Job, they rise to the occasion. They are resilient and subsidise the job with their own extra energy.

Soon, the condition of crisis and stretch become endemic. Like a migraineur's brain, which is misfiring due to a Cortical Depression Wave, it works inefficiently, thereby taking far more energy than it should. Still, the commitment to the cause is there and masks the structural deficit in the system. For a while.

Energy flags. The elasticity within the tendons fails. The rope between the system's goals of good universal healthcare fails. Good people who've subsidised a failing system with their own health become ill. They take sick leave, work fewer days, retire, or die too early. The health of all of us suffers. This is a chronic condition.

14

I've been disabled for eighteen months (and the decade before, if I'm honest) before the world stopped due to Covid. It was business as usual for me and the millions of other chronically ill citizens. I, like them, rolled my eyes at complaints about not being able to work, travel, socialise. These activities aren't human rights, they're the way millions live. We're grateful for tiny daily domestic victories like being able to make lunch or go for a short walk. This is the stuff of victory.

I had mixed feelings about those suffering from Long Covid.

I'd already passed through the mirror from being active in the world to the half-life of debility. I feel for them enormously because I know the hell of ill health and shock of losing everything. More positively, I welcome the promise of funding for research into the condition and support which will benefit the rest of us. But I can't stifle a snort when a professional person, unable to function for, say, three whole months. What, only three months? What about that hidden chorus of us who've been ghosts in our own lives for years?

If you have a chronic condition, not only are you repeatedly and daily experiencing ill health, that condition has replaced any alternative life that you might have lived.

> The unlived life has no scope, no dimensions. I am haunted by what could have been, by what did not happen. But can I truly claim to have a foothold in the lived life?[6]

Gradually, by tiny degrees, my epic sleeps reduce in number. I still go to bed as early as an infant but I'm now able to stay up during the day. I do a bit of online teaching and it goes well. I start to write again, which is brutally hard work but this is all I've ever wanted to do and I keep at it, even though my own clumsiness is humiliating. The cognitive fog begins to lift. I'm doing more than enduring, I'm able to take delight again in cutting the lawn, observing steam left on a table by a cup of tea.

Illness has humbled me and my goals are modest: to claw back the hours in the day that have been lost to malaise. I peg out the washing. I try and maybe fail to walk the dog. I grab ten minutes weeding out in the garden. I cook my neighbours a dinner that I promised them four years ago and I don't take days to recover. I finish writing a book that's been in my mind for decades. In between each of these sentences are months of perseverance and consistent self-care. Three years on, the new drug continues to improve my life.

I'm one of the risen dead. For now.

---

[1] The Etymologies of Isidore of Seville, eds Stephen A Barney, WJ Lewis, JA Beach, Oliver Berghof, Muriel Hall (Cambridge, 2006), p. 185

[2] Ibid, p. 125

[3] Ibid, p. 127

[4] Ibid, p. 127

[5] William Barclay, New Testament Words, (SCM, 1992) pp. 78-79

[6] Jan Grue, I Live a Life Like Yours, tr from the Norwegian by BL Crook (Pushkin Press, 2021)

THE SPACE BETWEEN

Kaite O'Reilly & Phillip B Zarrilli

2000-2020 LLANARTH

The studio...a place of hypothesis, and therefore a place of possibility...where something can come of nothing. Sound from silence. Light from darkness. Therefore, a liminal place, between[1]...

This 'place between' is where much of my work and that with the late great Phillip Zarrilli lies... Between cultures, between belief systems, between East and West, between the described and prescribed, the atypical and the normative, between practices and theories. Phillip Zarrilli himself occupied a liminal space between practice and theory, between teaching and doing. An internationally respected theatre director and scholar, Phillip won awards for his writing as he travelled the world directing and training actors, always returning to Ceredigion where he established his studio and did much of his reading, thinking and writing.

For someone coming from the wide open spaces of midwestern America, Phillip found the intense diversity of landscape and spectacular vistas in such a small nation as Wales astonishing. He was also attracted to the creative breadth and depth of the artists, craftspeople and individuals who made their home alongside us in the west. The Welsh studio was – and remains – an astonishing place to make work. For both of us it was a place of possibility.

Phillip trained in the South Indian martial art Kalarippayattu with Gurukkal Govindankutty Nayar of the CVN Kalari, Thiruvanthapuram, Kerala, and dedicated seven years to intensive training in South India, after which he was gifted the *pitham* – traditional stool – as a sign of his mastery. He was the first non-Indian to be granted Gurukkal (Master) status in Kalarippayattu. In India his ethnographic study *When the Body Becomes All Eyes: Paradigms, Discourses and Practices of Power in Kalarippayattu, a South Indian Martial Art* (Oxford University Press, India) is believed to have significantly contributed towards the resurgence of interest in the form. Whenever we travelled in Kerala this quietly dynamic American was treated as a celebrity, with film crews unexpectedly turning up at any public talk or event he attended.

Phillip devised a psychophysical approach to actor-training which utilised Kalarippayattu, taiqiquan and yoga, asserting that the work of the actor 'is based not on acting as representation, but on an 'energetics' of performance.'[2] In 2000 his private studio in west Wales was inaugurated as a CVN Kalari (studio for the training of Kalarippayattu) and Phillip initiated The Llanarth Group.

The Llanarth Group (2000-2020) was an association of theatre/performance artists dedicated to producing international theatre of the highest quality through Phillip's in-depth psychophysical training of actors from all cultures. Each production brought together a specific group of local and/or international collaborators relevant to the aesthetic of a specific project. I was the resident dramaturg, playwright and at times co-creator.

It has been the joy and privilege of my life to work so closely with Phillip over two decades – always separate and distinctive in matter and texture, we braided together to create one cloth. In the following pages I hope to reflect on a few of these intercultural projects, grown in Wales and then taken out into the world. As I do so, I will draw on some of Phillip's writing, so his voice continues to both harmonise with and be counterpoint to mine, which was perhaps the key to the success of our twenty year collaboration in life as well as work.

The studio... a place between, a location without coordinates, or answers. A place to map, temporarily, space-time along some continuum, but only momentarily, in that moment of performance... a place of erasure, of risk, of loss, and always, as anyone who steps on the stage knows, of potential failure...

As an artist/maker/writer I have always been drawn to risk – the ambitious challenge – that intoxicating "what if...?" I want to explore new form and interrogate the possibilities of performance and that relationship between the spectacle and the spectator. Once done, I have never wanted to repeat the same form, but to continue exploring, keeping my practice fresh. With Phillip Zarrilli I found the ultimate collaborator and conspirator – a scholar-practitioner not afraid of risk and failure, but one who would challenge and expand my own reach and understanding – like ecstatic children, we dared each other, egging each other on to undertake delicious and at times high-risk experiments. Throughout, active enquiry and analysis of the process informed by diverse philosophies, performance theory and cognitive science was his practice. It was important to both of us to engage with cultural journals and platforms such as *Wales Arts Review, TDR, Howlround,* etc. to initiate connection and share ideas and experience. As writers, teachers and theatre makers, communication was our modus operandum and Phillip's curiosity in others' ideas was as strong as his generosity in sharing his own.

He used both our Welsh grown and international projects as

seedbed for his theoretical writings, most notably in *Psychophysical Acting: An Intercultural Approach After Stanislavski* (Routledge 2008) and *(toward) a Phenomenology of Acting* (Routledge 2019).

What follows is a consideration of some of our co-creations, utilising his and my words.

2013. TOKYO[3]

The studio... A place to explore such fundamental paradoxes as (1) how to make the complex, simple; the simple, complex; (2) the relationship between space and time; between absence and presence; here/there; now/then; if/when; (3) the embodied relationship between in-spiration and ex-piration; (4) the relationship between the said, and the unsaid, or the must-be-said; (5) the relationship between "self" and "others"...

I knew I was a long way from Ceredigion when Takayuki Kako, the stage manager of Babylon Theatre Tokyo, asked us what our preferred procedure would be if there was an earthquake during one of The Llanarth Group's performances of *Told by the Wind*. Our safety was his priority, he told us, but tremors were frequent. Would it be best if he stopped the show if he thought any potential quake was dangerous, to lead us and the audience to safety? Yes please, I said, explaining that although I was running the show, I had limited experience of earthquakes and so might not be the best person to lead an evacuation, especially as I don't speak Japanese.

Thankfully no earthquake struck – or at least not during any of our performances. We were in Tokyo for a month long cultural exchange with Ami Theatre, to present our work inspired by Japanese aesthetics.

Told by the Wind was made in Wales, a collaboration between Pembrokeshire-based multi-disciplinary artist Jo Shapland, Phillip and I, inspired by the dramaturgy and principles of Japanese nō theatre, astrophysics and the aesthetics of Quietude. Throughout his career Phillip had an abiding interest in Japanese theatre and particularly the commentaries on acting by Zeami, the founder of Japanese nō during the 14th century, which he often cited in his writings on acting. Phillip and Jo had both trained with Kita nō school master actor Akira Matsui, with Phillip's intensive training early in his career concluding with him working with Matsui on two productions. This exchange with Ami – a company specialising in modern nō – seemed an obvious and exciting possibility, although we were clear in our work we were making a chamber piece inspired by Japanese aesthetics, but not reproducing them. A dialogue is the essence, whilst avoiding cultural appropriation and rather, inhabiting 'the space between'. Phillip was renowned for his intercultural practical and theoretical work, and I teach intercultural dramaturgy at ITI – Intercultural Theatre Institute in Singapore. We were both fellows for many years of the International Research Centre 'Interweaving Performance Cultures' attached to Freie Universitat and spent several months every year between 2011-19 in Berlin, reflecting on intercultural performance practices.

As Phillip described in an essay for Wales Art Review:
"As co-creators of *Told by the Wind,* we of course recognised that *none of us were specialists* in Japanese or *nō*, and that we therefore had no intention or interest of attempting to create a performance that in any overt way appeared to be *nō* or *nō*-like for the UK/Western audiences that would constitute our primary audience, and the vast majority of whom would have absolutely no familiarity with Japanese theatre or *nō*. We therefore took an

indirect approach to the source tradition [...] Unlike narrative or character driven theatre performances, *Told by the Wind* operates like poetry through allusion and suggestion, but in three space-time dimensions. Each of the performers [Zarrilli and Shapland] 'dances' an inner landscape. Like *haiku,* poetry in general, and Japanese *nō* dramas, *Told by the Wind* invites the audience to enter an imaginative space of possibilities."

This choice reflects the underlying Japanese aesthetic concept of *yūgen:* a term which suggests 'mystery and depth' or 'what lies beneath the surface'. "In our creative process" Phillip continues, "we constantly addressed "the hint", i.e., the question of "what lies beneath the surface" for the two figures. Dramaturgically, could the two onstage figures be constantly present to one another, yet could the presence of each to the other remain a question mark? O'Reilly framed and articulated this "question mark" as follows: who is "dreaming" whom? We interpreted "dreaming" as the active task of constantly "imagining" or "conjuring" an-Other. This question mark was central to the final development and overall aesthetic of *Told by the Wind."*

One of our artistic advisors when originally making the work in Wales was Mari Boyd, a Japanese academic and translator of the playwright Ōta Shōgo. Mari's highly recommended book, '*The Aesthetics of Quietude*' was influential in our thinking when creating the work, which uses embodied silences, spare text and slowed down motion. Making the work in West Wales enabled us to ease into stillness within the Spring-warmed stone walls of the studio, surrounded by fields and the courting calls of the birds, a recording of which made their way into an otherwise almost silent performance.

'Slow theatre' was something that intrigued Jo, while Phillip had directed Shōgo's non-verbal "living silence" dramas in the

UK, Norway and Singapore and had a long history and affinity with the late "quiet" work of Samuel Beckett.

As Mari Boyd has explained, "Quiet theatre" does not attempt to "aggressively transmit meaning to the audience"[4]. Rather, it turns down the often busy volume of theatre's multiple modes of communication, paring away anything non-essential. Together, we three co-creators sought to strip away the non-essential, working constantly with what lay "beneath the surface" – the subtle, the hint, culminating in Elisabeth Mahoney of THE GUARDIAN describing the performance as *'...hypnotic... [with] a haunting, painterly beauty...[and] the astringent purity of a haiku poem...'* Similarly the critics in Chicago at *SEE CHICAGO DANCE* and *CHICAGO TIME OUT* described the performance respectively as *'...minimal... mesmerising...evoking both later T.S. Eliot and haiku'*, and *'...Beckettian magnetic poetry...all dropped like shapeless stones into a moonlit lake of silence...'*

It seemed that the sparse, subtle work we endeavoured to create inspired poetic responses from our critics – and the breath, so important in Phillip's Psychophysical approach to acting, became present also in several reviews. I have never before read a critic describe their body and breath in space alongside a performance. I feel this is part of the 'attunement' Phillip emphasised both in his actor-training and direction and sign of the achievement Jo and Phillip created together on stage: to get the space to slow down and all to 'breathe' together, temporarily dissolving the divisive binary of audience and actors.

This short but powerful work premiered in Wales and toured internationally for eleven years to Portugal, USA, Poland, Japan and Germany, with a final performance at the Kerala International Theatre Festival in January 2021, to a house so full, audience members were sitting on the stage, in the aisles, and on each other's laps in an intense heat.

2014. TAIPEI

4/8/14. Travel notes[5]

'You can only cook if you turn on the fire and that's what your awareness is. That's why we train.'[6]

It's a sweltering black box studio in Taipei Arts University and Phillip Zarrilli is leading a masterclass in his approach to pre-performative psychophysical actor-training, using Asian martial/meditation arts.

'If we open our awareness in the exercise,' Phillip says, 'if we follow the breath, there's a certain quality in what you're doing which is tangible – without that awareness, you're just opening and closing your arms. It's the same with acting.'

I know what he means. I've seen performances where the actors just seem to be going through the motions, moving around the stage in a pre-determined score that seems oddly dead, like there's no ghost in the machine. There's little connection to the space, or other actors around them and they converse without listening to what the others say. How to keep it fresh, to 'enliven' an actor on stage has been a fascination ever since and sitting in on Zarrilli's masterclass as Guest Director at the Taipei Art Festival is illuminating. His approach seeks to 'enliven' actors when on stage, and to create 360 degree awareness.

'This training,' Zarrilli says on his website[7] 'begins by focusing on the development of the contemporary actor's interiority, i.e., how the actor might discover, awaken, shape, understand, and deploy "energy", awareness, focus/concentration, and feeling to the "matter of performance—the impulses, structure, contours, and texture of the tasks or actions that constitute a specific performance score shaped by particular dramaturgies... While the exercises are "traditional, the pedagogy is "contemporary".'

There is no suspicion towards the use of words like 'bodymind', 'energy', '*chi*', or '*ki*' in Taiwan. Unlike in the West, the importance of generating and circulating energy is accepted and everyday, at the heart of Chinese traditional medicine, and part of common daily practice.

The space between each breath is very important to Zarrilli, which is why he asks us to pay attention from the space of completion to the start of inhalation. That 'space between' is where he believes acting happens – the empty space – everything and nothing, filled with potential.

4/8/14. Notes

We are in Taipei for the 2014 International Arts Festival, where Phillip is directing the premiere of my post-dramatic text *the 9 fridas* in Mandarin with Mobius Strip Theatre and Hong Kong Repertory.

The 9 Fridas is a mosaic, a collage of impressions and stories reflecting the life of Mexican artist Frida Kahlo (1907 – 1954) and the fictional journey of 'F' through the 9 Hells of the Mayan Underworld. 'F' is accompanied by a chorus of figures who, like her, are and are not Frida Kahlo, but whose stories echo actual events from Kahlo's life: The political activist, the national emblem, the bi-curious lover, the would-be mother, the teenager severely disabled in a road accident, the fashion icon, the struggling artist...

5/8/14. Rehearsal notes

'The world will not be destroyed by those who do evil, but by those who watch them without doing anything.'
– Einstein, quoted by The Sunflower Protest.

The last living photograph of Frida Kahlo was taken several days before her death, participating in a political demonstration. She is frail and thin, pushed in her wheelchair by Diego Rivera, scarf wrapped about her head against the driving rain, her right fist raised in defiance, her left hand holding a reproduction of Picasso's 'Dove of Peace'.

Even before I reached Taiwan, I knew I wanted to rework what became known as 'the political scene' in my text, so it had resonance for a Taiwanese audience. In this intercultural exchange we felt it essential to acknowledge and engage with contemporary issues – the global and the local – as Frida Kahlo herself did, as an activist and political animal. In *the 9 Fridas* I've taken aspects from Kahlo's extraordinary life and reframed them in contemporary contexts. Bringing in recent Taiwanese political activity seemed an ideal opportunity to make parallels between Kahlo's activism and those of the Sunflower Protest.

On March 18th 2014, hundreds of students occupied the Legislative Yuan, Taiwan's parliament, to protest against the Cross-Strait Service Trade Agreement. Their action was in protest against undemocratic procedures pushing through this trade agreement between China and Taiwan without fully informing the Taiwanese people what it would entail. Many feared this would make Taiwan too dependant on China economically, isolating Taiwan from other allies, and therefore vulnerable to political pressure from Beijing. This quickly spread across the city, and soon thousands of citizens gathered on the streets outside the parliament, to support the students inside.

On March 30th, twelve days into their occupation, students organised a demonstration that saw more than 500,000 Taiwanese citizens taking to the streets in support of their non-violent cause. The support was across Taiwan and internationally, with demonstrations occurring in many cities across the world. With this support, the government had to listen and respond and the action ended officially on April 10th.

I'd been following the protest from the UK through translations of news reports provided by our translator Betty (Yi-Chun Chen). When I arrived in Taipei, I looked for people to interview who had been involved in the occupation – and didn't have to look very far. Along with Betty, cast members as well as our excellent stage management had been deeply involved. Lunch hours have been spent with them telling me their experiences and how significant the protest has been in politicising the younger generation. They fear Taiwan's independence will be absorbed by big neighbour Mainland China; recent developments in Hong Kong have increased the fear.

'It's the evolution of control,' one of my characters says in the script. 'Once, it was with might, now it's with economics.' The section concludes with a description both an act of protest at dawn and the awakening of a political consciousness: 'It was 4am, and we faced the new morning.'

The new material was drawn from my interviews with those involved in the action, which I then developed and fictionalised, retaining the central 'truths'. This scene would only be performed in Taiwan, as I often rework scenes citing localised activism, so the material has even more relevance and resonance to specific audiences.

One of my collaborators, Kuo Yi Chi, emailed me sections from her diary kept when she was occupying the Legislative Yuan, which she has given me permission to reproduce here, alongside her reactions to the script:

> You know, a part of me wants to stay, a part of me wants to run away, and that's the problem because I don't know who I really am（交錯地） 你知道有一部份的我想要留在原地有一部份的我想要逃離然後這就是問題的所在因為我不知道我自己到底是誰
> I guess I can't be happy ever after.
> ...I forgot to tell you something about 'It was 4 am and we faced the new morning'. At first, I thought it was very positive, hopeful. But one day I suddenly felt that it was so ironic because bad things always happen at the darkest moment even though it should start to shine at the same moment. I've been through a hopeless 4am once, on April 27 at Zhongxiao West road. When we were in raincoats surrounded by the police, knowing we were going to be sprinkled [by water cannons, and tear gas]. We hoped to see a new, safe, peaceful morning with our dry bodies, but we didn't have a glimpse to see. The sunshine came up just when news reporters were all expelled... However, 'It' didn't come at all. Of course the sun did rise, just like people keep moving on or keep forgetting, but the morning we expected didn't come. We were abandoned by the government that night, that morning. But we don't give up. So yes, it was 4am and we faced the new morning, but not 'The' morning we want.[8]

8/8/14. Rehearsal notes

'Nothing is worth more than laughter. It is strength to laugh and to abandon oneself, to be light. Tragedy is the most ridiculous thing.'
– Frida Kahlo journals.

I shared this quotation with the actors today, to remind them of Frida Kahlo's defiance in the face of pain and adversity. It is easy to see her as 'tragic but brave' and her life as one long miserable drag of one peg leg after the other, but as a disabled woman and feminist, I reject this. One reason why I chose to make this multi-layered text was a desire to reclaim Kahlo as a disability icon and inspiration, rather than the pity-inducing mainstream representations of recent years that have reduced her to a fragment of her biography, and the little broken betrayed wife at that. Before we coined 'crip culture' she was living it...I adore her for her refusal to be constrained by what could be viewed at the time as the limitations of her gender and impairment – for the fact she created extraordinary art the likes of which had not been seen before – for her laughter, her anger, her attitude in her paintings – what Andre Breton called *'the pretty ribbon tied around the bomb.'*

12/8/14: Travel notes

As a Mexican, death would have been a constant companion to Frida Kahlo, and not taboo, nor as feared as it is in so many other cultures. In the script I use references to the ancient Mayan belief system which Kahlo quoted in diaries and letters: the sense all has spirit – even the rocks and cacti and hummingbirds – and that death is a natural state we return to after living. It can be challenging and unsettling, dealing with issues of the journey of the soul after death, and the 9 hells of the Mayan underworld during August – Ghost month – the 7th lunar month – when the door between hell and earth opens from twilight until dawn. In Taipei it's a time of ancestor worship, remembrance and placation of the hungry, jealous ghosts.

August 10th is Taiwan's Day of the Dead, with rituals across the city, but particularly in the north of the island, where huge burning boats are set sail into the night. I walked the back roads behind the apartment where I'm staying, finding a side road blocked off, a massive marquee stretching across. Inside hundreds of placements for a lavish meal were set, with offerings of food, fruit, cigarettes, and the ever present green tea – a feast for phantoms – a banquet where the diners are present, but invisible. Meanwhile braziers burn in the streets, fuelled by thousands of notes from The Bank of Hell, 'posted' to the dead via flames.

I followed a saffron robed monk as he dog-trotted through the back lanes, blessing the makeshift altars the businesses and restaurants had set up outside their premises. A man carrying a yellow lantern was in the vanguard, with various animals and children following in his wake.

14/9/14 Rehearsal notes

The script is becoming more familiar to the actors, who are interrogating the content, asking questions, seeking clarity. It's a hugely exciting time as the text begins to breathe and take shape. I am constantly editing and tightening the text. What may work on the page can trip, divert, or slow when put 'up' – the dynamics of individual moments, as well as sequences and the flow of the whole piece needs to be taken into consideration. Tempo-rhythm, dynamic and flow is of great importance to me, especially at this point in the process.

Issues of translation: 'Can you translate 'cheeky' into Mandarin?'

My work is very musical and dependent on tempo-rhythm for tone, emphasis, and to help create meaning and flow. Punctuation is essential and I think every director I have worked with has commented at some point on the precision of my signification of pause, beat, or length of line. In translation, it becomes complicated. One word in English can become six in Mandarin, therefore there is an issue of balancing the line – there can be an emphasis on part of a sentence I hadn't intended. As an example today, the balanced line in English we were working on was: 'I lived, dying.' In Mandarin the equilibrium is gone – it becomes in effect 'I lived, but in actuality I was dying' – which gives too much emphasis to death, thereby weighting the meaning too much in that direction, and bringing a more sombre tone. We changed the translation to be more balanced – 'in life, there is death,' re-establishing the equilibrium I had sought in the original. Everyone has complimented the translation by Betty Yi Chun Chen, but additional help has come from our outstanding cast.

16/8/14. Travel notes

Asked by the British Council to give a workshop in writing and then a public lecture: 'Representations of Impairment in the Western Theatrical Canon'. This has been an area of my research for some time, developed partly during my on-going fellowship at Freie Universitat's International Research Centre: Interweaving Performance Cultures in Berlin, where I'm reflecting on my work between mainstream culture and disability culture, between hearing and Deaf cultures. I'm encouraged by the responses to the talk, especially the understanding that disability is a social construct. It is not my impairments that disable me, but the prejudices, fears, physical and attitudinal barriers of a society with little value in human variety that are disabling.

In the dinner hour between the events I and my spontaneous girl gang – a group of fabulous creative Taiwanese women – head for fermented 'stinky tofu' at a street cafe and the auspicious temple for match-making nearby. I am introduced to the local gods by name, and promised divine protection in my travels around the city if I buy a blessed charm of a fierce looking 'god gangster' for about £1.20. Bargain.

18/8/14: Rehearsal notes

A great silence fell over the rehearsal room today when our extraordinary costume designer, YS Lee, brought in two reproductions of Frida's corsets. One is leather, the other plaster, with the tender depiction of an embryo curled beneath a defiant hammer and sickle. I saw the original at an exhibition of Kahlo's work in Berlin some years ago, and it looks identical. The sweltering room became chilled as Mobius Strip co-artistic director and performer Faye Leong was strapped into it.

YS Lee's work is phenomenal and he and designer YY Lim are having the time of their lives working on this project. Their work is visually stunning.

26/8/14 Travel notes

Gearing up to show time, but the time difference between Taiwan and Europe allows me to work a full day in Taipei, then skype into rehearsals at Forest Forge Theatre Company in the UK, who are beginning rehearsals on my new play *Woman of Flowers*, a reinvention of the story of Blodeuwedd from the Fourth branch of the Mabinogion. This magnificent medieval treasure has inspired various performance texts I've written over the years – *The Wild Girl*, at the Sherman, *Perfect* directed by John E McGrath in 2004 at Manchester's Contact, and now, in spoken, projected and visual languages, my third iteration of owl faced Blodeuwedd for a national tour. 'I' am present and active in rehearsals via the screen of a laptop placed on a chair, facing the actors. Performer Sophie Stone and I practice signing to each other over thousands of miles and director Kirstie Davis and I relish our conversations, with me seven hours into her future. It is exhausting but strangely exhilarating, and at night in my dreams Frida tangoes with Blodeuwedd to a sound track of owl calls and the sexy smoky croak of Chevela Vargas.

5/9/14. Opening

Our performances at the Taipei Art Festival have been sold out for more than a month and we're slightly surprised to see a handful of Kahlo fans turn up dressed in Day of the Dead outfits. Although officially the most famous female artist in the world, we weren't sure how well known she was in Taiwan.

Tears, laughter at the filmed sequences, gasps at the multiple live reproductions of 'The Two Fridas' and an impromptu speech of congratulation from the former ambassador to Taiwan, Jorge Pinto, 'the only Mexican in Taipei.' Some were nervous about how accessible the Mexican and Mayan cultural references might be to the Taiwanese audience, never mind the complex post-dramatic script, multiple protagonists, and psychophysical approach, but all fears are proven unnecessary. In the after-show dialogue, Keng Yi Wei, director of the festival, spoke of Phillip Zarrilli's long experience of 'multi-layered intercultural work' and how welcome that is to the Taipei Art Festival. There are talks of a transfer to Hong Kong, and further tours around Taiwan and perhaps Mainland China, and there are plans for the publication of the script in Betty's Mandarin translation.

7/9/14 Travel notes

We head for the airport after the last show and a celebratory banquet, a crowd of Mobius Strip Theatre Company, the Taipei Art Festival, new friends and Phillip's former students all waving us off in our taxi. All I feel is gratitude for this experience – the generosity and welcome I have encountered, the talent I have witnessed and the understanding I have had enhanced. I am tender-hearted leaving Taipei and the extraordinary people I have met, but yearning for that particular Welsh landscape which somehow opens me like a clean cut wound.

2017-18 SINGAPORE/WALES

The paradoxical places that the theatre inhabits, those places where creativity is launched, where discovery unfolds, where vibration flickers between...are sites of transition, and therefore tension between...sites of both playfulness as well as danger; therefore, sites of potential power.

I have been angry most of my life[9]. Identifying as a working class Irish immigrant disabled female sounds like the start of a right-on joke, and the jostling identity politics certainly creates friction, a blistering energy I've found best directed into cultural pursuits. Beyond bigotry, intolerance and the socio-political status quo to rage at, I'm angry at stereotypes and the lazy representations of difference in our media, stage, and screen. I get apoplectic by the churning out of lies representing disabled peoples' existence:

tragic but brave, benefit fraudsters, inspiring over-comers, or helpless figures of pity.

Since the Ancient Greeks, the vast majority of disabled characters in the Western theatrical canon are tropes, reinforcing limited notions of what it is to be 'normal' rather than embracing all the possibilities of human variety. So common is the atypical body in our stage and TV dramas, the audience(s) assume they know and understand the realities of these individuals' lives, yet few of these narratives are informed by lived experience, and so misconceptions and ableist notions of difference, shaped by the medical and charity models of disability, are reproduced and reinforced.

As a playwright and dramaturg who identifies as disabled, I have been working for several decades across and between so-called "mainstream" culture and what I coin "crip" culture, informed by the social model of disability. I consider disability a social construct—I am a woman with a sensory and physical impairment, but it is society's attitudinal and physical barriers which is disabling, not the idiosyncrasies of my body.

In my work I am interested in creating new protagonists, with different narratives, and with different endings. I believe reimagining disability opens up creative possibilities in aesthetics, form, and content—changing the stories we tell, how they are told, and the people who tell them.

Victims, villains, metaphors, parodies, benefit scroungers or inspiration porn stars...I was tired of the way disabled characters were portrayed in the media and frustrated by the limited range of parts available for disabled and Deaf actors, so decided to do something about it. I began my explorations of the monologue in 2008 on a Creative Wales Major Award courtesy of Arts Council Wales. My first 'd' Monologues, *In Water I'm Weightless*, was directed by John E McGrath for

National Theatre Wales as part of the Cultural Olympiad celebrating the 2012 Olympics/Paralympics. *And Suddenly I Disappear: The Singapore/UK 'd' Monologues,* directed by Phillip Zarrilli for The Llanarth Group, was the most recent manifestation, an Unlimited international commission in multiple languages, inspired by lived experience.

Following the interview model I established in 2009, my Singapore collaborators instigated a series of interactions with disabled and Deaf Singaporeans, many of whom had never been afforded such interest in their lives before. These raw conversations inspired fictional monologues I wrote, mixing Mandarin, Cantonese, English, Welsh, Singaporean and British sign languages, thanks to our talented, multilingual cast. A triumph at its world premiere in Singapore in May 2018, this Deaf and disabled led intercultural production was hailed by the British Council as "a real game changer."

The company consisted of pioneering artists exploring new form, with the aesthetics of access – audio description, captioning, visual language – at the very heart of the work. The show wasn't about access, but the innovative use of theatre languages, mixing visual and spoken storytelling in dynamic form. In order to begin the process of professionalisation of disability arts in Singapore, I brought my muse and leading Welsh Crip' performer Sara Beer with me, and actor-trainer director Phillip Zarrilli, who also identifies as disabled. We offered training and professional experience to emerging Deaf and disabled Singaporean actors, alongside chief collaborators Grace Lee Khoo and Natalie Lim of Access Path Productions, and Peter Sau, hoping this collaboration would 'fast track' these pioneers of disabled and Deaf led work in Singapore.

These new monologues were in a variety of styles – pithy, funny and painful, reflecting the experience of disabled people in the UK and Singapore. These texts, alongside others written over the past decade, were published by Oberon as The 'd' Monologues. Together with the perspectives from Singapore, the performance montage creates, I hope, a symphony of experience – sometimes harmonious, other times discordant, with pace, tempo-rhythm, lyricism and counter-point. It is a snapshot of our times, a dialogue across multiple languages from one small nation to another.

Coda... to no end...

[...] suspended between the in-spiration and ex-piration... [...] that necessarily (un)known place between... where absence has the possibility of becoming presence, but can be so only when it denies itself... and keeps the traces of its absence... in the silence

The Metaphysical Studio. Phillip B Zarrilli

---

[1] All quotations in bold italics: Inspiring to Con-spire: The Metaphysical Studio by Phillip B. Zarrilli TDR/The Drama Review 2002

[2] Psychophysical Acting: An Intercultural Approach After Stanislavski (Routledge 2008) Phillip B Zarrilli

[3] Taken from my travel diary and blog www.kaiteoreilly.wordpress.com

[4] The Aesthetics of Quietude: Ōta Shōgo and the Theater of Divestiture. Mari Boyd. Sophia University Press July 2006 ISBN: 4324078866 C3074

[5] Kaite O' Reilly opens the pages of her travel and rehearsal diaries to reflect on six weeks in Taipei, staging the 9 Fridas at Taipei Arts Festival, September 2014. https://www.walesartsreview.org/notes-from-a-rehearsal-diary-the-9-fridas-at-tapei-arts-festival/

[6] Phillip Zarrilli – comment in workshop at Taipei Arts University 29 July 2014.

[7] www.phillipzarrilli.com

[8] Email. © Kuo Yi-Chi. August 2014.

[9] Freely adapted from the Introduction to my collected The d Monologues

LEADER OF THE PACK

P.J. Morris

Zulu is a perennial Christmas TV favourite: eminently quotable, it forms a matrix of reference points that facilitates a multitude of immediate intimacies between men. In particular, Welshmen – for whom the trials of war have, for generations, been experienced vicariously through schoolboy comics and Playstation video games.

The screenplay for the film was based on an article; one of a series on the topic of battlefield courage, written by the historian John Prebble, who peppered his subsequent script with occasional sideswipes at the savagery of colonial war. Such nods to the anti-war spirit of the nineteen-sixties, however, sit awkwardly alongside the Kipling-esque thrills of imperialist adventure that provide the film with its dramatic and emotive charge.

Zulu venerates the martial bravery and supreme self-discipline of an indigenous African people, but it also stands – for good, or for ill – as an unabashed nationalistic celebration of the Celtic warrior spirit. One of the most jarring aspects of the film is that, in spite of its title, the heroic function of the film belongs to a small contingent of redcoats who hold out against successive tides of nameless black hordes, whose voices are raised only in thunderous pre-battle chants. Circumstances are further compounded by this imperialist myth having been shot, almost entirely, on location in South Africa, and in full compliance with the apartheid laws, by a formerly blacklisted Hollywood liberal, Cy Endfield, and the Welsh socialist actor-producer, Stanley Baker.

The film is an enduring classic; expertly crafted, epic in scale, with enough attention paid to the delineation of complex characters to provide Stanley Baker and Michael Caine with career-defining roles. A supporting cast of brilliant character actors, including Jack Hawkins, Patrick Magee and Nigel Green, flesh out a gallery of memorable characters, most notably the latter creating an indelible impression as the steadfast Colour Sergeant Bourne. John Jympson's innovative editing allows Cy Endfield's assured direction of the action sequences to unfold with electric pace and all in sumptuous Super Technirama 70mm film. John Barry's memorable and superbly orchestrated score, which was inspired by recordings of Zulu music he had researched, amplifies the grandeur of the conflict and the Drakensberg Mountains where the film was shot. Both in creative and technical terms, *Zulu* is a formidable film-making achievement; yet it is this very excellence that should compel us to examine its inescapable ideological flaws.

The broad facts of the story are dramatised with reasonable historical accuracy. The film opens with the annihilation of a column of fifteen hundred British soldiers by an army of twenty-thousand Zulus at the Battle of Isandlwana. Later, that same day, a force of four-thousand Zulus is seen marching on Rorke's Drift, an army station-post manned by a meagre force of Royal Engineers and members of the twenty-fourth regiment of foot. News of the earlier disaster, and the prospect of imminent death, prompt the two commanding officers to have this sardonic exchange:

Lieutenant Chard:	The army doesn't like more than one disaster in a day.

Lieutenant Bromhead:	Looks bad in the newspapers and upsets civilians at their breakfast.

These lines suggest that rather than being dedicated to the military and ideological aims of British imperial policy; both officers are estranged from their fellow countrymen by a curious blend of cynicism and fatalism – the eternal excuse of the soldier intended to absolve him of his crimes, *I serve at her majesty's pleasure*. In a later exchange, a young private demands of his wise old NCO:

Pte. Cole:	Why is it us? Why us?
Colour Sergeant Bourne:	Because we're here, lad. Nobody else. Just us.

The realpolitik of imperial conquest is thus glossed over with the soldier's shrug: *theirs not to reason why, theirs but to do and die*. In contrast, the Zulu warrior does not even get to pose his question, never mind receive an answer. It is startling that the single utterance of a black character in the film is made by King Cetewayo, with the order of summary execution of a warrior who has man-handled the daughter of his guest, the white missionary Otto Witt. The moment attests to Cetewayo's immense power, but also to his otherness, his barbarity, his supposed lack of civilisation. Cetewayo's political aims and emotional ties to his country remain unexplored, a mystery – they are evidently unimportant to the screenwriters and film-makers. The voiceless grievances of the Zulus – who, let us not forget, have had their lands invaded by the British – loom in ominous silence over the film. No one appears interested in why they are fighting or why they have to be killed. The bravery of the Zulu is certainly acknowledged, even admired by the British (and the Boer Adendorff) but, ultimately, the presence of the Zulus serves only to contextualise the bravery of their Welsh enemy.

The silencing and over-simplification of the Zulu are given added bite by the casting of Chief Mangosuthu Buthelezi in the role of his great-grandfather King Cetewayo. Buthelezi would later lead the Inkatha Freedom Party, which became notorious for its collaboration with the Afrikaaner National Party in its fight against Nelson Mandela's ANC. Stanley Baker might not have predicted Buthelezi's future political career, but according to Baker's widow, Ellen, the Sandhurst-educated Buthelezi was 'treated very differently by the [South African] government' which should have given Baker some inkling.

The Sharpeville Massacre had taken place a week before principal photography. Ellen Baker maintains that the South African security police (BOSS) were present on set throughout the shooting of *Zulu*. Given this political context, and the strictures imposed on the producers by the apartheid regime, the casting of Buthelezi and the lack of dialogue in the film for its black characters, seems at best naïve, and at worst complicity. Perhaps the exigencies of film production contrived to dull Stanley Baker's politically liberal instincts, as James Booth, who played the iconic Private Hook, recalled twenty years later, "It is fun when you're boys playing at soldiers."

Historical epics require a little artistic licence if they are to work as dramas, and the minor historical inaccuracies in *Zulu* will not be listed here, as most of them concern changes to certain characters' backstories. Yet in one notable instance, the interpolation of an invented event, the paradoxical wrong-headedness of the film is vividly illustrated. Prior to a final charge, the Zulus begin a war-chant to summon up their bloodlust and intimidate their redoubtable enemy. Chard, played by Baker, approaches Private Owen, played by the Welsh singer Ivor Emmanuel:

Lieutenant Chard:	Do you think the Welsh can't do better than that, Owen?
Pte. Owen:	Well, they've got a very good bass section, mind, but no top tenors, that's for sure.

In the eyes of these men, the Zulus lack polyphony – they lack the complexity and sophistication of Western music. They also lack that other signifier of Western prowess, the Martini-Henry repeating rifle. For lacking both, the Zulus must die.

In the most celebrated scene of the film, the predominantly Welsh defenders of Rorke's Drift break into a spontaneous and polyphonic rendition of the Welsh anthem *Men of Harlech*. Yet there is no historical record of soldiers singing during the battle. Only fifteen per cent of the British soldiers present were actually Welsh. Indeed, over a third of them were English. The regimental song of the soldiers at Rorke's Drift was, in truth, *A Warwickshire Lad*. The question then arises as to why *Men of Harlech* features so prominently in Cy Endfield's film. A new set of lyrics for the song was written especially for *Zulu*. They are worth quoting in full:

Men of Harlech, stop your dreaming
Can't you see the spearpoints gleaming
See the warrior pennants streaming
O'er the battlefield
Men of Harlech, stand ye steady
It cannot be ever said ye

For the battle were not ready — Welshmen never yield!
From the hills rebounding
Let this war cry sounding
Summon all at Cambria's call
The mighty foe surrounding
Men of Harlech, on to glory
This will ever be your story
Keep these burning words before ye
Welshmen will not yield!

The original lyrics were written in the late eighteenth century and reportedly celebrate the heroic defence of Harlech Castle by Welsh soldiers under the command of Dafydd ap Ieuan from 1461 to 1468. Other sources claim it refers to another siege of the same castle, involving Owain Glyndwr in 1404. The important point to note here is that this song, which refers to anti-imperial resistance against the English, is sung by Welsh soldiers wearing the uniform of their colonial masters in the act of conducting imperialist aggression against people who are themselves expressing their resistance in song. In this crucial scene, Baker's Welsh chauvinism has allowed him to present the defenders of Rorke's Drift as Welshmen notionally protecting their little patch of Wales located in the middle of the Drakensberg Mountains. The station-post is no longer Zululand; it belongs to the Welsh who will defend it to the death.

Some may argue that John Jympson's expert cross-cut editing between the opposing ranks of singing soldiers in this scene, establishes some form of moral equivalence between the two forces – their respective bravery appears to evoke some form of mutual respect. Yet while this spurious equivalence credits the Zulus with immense physical courage, it ignores their moral right to their land. The film climaxes with the Zulu army departing the field, but not before saluting their fellow braves inside Rorke's Drift. No such salutation is mentioned in the historical records, and it's most likely that the Zulus made a tactical retreat after spying a British relief column on its way.

Before the credits roll, the sonorous tones of narrator Richard Burton list the recipients of the Victoria Cross who fought in the battle, before *Men of Harlech* is reprised. The final words of the song boom out 'Welshmen will not yield!' The historical reality of the aftermath of the battle was more sordid and prosaic, as the historian Ian Knight describes: '*When the battle was over, the garrison and relief column went over the field, and shot or bayoneted all the wounded Zulu they found there.*'

There is one exchange in which the cruelty of colonial aggression is acknowledged:

Lieutenant Bromhead:	...I feel ashamed. Was that how it was for you? The first time?
Lieutenant Chard:	The first time? Do you think I could stand this butcher's yard more than once?
Lieutenant Bromhead:	I didn't know.
Lieutenant Chard:	I came up here to build a bridge.

This seems to be a rather disingenuous case of trying to have your cake and eat it. Baker's Chard wants to distance himself from his role within the imperial military machine, whereas the historical Chard continued to serve for many years in the British army after receiving his Victoria Cross, as did Bromhead. *Zulu* tries to present both the British soldiers and Zulu warriors as victims of a one-off historical happenstance over which neither had much control. They appear to fight each other reluctantly, yet bravely – indeed as 'fellow braves.' The reality was genocide. *Zulu* is not an anti-war film, nor truly is it a historical epic, it is a cavalry western in the old Hollywood style, in which white men kill indigenous people in order to steal their land, and are deemed heroic for doing so.

The emotive power of *Zulu*, its ability to inspire within Welshmen – and it is predominantly men – a yearning for past military glories is largely attributable to the skilled filmmakers who made it. Yet Cy Endfield's film stands as a warning about the insidiousness of those old myths of empire and conquest. It is also proof that even those with a progressive political and social consciousness can be tempted into sacrificing their values in the pursuit of telling a 'good' story.

NEFAR IN IWROP / NEVER IN EUROPE

Siân Melangell Dafydd

I am telling a story in English. I am tired, but I am telling a story, walking down North Street, St Andrews. Who knows what story, but it's cold and my breath is visible. We are headed 'home' to halls of residence after a midnight cinema screening. My wallet falls out of my pocket as I stride. I abruptly stop the story, take a few hurried small steps to hurry back to pick it up, and then, once back between my friends and facing home again, I pick up the story where I left it. I keep telling the story. We all walk into the wind. But then I stop. My friends are slowing down, they are silent but not in the way of listening. They have, without a doubt, stopped listening but I'm not sure how that became obvious to me. I am telling the story in Welsh, now. Not English. Nobody understands me.

It only takes a break in concentration and I revert to the language in which everything else is rooted.

Bilingual people engage the same brain region that monolingual individuals use to put together words even when combining different languages, according to recent research. Their neurological patterns are the same. This allows the bilingual person to switch languages (or 'codes') freely, to juggle their languages. Yet, my experience is that intentional 'code switching' or language-switching – when I'm alert and focused – might indeed be possible. Teaching a bilingual yoga class and flipping from one language to another? No problem. But what about this deeper language experience? If I am interrupted, woken up quickly, surprised, injured; there is one dominant language of the self and only one. It is Welsh (in my case). It reminds me of my grandfather, ill in hospital at one stage, and I tried to explain to a fellow writer: 'you can't be ill in your second language'. Code-switching is far from possible then. There is only *mamiaith,* mother tongue. The true self 'escapes'. The rest is performance.

*

I am in the living room of my student accommodation, a house with a blue door and a long, long garden at the back. It has the tiniest kitchen I have ever seen (I've not yet lived in Paris!). From that tiny kitchen on the east coast of Scotland, I hear the television and I'm convinced that it's Welsh. How can it be? Something in my shoulders relax. I remember looking at the morning glories growing blues and violets outside and then leaving everything for the TV. Something was well again. I was glad. I was connected to that television and there, in front of it, I was able to listen better. It was no longer Welsh. Its music had been familial, the up and down and length of vowels, all of it from the kitchen was Welsh, but close-up, I couldn't make out the words. Somehow, the Gaelic news had come on and nobody had been in the room to switch it off. I hadn't even heard the English of the television before that. It had been noise, it was present, surely, but I wasn't aware of it being there. Only when sound became the vowel-lengths and percussion of consonants that I'd been brought up with, was it language. And yet, it wasn't a language, when I approached it. It was 'just' sound again.

*

Being Brought Up
Cael fy nwyn i fyny
We *do* say this, in Welsh, or at least some do. It has slipped into the natural expression of many. The act of bringing and the direction of upwards curiously put together in an image that pictures someone else gently bringing us (not taking, pushing) so that we reach our full height – upwards. A phrasal verb, a quirk so unique to the English language. In the short period I spent helping French individuals find their natural expression in English, phrasal verbs caused the most giggles. What has the act of turning and the direction of downwards to do with rejection? What has the act of running and the preposition 'into' to do with a chance meeting with someone? Why, oh why, do we need to use phrasal verbs when decent verbs exist that go directly to our intended meaning?

Head scratch. Laughter. *Seriously? Do I have to?*

No. But using the verbs rather than the phrasal verb might mean that your overall speech will sound more formal, somehow undetectably foreign.

Often, we are not so attuned to the oddness of the occasional English phrasal verbs in Welsh. They are used without causing the same furrowed brow as it most certainly would if a French person was to say *apporter en haut* rather than *élever.* Yet, it is no less foreign, in reality. It's just that, as a Welsh speaker, despite my dislike for the school English classes and total frustration with the word 'the' for not being spelled in what I considered logical as 'ddy', the English language is a living, daily language for us too. We are just as accustomed to the phrasal verb as an English speaker, so much so that we don't always spot them when they pop up in our own language.

Magu, on the other hand. A bolder word than *dwyn i fyny*. Better, too. To the ear, for me at least, *magu* has the *ma* of *Mam*, of *maeth* (nutrition) and *maethu* (to nourish or to foster). It is about care and parenting, not the destination. *Magu* can also be used for the nurturing or developing of things other than human, or confidence (*hyder*), or strength (*nerth*). It speaks to the true meaning of growth.

Cefais fy magu... I was raised saying 'chips' for *sglodion,* 'spinach' for *sbigoglys* and 'aubergine' for *wylys* like many others. Food names, especially, suffered from slipping into the English. Was this because in the 70s and even 80s, most recipe books accessible to us were in fact in English? This has been rectified now, with many excellent and varied cookbooks in Welsh, and here we are, using the words we actually always had. I was an adult when I first used *wylys,* having heard someone use it and then, as though teaching me a way to remember it, declared: '*Wylis, wylis, Lywelyn'!* This is sacrilege, you might say. The first words of Gerallt Lloyd Owen's iconic poem 'Fy Ngwlad' ('My Country') reduced to a joke in the swift shift from *wylit* to wylys, from 'you would weep' to 'aubergine'. But I haven't forgotten the right Welsh word for that vegetable since, and somehow, I think Gerallt Lloyd Owen might, after all, be glad of that.

Cefais fy magu, also, *not* saying 'tights' for 'tights' like everyone else around me. It wasn't until last week that I found out, the rather brilliant *clos-sanau* I had always used, can't be found in dictionaries or conversations for good reason ('trousersocks – 'clos' is a rather old-fashioned word for 'trouser' mind you). Expressing my absolute frustration that nobody seemed to use this excellent word, my father said, '*O, fi fathodd hwnnw*' ('Oh, I forged that'). It only took over forty years for me to get to the truth about that one! And so, as I always knew, deep down, each of us has our own Welsh, our own English, our own quirks and ways with whatever we consider our language(s). If anyone would like to start using *clos-sanau*, let's start! Language at its most vibrant is local. Language is made and re-made around family dinner tables, in the bar and in the margins of books.

*

In *Sidewalks*, a book of essays taking us around Mexico City by bike, Valeria Luiselli writes about a conference she attended, in which the Portuguese word, *saudade* is discussed. Someone argues that *saudade* is 'one of those untranslatable words which can only be understood by those who love, experience, pleasure and suffer in Portuguese.' Later she says it is 'homesickness, lack or longing'. These are the very same three words that people use to *try* and translate the untranslatable Welsh *hiraeth*. Then Luiselli lists the Finnish *kaihomielisyys* 'though it contains smooth, mellifluous sounds – expresses only its most desolate sense', the German *Sehnsucht*, the Icelandic *söknudur*, the Polish *tesknota*, the Czech *stesk*, the Estonian *igatsus* as possible fellows to *saudade*, all connected in meaning. So many of them! So, not untranslatable, then?

I read and stop. I scribble in the margins.

What about *hiraeth*?

I want to take issue with her for leaving out *our* untranslatable, our not-quite *saudade* from this international gathering of almosts, this conversation between those who can claim a unique national feeling and the existence of a word that captures all of its particularity. We have a feeling that others do not: we have a word for it. How did she not find us and *hiraeth*? It unnerves me that we were invisible or inaudible to her, as though a cherished author of mine should have somehow known. Nonetheless, the Welsh language wasn't part of that conversation.

I feel left out of the conversation again when I read the Bulgarian author, Georgi Gospodinov's *The Story Smuggler.* Another of my favourite authors, and I'm left out in the cold, trying to insist that I, (that we) deserve a little 'excuse me, but'...

Here, Gospodinov offers the Bulgarian word *tbra.* 'It is not *sadness,*' he writes, 'nor exactly *sorrow*, nor is it *melancholy.*' He compares it to the Turkish *hüzün* and the Portuguese *saudade,* but claims that these are 'sorrows or melancholies of empires, of former empires; their sorrow is born of what once was owned and now is lost'. I want to offer up our *hiraeth* to slot into this new consideration. I want to suggest that our word, too, might spring from our relationship to our neighbours rather than our relationship to ourselves. The sorrow of a former empire: no, we cannot claim that. We cannot saddle up to the Portuguese and Turkish words, in Gospodinov's understanding of them. Neither can we claim that *hiraeth* is a sorrow for something that has never and will never be possessed, like Gospodinov's *tbra,* when his mother longs for Paris which she never saw and never will. I find myself defining *hiraeth* by what it is not. We have not lost an empire, but we have lost something. We are always, always in danger of losing more. Is that it – what gives flight and bellyache to *hiraeth*?

Hiraeth is the moment when I see the morning glories, when the life I am living cracks to reveal what music I'm really made of. It *is* a longing for something lost, like our own childhood. It's something you learn to live with. Only those who know you very well might see a glimpse of it – those who see you in your pyjamas, before the brain has really woken up and the mouth has already said, *bore da, faint o'r gloch 'di?* (good morning, what time is it?). It is, like *tbra,* a feeling that 'doesn't topple you like a wave; her waters are placid, her poison is slow, enfeebling'. Untranslatable: maybe it is after all. Despite our need to find family and familiarity by comparing our unique words from country to country, none of them are actually comparable. It's the discussion we need. The thing is, I can't believe that I'm spending time with a word that has become irritatingly cliché. Memes are made of it. There are probably cushions out there with this word on it. But still, the discussion allows me to come home, albeit the long way round via Bulgaria and Mexico. It is Goethe who claimed that 'left to itself every literature will exhaust its vitality if it is not refreshed by the interest and contributions of a foreign one.'

In *The Bhyabachayaka and Other Wild Poems,* Sampurna Chattarji writes a poem to Hiraeth. It has to first be explained that in this book, she and fellow poet, Eurig Salisbury draw on each other's languages (Welsh and Bangla) by gifting each other words from their respective cultures and writing poetry for children, aiming to 'bring languages and their traditions to a wider audience'. What we have is a fun, 'cross-cultural smorgasbord of nonsense' to entertain, to challenge the idea of culture being territorial, to encourage play.

Hiraeth then, 'is it the lion / you just saw?'

Not morning glory flowers?

I may need to give myself permission to allow my *hiraeth* to be louder and more predatory than I'd previously imagined it.

> human as *insaaniyeth*
> real as *asliyeth*
> clear as *koifiyeth*
> that old homesickness *hiraeth*
>
> diamond-bright as tears

The italicised words in the first three lines quoted here are words in which the Welsh *hiraeth* can somehow be heard singing and are derived from Urdu. *Insaaniyeth* means 'humanity' for Hindi speakers. *Asliyeth* means 'reality', again for Hindi speakers. *Koifiyeth* means a kind of explanation, this time for Bangla speakers.

Hiraeth, maybe, is the moment of clarity when we realise that we are only human. That we cannot be everywhere in all our life's experiences with all of our loved ones and all of our joys all at once. And so, with our mere humanness, we feel *hiraeth.* We have to be here, now. *Hiraeth* tugs at that from time to time – as Sampurna Chattarji's lion with its 'maw/trimmed/jet/black' or it tugs at us like a song on a TV, but it takes us elsewhere and makes us fallible.

*

I go to the main Gallimard office, rue de L'Université, Paris, first by bike and then on foot, past the Louvre Pyramid, the tourists standing on bollards to be photographed pinching its tip, past the plastic water bottle vendors and the plastic Eiffel Tower vendors, and over Pont du Carrousel. I do this once a week on a Thursday to talk about books with an editor there. We talk in English. It is not his language nor mine, but I am there so that once a week, over lunch, he can experiment with that language and make mistakes without getting embarrassed. I usually don't eat because I can't afford it. So, he does the eating and the talking. I correct or offer expressions, especially when he seems to need a pause.

It becomes a personal joke, to spot the new pronunciation of my name by the receptionists. It is often someone different every time. I say who I am, and for whom. Then I hear the repetition – 'c'est...' and then she informs my student who is waiting for him. On the rare occasion that I find the same person in reception week after week, embarrassment sets in. Eventually I introduce myself as Madame David, which only confuses my editor-student even further. Who is Madame Davide? he asks, sharing my joke, not understanding that this time, the receptionist had mimicked me perfectly. It's just that I had given up being Welsh. In the heave from street to sleek interior as I open the giant door-within-a-door of that iconic publishing house every week, I too am translated. I don't know myself here.

During one of these lunchtimes in the 5ème arrondissement, he stumbles when wanting to express that he never, ever wants to do something. Never, what, I wonder? That's not the detail I remember. He wants to express an emphatic 'never'. I offer an expression that I think he might find humorous. As I explain, I write the expression down in my notebook to later type up in his weekly notes. I write,

Never in Europe

He repeats it in perfect English and with doubt. Was I, again, joking? What did Europe have to do with it?

I am on the way back towards the Louvre, stalling as I do every week at a building site where they are saving a beautiful façade and demolishing the entire building behind it. There, in front of two stone lions, I realise that I have made a mistake.

Nefar in Iwrop, I say to those French lions. I think I just taught him something that isn't after all English. Never in Europe. Those three English words make a Welsh expression. Half a century ago, it's possible that even to a Welsh person, the expression would have carried little meaning, but they had always been a part of my bilingual world, and since the words themselves are English, surely it is an English expression? No. I remember where they had come from: a Welsh comedy show for children, following the antics of two left-footed, ridiculous characters who went by the names of Syr Wynff and Plwmsan and rode a motorbike with side-car, recklessly.

You need to say the words like this: *nev-ar* (with a rolling 'r') and *in Ewrop* or *Iwrop* (again with a rolling 'r'). *Ewrop* is the Welsh word for Europe. I could get away with saying that the expression is one-word Welsh and two-words English, even. Still standing at the chipped lions, I wonder, like my student had said, 'Why Europe?' The European Union was formed a few decades after the television comedy. Europe, at the time of writing the expression, was a complicated place with many languages, currencies, road passes and border controls.

Still, I try to understand, what was it, other than the rolling 'rs' that allowed that idiom to roll? And then to stick? It's as though the amplitude of the 'never' we want to express is so huge, it covers the largest thing we can think of, it reaches the very periphery of our known, complicated world: Europe. It isn't 'Never on Earth would I do such-and-such'. It isn't either 'Never in this Galaxy would I do something-or-other,' but Europe. Huge, huge Europe with its lovely 'rs'.

*

We don't have proper nouns for Grandmother and Grandfather that distinguishes if they are from the paternal or maternal line in Welsh, unlike some languages like Swedish. We do, however, have a habit of naming all people by the house they were raised in or the village or town they came from. You need only turn to Caradog Prichard's *Un Nos Ola Leuad* (or its translation by Niall Griffiths, *One Moonlit Night)* to see this at play. And so, each grandmother, for example, would be named by her home, not her husband's surname, in real usage – Nain Tŷ Tan Dderwen, Nain Bryn. This, I rather like. But I have been lucky. A third grandmother appeared in my life and she went by the proper noun of Nonna Gilda. She lived close enough to Venice to never bother going there. She was the wife of a prisoner of war who spent time in Wales during and after the Second World War. Although better work was to be had here, she and her husband decided to leave Wales and return to Italy after all. She was pregnant with her second child who was christened Glenys – a Welsh name. They left because their son, Lino, wasn't speaking Italian. I understood this. I would have sought home too.

Nonna Gilda's family is, as far as I'm concerned, my family. One daughter-in-law affectionately refers to the Welsh language as that 'chi-chi-cho' language. The impossible one. If it wasn't for the love between us, I might become tired of this joke at the expense of my language.

*

My neighbour in France, who lives on the barge facing the house says,

'But Welsh is a dialect of English.'

It is not a question. It is his fact. I correct him, gently. He doesn't believe me, I can tell. He moves to another topic. Some weeks later, overhearing me speaking to my new-born baby in Welsh, he says,

'Oh, the poor thing, he has to put up with you speaking to him in English?'

I have no words, in any language whatsoever. I should, really, have let lion roar.

*

I listen to hours of the poet Andrea Zanzotto talking in Solighese. My novel, *Filò*, is partly situated in his hometown of Pieve di Soligo, northern Italy. My narrator is from that little town on the banks of the Soligo river, a place I feel a level of *hiraeth* for, as though I had lived there. This town was my first ever foreign destination as an eleven-year-old clutching a phrase book and marvelling at *grissini* bread sticks in the shops.

I listen to Zanzzotto on a loop to bring the sounds of his language to the writing of my Welsh novel, to the voice of my Solighese-infused-Welsh. I listen while I write and let it guide how I feel inside my Welsh sentencing.

Solighese could be called a dialect. When it comes to dialects everywhere, we assume that they are deviations from the standard language or form of speech. The thing is, for many in Nonna's generation at least, and those I knew of that generation in Pieve, their 'dialect' was the only natural way of communicating. It is their language. And I, with my studied-Italian peppered with unaware bits of various dialects – dinner-table dialetti from Pieve to Roncade nearer Venice and Trentino (married into Nonna's family) – still really struggle to follow any one 'dialect'. They are so distinct from each other and from Italian.

While spending time in Pieve, once in a while, someone would say, 'but our languages are the same. We are Celts too, the Solighese.' Theirs (their language) is more Leponic than Roman, some claim. And of course, it is typical of the northern Italians to identify themselves as 'other' than Roman, 'other' than the southerners. I, a Welsh woman, am kin. The Lepontians are peoples who inhabited the valleys of the Southern Alps in the first millennium B.C., making Lepontic the oldest attested Celtic language. When I briefly studied in Udine, I experienced a similar kinship with those who spoke Friulano or Furlan. Was it the struggle to survive as a minority language in Europe I connected with only, or did something of its song resonate? I come home clutching CDs and pamphlets in Furlan. All my money went on those. I remember the wine-stained white socks of a man I tried to understand. Was I too close to him, like the television in St Andrews? Did I need to stand back, listen without looking?

So, I listen to Zanzotto and I seek patterns of similarity, of a song I might mistake for my own. I hear the quip of words, the abrupt endings and vanished vowels at the end of words. *Pes*, not *pesce* as though words are being eaten. I hear more 'Sh' or 'ch' than I expect from reading. ('ch' of 'chair' not the Welsh 'ch' like *chwilen*). Is this a 'chi-chi-cho' that unites us?

'Vécio Parlar' ('Old Tongue') is ve-chio in pronunciation, not like the 'k' sound of 'cch' in the same word in Italian *Vecchio* (old). 'Io parlo in questa / lingua che passerá' he writes in 'Caso Vocativo' ('I speak this language / which will pass'). That's it, really. Not in sound or word or song but in the *hiraeth* or fierceness that drives poetry, I finally understand my need to connect to Andrea Zanzotto and to Solighese. Everywhere I have been, from India to the Dolomiti, I seek 'Vécio Parlar' and it finds me. I think this is part of what it means to be a Welsh speaker in the world. We find the other old tongues and we feel recognised by those who speak them.

*

While I listen to Zanzotto, I receive a text message from a South Walian friend who now lives on Ynys Môn (Anglesey). She is re-learning Welsh and is navigating what she remembers from the south-west, from school, what people around her now say, what Duolingo suggests and what is written in her children's books. I often get out-of-the blue questions like 'Send me *ysgwyddau*' and I send a voice recording back. Today she asks, how do I actually say 'look!' (imperative)? I send her a list, a joking face emoji, and follow it up with a phone call.

> Yli! [Bala]
> Sbia! [around you: Ynys Môn]
> Edrycha! [anywhere]
> Wele! [Biblical]
> Watcha! [Wenglish]
> Dishgwl! [South]
> There will be more... I'm sure.

*

In a foreign city I won't even name here, a gaggle of Welsh and international artists and those who represent artists for a living, all sit for dinner. The table is large but is too small. We sit on piano stools, we share chairs. Some step out to smoke and bring the evening chill back into the room on their clothes and sit back among us. We are hot and cold and chatting. There is wine.

'But of course, the Welsh language will die, one day,' someone says.

I look towards the person who has spoken. I wait for something else to come from their lips.

'But of course, it will,' they say, 'by the time of our children's children's children. Eventually.'

I know, right then, that not one of us would have dared say that if we were not abroad. Not one of us would have nodded. Each of us, in some way or another, gave our working and leisure time to work in the Welsh language, or another equally threatened language. However, being away from home is standing back, is more objectively seeing that between 1950 and 2010, 230 languages went extinct according to the UNESCO Atlas of the World's Languages in Danger. Today, a third of the world's languages have fewer than 1,000 speakers left. We might do all we like, but our descendants in generations to come would in fact, realistically, probably not speak this language, or at least they wouldn't speak this here Welsh, in the same way as us. While *in* Wales, we think of other statistics, those of the Senedd's Work Programme for Cymraeg, aiming to reach a million Welsh speakers by 2050.

I let the words slip under my shirt, I hide them right next to my skin, so near and full of warmth that I'm not sure if they keep me warm or sting. Either way, I hide them. I have carried those words ever since. This problem. This conversation should remain between the four walls of a foreign apartment, and should not, in fact, be repeated.

*

I came home to Wales for many reasons, one of them, like Nonna Gilda, so that my son would hear and speak my language.

He is telling a story in Welsh (sort of). It sounds like a songline, a land-memory-song to record the path we're taking. He sings *cerddinen* (rowan) and *eithin* (gorse) which I know he loves to start with because they rhyme, and rhyme is the best thing in the world at the moment. Then, *mieri* (brambles). We sing past the *llys heb lys* (bilberry [bushes] without bilberries) and the *nyth rhedyn* (bracken nest) – a well, made in the bracken which has become our play-den. Then he adds a new addition to the usual songline. I don't understand it, but that's ok, he will always sing it more than once. *Cerddinen, eithin, mieri, llys heb lys, nyth rhedyn...* He's pointing at the spot between gorse bushes where a family of white rabbits lived this summer. I catch his words, eventually. He's saying *cwningod yn llanastio.* He has made a new verb. This is where the 'rabbits make a mess' – *llanastio.* In language building, he has learned that a noun becomes a verb with 'io' at the end: *naid* is 'jump' and *neidio* is 'to jump', *llanast* is 'mess' so *llanastio* must be 'to make a mess'. This makes sense. We both sing of *llanastio* as we head up the hill until we pass lichen blown in the wind, mosses and owl spit. They are all strung together to make today's song.

IMAGINING EUROPE

Grug Muse

SPRING, 2021, ARFON, WALES

A man approaches us on a hillside. A gorse fire is burning on the slope below us as the emergency services battle to contain the flames. The approaching man complains about how the emergency service personnel asking him to stand further from the fire spoke to him in Welsh, that it was terribly irresponsible of them, that the time it took for them to switch to English could have cost him his life. We suggest that in a majority Welsh speaking area, it is not such an outrageous thing for a person to do, that they were not to know he was from England and did not speak Welsh; we point out that he was clearly not in imminent danger, that the time it takes to say 'Symudwch oddi wrth y tân plîs – move away from the fire please' is not so long. The man flies into a rage, rants about pilots in Cardiff airport and health and safety, shouts 'English is a universal language', screams 'fuck the Welsh, fuck the Welsh' as he charges off into the flaming night.

English is not, of course, a universal language. Nor is music, love, or maths. Very, very few things are truly universal, and the English language is certainly not close to being one of them. More common than the ability to speak English, is the experience of multilingualism. Movement between different systems of signs, symbols, and signifiers. Sol-Fah, coding languages, knitting patterns, maritime jargon, slang and emojis; the experience of moving fluidly and effortlessly between these dialects and languages is more common than the experience of speaking English, and English only.

In 2016, when Wales, like England voted to exit the European Union, my grief was not over losing out on Regional Development Funds, or laws protecting environmental standards, or access to the single market, but on losing out on the right to be part of a community where multilingualism was a norm.

Five out of twenty two Welsh voting areas voted to stay in the European Union in 2016. Three of these – Gwynedd, Ceredigion and Cardiff – are some of the areas with the most linguistic diversity in the country.

*

PRAGUE, 2013

I arrive in Brno late at night, and somehow find a taxi to take me to the student halls on the other side of town. The security guard examines my paperwork, matches my name to a name on a list and hands me the keys to my room, a twin bedroom with a small kitchenette that I am going to be sharing with a German student who arrives tomorrow.

As I lie on my bed, the last of the adrenaline and nervous energy that has allowed me to keep my nerve on my trip from Gwynedd to London to Prague to Brno dissipates. Fear and fatigue hits like a ton of bricks and I cry myself to sleep. I am in Brno, a small city in the Southeast of the Czech Republic to take an intensive Czech course, before beginning my Erasmus placement in Prague in October.

On our first day, we are split – the Slavic students are sent to a separate class, since they are likely to have some advantage with grasping the language. The rest of us are beginning from scratch. The class includes maybe half a dozen French students, half a dozen Spanish, three Hungarians, a guy from Finland, two guys from Turkey and a couple of Germans. I am the only one from the UK and, it turns out, the first British citizen to take the course in 4 or 5 years, despite Britain sending its fair share of students to the Czech Republic. I become a kind of curiosity. Until they learn that I am not British but Welsh, and that my first language is not English. That, apparently, explains things.

A few weeks later, newly equipped with my clumsy Czech, I arrive at Prague, and the student halls in Hostivař, old student dorms at the outskirts of the city, where the international students are kept. My roommate is a Catalan medical student. Every week we meet at our friend's apartment in Anděl, where we all take turns preparing a shared dinner. 'We' are from Montenegro, Bosnia, Germany, France, Hungary, and Spain. The major religions represented are Catholicism and Islam. At least nine languages are spoken between us. I try to make lobsgows but can't find stewing cuts of the necessary red meat. I try to make a roast chicken, somehow turn the roast vegetables into a sort of vegetable soup. It's strange and delicious. I make Welshcakes, use a wine bottle as a rolling pin. I am trying to fit my identity, my culture on a dinner plate. I want it to be delicious, I want them to like it.

*

The Erasmus programme was approved by the European commission in 1987, named after Desiderius Erasmus Roterodamus (1466-1536). Erasmus was a Dutch philosopher and theologian, and a prominent intellectual of the European Renaissance, who engaged with a pan-European community of thinkers. He spoke many languages, worked at many universities: an ideal model for the EU's academic mobility scheme. By 2020, an estimated 10 million students would have participated in the scheme, and one of its key architects was Dr Hywel Ceri Jones, a Welshman who served as the EU Commission's Director for Education, Training and Youth during the founding of the project. The purpose was yes, to enrich academic experiences through exchange and travel, but also to build a European citizenry through cultural exchange.

In a much-quoted article on European identity, Umberto Ecco describes Erasmus as a method of creating a European identity through sex:

'Erasmus has created the first generation of young Europeans. I call it a sexual revolution: a young Catalan man meets a Flemish girl – they fall in love, they get married and they become European, as do their children.'

The comment was made in 2012, one year before I left for Prague on the scheme. What struck me about this idealised vision of a new European demos was the way Ecco identified the young Europeans; Catalan and Flemish, rather than Spanish and Belgian. Members of Europe's stateless nations, speakers of minoritised languages.

For me, a white, middle-class, Catholic Welsh speaker, it was an experience of a new type of belonging that I had never experienced before. For the first time I experienced Catholicism as a majoritarian rather than minoritised experience, cultural references that had never been shared outside of my family suddenly common references shared with people from all over Europe.

And linguistically, suddenly, after a year studying in England,

I was not the one person in the room with the difficult accent and bad English. We all had beautiful, bad English, and we were equally foreign in the language. We all had mother-languages that we would be more comfortable and eloquent in. There was an equality to it. A space of constant slippage and spillage, where conversations moved between languages depending on who is speaking, who is listening, who is drunk, who is homesick.

Monolingual English speakers seemed to feel ill at ease in these situations, as a rule. The mostly white American and English students formed their own cliques, had their own parallel social circles.

A key part of the multilingual experience is the experience of being misunderstood; of not being able to express yourself as you would wish; of the breakdown of understanding; of not speaking the language at all, of zoning out as the conversation moves between English, French, Spanish, Serbo-Croat. It is, if not being at ease, being used to not understanding. It's knowing that perfect understanding in translation is not achievable, and not stressing about it. Our monolingual fellow students seemed less at ease in these situations. Monolingualism seems to breed a specific sort of main character syndrome: a sort of expectation or assumption that whenever another language is being spoken in their presence, it must either be about them, or to intentionally exclude them. It does not naturally occur to monolinguals that there may be many different storylines being acted out at once, and that not everyone has to have a speaking part all the time.

And like those girls who 'aren't like other girls', I was more than happy to be counted as 'not like the other Brits', but as a European, i.e. chill about other languages. As M. Wynn Thomas describes the phenomenon of 'Euro-Welshness':'To be a Welsh

European is, among other things, an effective means of not being English' (t.8). That is, an easy way to reject negative associations or traits of the British and Britishness, without needing to reflect on Welsh complicity. The Erasmus student hostel was then a place where I could invent my own Welshness, where multilingualism (between European languages at least) was normalised, and where Britishness could be shed easily and without question.

*

'Wastod yn mynd i Lydaw
byth yn mynd i Ffrainc,
wastod yn mynd i Wlad y Basg
byth yn mynd i Sbaen'

['Always visit Brittany,
never going to France,
always visit the Basque Country
never going to Spain']

Dave Datblygu's words in the song 'Cân i Gymru' capture a cliché of Welsh attitudes towards the continent. It represents a worldview that places Wales firmly in Europe, as part of a community of minoritised linguistic groups, and sub-state nations: Brittany, Galicia, the Basque Country, Catalunya. It is a worldview that seeks to construct a 'Europe of the regions' through sheer force of will: it is the Europe I recognised in Umberto Ecco's words. It is the ideal of a Europe that respects the autonomy of small cultures and nations, respects linguistic diversity, celebrates the small (small being a relative term: while Latgalian speakers in Latvia number around 164,000, Catalan has closer to 10 million; both are minoritised in their national contexts).

In a recent book, *Eutopia*, M. Wynn Thomas examines different ways Europe, and Euro-Welshness has been expressed and imagined, between 1850 and the 1980's. It describes the many pro-Europe attitudes that emerged in Wales from the home-rule nonconformists of the 1800's, that saw potential models of autonomy in European leaders such as Mazzini of Italy and Kossuth of Hungary; to the small-nation solidarity of the first world war, which fostered solidarity between Wales and countries like Belgium and Serbia. From there, the mid-twentieth century visions of Wales as the inheritor of European culture by Catholics such as Saunders Lewis, or as a space of liberation and expression for female writers and artists. These stances towards Europe, shaped by their times and political contexts, seek to identify Wales with Europe in different ways. Many are explicitly interested in the question of what Europe can offer Wales in terms of self determination. But they are also fringe movements, dialogues held between comparatively small groups of intellectuals and thinkers at different times. They represent passionately held views, but views that never spread beyond a small core. As Thomas himself puts it:'[Euro-Welshness] has remained a fringe movement, the preserve of middle-class academics, writers and intellectuals, many of whom have been working in the Welsh language' (t.6).

Raymond Garlick published *A Sense of Europe* in 1968, the year before Charles De Gaulle's resignation from the French presidency would allow the UK's attempts to gain membership of the European Economic Community to succeed, as they did in 1972. A pan-European republican, Garlick's European poems lay out an argument that Wales is culturally integrated with Europe – Northern and Western Europe, mostly. In the poem

'Capitals', Garlick slips Cardiff into a list of the great European cities, before closing with a recap of Welsh interaction with the continent:

Europe:
young ap Iwan's yard,
Gruffydd Robert's vision's scope,
Morgan Llwyd's hoist petard:
source to which our ballads grope –
context, compass – card
and hope.
(1968, t.66)

Referencing writers, scholars and religious figures, the poem places Europe in the imagination of the intellectuals, if not an ivory tower, an ivory continent, associated with high literature and culture. In referencing the past, Garlick is trying to summon a possible future where Wales is not simply integrated politically and economically, through the ECC, but embedded culturally. Like the class of thinkers he references, and the wider landscape of hopeful Welsh Europhiles, it is a future imagined by a middle class, for a middle class. Similarly, I wonder if the Erasmus scheme, which offered most of its opportunities for cultural exchange to those in university education, ultimately achieved the same effect: creating a middle-class, pan-European identity that failed to extend beyond a certain privileged class?

In one of few accounts of Euro-Welshness to take a conscious class stance, Cyril P. Cule writes of his experiences in Spain on the brink of the civil War. He draws comparisons not between Welsh and European scholars, but between the coal fields of the Rhondda and Asturias. As Thomas writes in *Eutopia*: 'Cule always positioned himself as a Welsh-speaking product of the south Wales Valleys who felt a natural solidarity with the Welsh proletariat and viewed contemporary Europe through the eyes of their experience' (Thomas, t.159).

Some 200 Welsh volunteers joined the international Brigade to fight the fascists in Spain, mobilised mostly by the South Wales Miners' Federation and the Communist Party. And so there have been working class iterations of European solidarity, however they have been fewer, and such class-solidarity was not put forward as an imagined future in the Brexit Remain campaign.

*

The EU has never been a Europe of the Regions, for many reasons. The EU remains the organ of the states and their governments, none of whom see it in their interest to empower regions at the expense of their states. The Committee of the Regions remains a toothless talking shop and regional representation remains ad hock in Councils. Separatist movements in Scotland and Catalunya are met with nervousness and hostility by the European Council.

In summing up the extent to which the political dreams of Euro-Welsh idealists were realised, Thomas concludes that the European Union did not become the organ that was hoped for: 'As far as its political structure was concerned, it became a bulwark of the established order of nation states, led, as ever, by the most powerful. While 'regionalism' was certainly recognised, and catered for, this Europe had no sympathy with any genuinely advanced empowerment of minority peoples, let alone with a deliberate shift towards a politico-cultural pluralism much greater than ever before' (Thomas; t.17-18).

Given that many Welsh intellectuals saw Europe as a space

where the threat of Anglo-centrism to the distinctiveness of Wales – its language, politics and culture – could be withstood, the European Union was ultimately not the organ with which to realise this ambition. Instead, the EU became synonymous with European-ness more generally: institution became identity.

*

MÜNCHEN, 2014

It is winter, and I am travelling from München to Prague. The train is an old one, each carriage made up of small compartments, with seats facing each other. The train is quiet, and there is only one other person in my compartment, an older man with a walking stick. We pass through the dark forest, thick trees for miles and miles, the forest floor covered in bright red leaves.

I am half asleep when the train stops at a small border village. Police enter the train, moving from compartment to compartment to check documents. They look briefly at mine, and that of my fellow passenger, before moving to the next compartment. This time, there is more noise. Low talking, then voices raised, weak protestation. Through the frosted window of the compartment, we watch as a young man is escorted out of the compartment. They come into view, two policemen in dark uniform arguing with a young man with brown skin and a white t-shirt. They are instructing him in broken English, he is weakly protesting in equally bad English. He is about my age, with a small rucksack and no coat. They tell him he cannot cross the border; his visa is about to run out, he points to the document, he still has time. The exchange is brief, and they quickly disappear off the train.

As the train begins to move again, on towards Prague, the man begins to talk to me. 'Ich spreche kein deutsch' I say politely, but he either hears, or ignores me. He is gesturing angrily at his documentation and is getting angrier and angrier as he speaks. I pick up some words, the name of the German parliament, possibly something about the European Union. But I cannot understand what he is saying, I just listen, making sympathetic noises every now and then. Finally, he runs out of steam, looks at me, frustrated by my silence.

*

Although plenty of Welsh Europhiles indulged their passions from home libraries or studies, much of the 'Euro-Welsh' identity was constructed by Welsh travellers to Europe. From Emrys ap Iwan, Ned Thomas, the Davies sisters of Gregynog to Cyril P. Cule, many spent time on the continent. Some, like O M Edwards captured those experiences in print, in books such as *Tro yn Llydaw* [A while in Brittany] (circa 1888) and *O'r Bala i Geneva* [From Bala to Geneva] (1886), and constructs relationships between Welshness and Celtic or Protestant Europe.

Another writer who uses travel in relation to identity is Johny Pitts in his book *Afropean* (2019). Pitts spends six months back-packing through Europe, to Paris, Brussels, Amsterdam, Berlin, Stockholm, Moscow, Marseille, Madrid and Lisbon, searching for what he terms 'Afropea'. A term to connect Afro-Europeans, or black Europe, aspirational but reflective:

'Afropean' as aspiration was one thing, but as I was writing about an interplay between black and European cultures, I realised this utopian vision of a black European experience would mean wilfully ignoring the realities shared by a majority of black people living in Europe. It would mean making the numerous groups of unemployed black men I saw at train stations, or the African women cleaning toilets, or the disenfranchised communities struggling in the hinterland of cities, completely invisible (2019, t.4).

Pitts's Afropea is frequently celebratory and joyous, but also necessarily dark and brutal. From the dire situation of black students in Russia, to the Tervuren museum that holds the gruesome archive of Belgium's brutal colonial legacy in the Congo. In the Netherlands, Pitts observes the white amnesia surrounding the figure of Zwarte Piet, a racist caricature that is part of the Netherlands' Christmas celebration. The denial of its racism is, in Pitts words, connected to what Gloria Wekker defines as 'White Innocence', and associated ideas about the Netherlands' identity and self-image:

This is a self-image woven around the Netherlands' status as a victim of German occupation during the Second World War, which embraces innocence and defends its innocence so vehemently that when struggling black communities, who, in the case of the Surinamese community, are physical evidence and an uncomfortable reminder of the history of Dutch slavery, are seen and heard, they must be silenced (2019, t.160).

This is the same Netherlands that features prominently in the work of Raymond Garlick, who lived for many years in the country, teaching at Eerde Castle school. In M. Wynn Thomas' words, the Netherlands for Garlick represented a 'physical palimpsest of European history' (2021, t.317). While for Garlick, this seems to have meant Louis XIV, land reclaimed from the sea through human industry, and the Nazi occupation (t.317-319). The mirror image however, of what Garlick and many others recognised and identified with is the darker context that is the blind spot, or the missing piece of the puzzle, so easy to leave out since it all happened so far away; the history of the colonialism and exploitation that funded and built so much of what is widely admired in Europe.

The concept of 'White innocence' is as relevant to Wales as the Netherlands, and is maybe what ties Wales to Europe as strongly as any historic cultural tie, or aspiration to nationhood.

In her book, *White Innocence: Paradoxes of Colonialism and Race* (2016) Wekker examines certain myths around Dutch national identity, challenging the Dutch exceptionalism and its self-identity as 'gentle' and 'ethical' by exposing the underlying paradox: coexistence of racism and colonialism, with the myth of exceptionalism based on the perceived victim status of the Netherlands following the Second World War.

It brings to mind the polarised debate on the legacy of Welsh Patagonia, and the widely celebrated 'Welsh colonial exceptionalism', that is based on an exaggeration of Welsh victimhood vis-à-vis the British state in 19th century Wales. While the acts of Welsh settler colonists are not comparable to the violence of European state-led empires and their colonial wars, an insistence on the innocence of the Welsh enacts a contemporary violence on the survivors of the colonisation of Patagonia. When we centre the early 'friendship' between the Welsh settler and the indigenous population in 1860 as a central and timeless narrative, we necessarily silence the indigenous voices today who paint 'Petü Mogeleiñ' ['we are still alive' in Mapudungun] on Welsh monuments to the Mimosa. We confound the celebration of Welsh-Patagonian culture with the celebration of Welsh colonisation; in Wales, we celebrate the Mimosa but do not commemorate and celebrate the indigenous people whose land the Welsh settlers benefitted from its occupation.

*

To be multilingual is to hold many realities in our heads at once.

I want to be able to mourn our loss of EU citizenship and the dream it represented for many Welsh-speakers of the normalisation of a multilingual identity, while recognising the white supremacy and capitalist forces that dominate the institution. Not to reconcile them, which means 'to make consistent', but to hold both as they are.

For Wales, we must see our Europeanness as not simply a generative space where we can imagine a better future, but a space already inscribed by the forces of racism and capitalism that Wales played its part in inscribing. In can be a space for imagining realities beyond those of the British state and the binary of England-and-Wales, while also reflecting critically on the realities of a shared European history of colonialism and violence.

References

Cule, Cyril P. (1941) *Cymro ar Grwydr* Llandysul: Gwasg Gomer.

Eco, Umberto (2012) 'It's culture, not war, that cements European identity' in *The Guardian:* https://www.theguardian.com/world/2012/jan/26/umberto-eco-culture-war-europa

Garlick, Raymond. (1968). *A Sense of Europe.* Llandysul: Gwasg Gomer.

Pitts, Johny. (2019). *Afropean.* London: Penguin Books.

Thomas, M. Wynn. (2021). *Eutopia: Studies in Cultural Euro-Welshness, 1850-1980.* Caerdydd: Gwasg Prifysgol Cymru.

Wekker, Gloria. (2016) *White Innocence: Paradoxes of Colonialism and Race.* North Carolina: Duke University Press.

WANTED: WELSH TRAVEL WRITERS

Horatio Clare

Wanted: New Welsh* Travel Writers
Qualifications: None (*applicants do not have to be 'Welsh'.)
Essential: Joy, Humility, Curiosity, Pen
Desirable: Courage, Reading, Paper
Salary: Variable
Start date: Vague

In haphazard fashion Wales turned me into a traveller and a travel writer. Does anything meaningful ever happen in a straight line? I am still proud of my first piece, though it was never commissioned and never published. It was never even sent out for rejection. But everything changed, that hot evening, when it found me. I believe that books and pieces find people to commission and write them. Art finds makers.

I was a year out of university, not exactly trumpeting my low 2:1 in rizlas and roaches, going further into debt doing unpaid and bashful work experience at *The Western Mail*. The best thing was sitting opposite the Chief Reporter, Andrew Buncombe, who was destined to leave Cardiff for *The Independent* and become a foreign correspondent.

Andy picked up his phone and said things like, 'And how *is* the finest police officer in South Wales?'

And then, 'Well the thing is, what they're saying doesn't

really make *sense* to me. Can we just go over it again? Off the record? No, no, no, no – I mean *really* off the record?'

The distant editor and terrifying news editor, cursing him affectionately, would hold the front page. At the last moment, Andy would deliver.

Reporting, I observed, was all about delivering, even if that meant hanging the disintegrating spine of a long-dead sheep on a fence, with a headline asking, *Slain by the Beast of Borth*?

'Clearly not,' is clearly not the point of news.

I found Andy's doings bewitching. He spoke to the powerful of Cardiff as though he were a rogue young version of them. You could tell they were fond of him. Eavesdropping conscientiously, I learned he did something called Boxercise with some of them. I just knew that no one of civic significance would ever consider Boxercise with me.

And if the mere thought of Boxercise made me feel giggly and truant, perhaps I was not made to be a reporter? I was mulling this, dithering around Cardiff Bay, when my life was transformed (though I did not know it for years). I came across a circular sculpture marking something, and a plaque. The Taff Trail, it said, began in Brecon and came south across the mountains and down the valleys via Cefn-coed-y-cymmer, Merthyr and Pontypridd.

I re-read it and found I was grinning.

'*Who in their right mind..!*' I exclaimed.

This was the end of the last century, you see. No one had heard of Wellness. You couldn't pay more than a couple of hundred quid for a hotel room in Wales then, even if you had the cash. Depression, anxiety and mental health did not exist – at least the words for them did not. No one had a mobile phone and none of the papers I work-experienced on that year had the internet, though we'd all had it at uni, in 'computer rooms'.

Like therapy, exercise for the sake of feeling good was for Americans and eccentrics. It was a simple world, and it tickled me that persons unknown had thought to furnish it with a long-distance trail through Merthyr and Ponty.

A week or so later Tony Blair had become Prime Minister, the world was going to be a better, safer, fairer, joyful and united place, my work experience was up and I was waving goodbye to my mother as she dropped me off on the Taff Trail.

Hindsightfully, my decision to skip the first part of the path, from Brecon along the canal to Talybont, seems a mistake. But I was hungry to see the worlds I didn't know – the other side of the Beacons – and not interested in trogging along the valley from Brecon, so I gaily cut out one of the most important sections of any journey and any story of journeys: the start.

Turns out, there was a good lesson there. If you are not being paid – not being paid *yet*, hopefully – and you do not have a commission, you have no one to answer to but the page, and responsibility only to your pleasure. To win that kind of freedom when you are under commission and writing for an editor you have to go right to the other end of the scale. You have to be A.A. Gill or Jan Morris. Both wrote with exactly that sense of joyful and fearless liberty most of us reserve for writing to entertain ourselves. I think it was their secret. If you would write, steal it.

Past the Talybont waterfalls I went, up and over the Blaen y Glyn pass across the Beacons. In the woods was orienteering, outward-bound Wales, young people milling about in orange hard hats. I liked it. I liked the instructors and teachers, and the shouts, and the minibuses. At the top, I liked the coach with grey heads in all the windows, and the peering expressions on the faces, and the little railway. Over and down I went, in sun, through pink featherings of rosebay willow herb. I was having a fine time! The swing of the world under your feet. The way the eye sharpens to new views. In Cefn-coed the kids hung around opposite the shop, blasting the Spice Girls on a stereo, telling the dusty road and the valley that what they really wanted was a zig-a-zig-aaa... The mountains I had crossed were watersheds between different universes. Here was a car culture, roaring pimped things like Star Wars ships; here were bars where men like me were muppets and the look you really wanted was two-tellies. There was the Castle Hotel, Merthyr Tydfil, where they shot down the protestors during the Merthyr Rising in 1831. Here they first raised the flag of Revolution Red! Here *we* first raised it. I knew in those days that I was from a valley and a hill that happened to be in Wales. It took many years and a lot more writing and travelling to discover this made me Welsh.

The Castle was shut or full. I stayed in a B and B around the corner. I love those places, now that I can sometimes stay in better – you know, where there really are China dogs and mad net curtains doing lace tribute acts and set fried eggs like happy farts and the sausages and tinned toms take turns to flob on you. At breakfast there were some men from Birmingham working in construction, and other travellers from Wales. The TV was on, Sky, never a good choice – in BBC news they call Sky 'Never wrong for long!' This morning Sky had a report based on a survey commissioned by a company recruiting people for call centres. (I know! They were still here, then.) Even as a fledgling journalist I knew that such surveys tend to be unreliable, created by the PRs promoting the company. In fact, a PR turned journalist told me, later, they simply and entirely make them up. This one had made up this statement, which Sky now broadcast to us – as we worked away at our farts and flobs – authoritatively, as 'news'.

'Geordie accents are the most trustworthy, according to a

survey by (who-the-fuck-ever), with Scottish voices coming a close second. The survey also found that the least trustworthy accents in Britain are Brummie, and Welsh.'

There were small flickers in our gazes as the Brummies and the Welsh in that plucky little dining room surveyed each other. I'd love to recall the rich West Midlands voice answering Sky with a 'Well fok yow!' and a phlegmatic Welsh accompaniment – 'Cheers, butt.'

No one said a thing. It was too early. It felt like something, at the time: something comic, absurd, something rather melancholy; those men, away from home, being mocked, not for the first time – it felt like something you would write down, which I did.

But if you look at what happened then, with Tony and Gordon coming to power, and Tony taking us to war, and Gordon's own fatal misadventure in Rochdale where a Sky news mic (what else?) caught him, in his trustworthy Scottish tones, calling that honest Mrs Duffy (who only wanted to know where all the Eastern European immigrants were coming from, a straight question crying out for a pithy answer) 'some bigoted woman', and if you look at the long sad fall of the socially-minded left, who never could quite eat breakfast with unprivileged people like unprivileged people (remember Ed Miliband and his bacon butty?), who never could quite convince accented regional society that they – that *we* – trusted them, or that we could be trusted, if you look at all that followed from that, from Iraq to Austerity to Brexit and Boris, Boris with his 'Your deference, your duty and your daughter are mine by divine right' sort of accent, well, you can see what it is that I love about travel writing. Right there, over the Nescafe and builders' tea, *I saw the whole thing*. I saw a good thirty years of the future!

Below the B and B, on the banks of the Taff, in a great patch of builders' mud where the Brummies and their mates were making Merthyr Tydfil College, there was nothing but an army recruiting trailer. Only looking back on it now, writing this, does the sudden sick feeling come. Blair had just got in... I hope one or two of those young men at breakfast trained as lorry drivers. I hope none of them signed up, much as I like and admire soldiers. I hope it's them I've just read about, being hunted in greasy spoons by supermarket reps desperate to offer drivers 70k and a two grand signing bonus, now that the Brexit they voted for, mainly to stick it to the Man, turns out to be the Man sticking it to them, again.

Because I was telling myself I was writing a travel piece about this foreign land, my country, I happily wrote it all down and strolled on, on to the turrets and follies and tombs of the industrial moguls, to the coal kings and the iron barons and Robert Crawshay under his slab, which orders, rather than asks: 'God Forgive Me.' It seemed dire then, but time has shown it a far more honest and self-aware parting shot than anything the gangmasters of our zero hours universe will manage, one suspects. Their last thoughts and words will all be tax related.

There, now, that's the Valleys talking. Except it isn't. The Valleys said one of the loveliest things. Like the lady I asked, near Aberfan – 'Are you from here, then?'

'Oh no!' she said, 'I'm from over there!' And she pointed, I swear this is all true, a little way up the road.

I paid my hopeless homage to the place. I remember the stones and the silence. I remember the way my parents told it, the way they said the word. It wasn't like any other word. Nothing else they told me about, in all my childhood, had the sound of that. It seemed to tear right through them just to say it. Aberfan.

Now we know it was one of those hells, like Zeebrugge, like

Chernobyl, like Grenfell, that greed and incompetence and lies unleash on a people, on an era. Their memorials march through time, indicting the same ills. The question they ask is not how did this happen – we know exactly how they happen – but what will you do to stop us? Part of the answer, at least, comes from reading their plaques, and writing them down, and trying to ensure their testimonies will never be lost or forgotten.

I plugged on, thinking about Lloyd George and Aneurin Bevan, about Michael Foot, about leaders who could stand in a town square and speak frankly to the needs of hundreds, thousands, millions, without notes, without spin doctors, without fear or evasion.

Eventually I came to Pontypridd, to the Morning Star Inn. It was the end of the day. This pub offered bed and breakfast. They were amused and they were very welcoming. We had pints. They asked what I was doing. I told them. They were more amused. That evening, in a room that slanted with a wardrobe that leaned and a window that sort of opened, I wrote the first words of what became, ten years later, my first book. I was no Proust, but the same thing seemed to happen to me in the Morning Star that happened to him with his tea cake. The taste of it summoned his entire childhood, and he knew instantly that he could write it. I looked out on a green Welsh evening coming in, and saw and felt suddenly that I could write down mine.

I followed the Taff the next day, through a valley which became a huge cemetery, which became roads, with woods and fields, which became eventually Cardiff and Sophia Gardens and the city. All the way down to the Bay I followed the river, to the sculpture at the end of the trail. My feet were sore and blistered and I felt knackered and fantastic. I would go on to work experience on other newspapers in other towns, and eventually to the BBC, and even on to doing the newspaper reviews on Sky News (they sacked me off when I proposed that evidence in a piece in the FT about Dick Cheney and torture put us and our allies in the War on Terror in the same camp as the Nazis). But inside me something had shifted.

When I teach writing now, I say it is 90 percent will, and that's true. But the lovely thing about travel is that really, it's 100 percent, all and only will. There are plenty of travel writers who have no special arty gift or care for a sentence, or an image. But they pack a bag, and go out into the world, and that is all it really takes, along with a pen and a willingness to use it. Reading, rhythm, something to say and somewhere to say it about: this is all the specialist knowledge and equipment you need.

Being odd, being off to one side, perhaps feeling you do not wholly belong to your own or any tribe and coming from Wales is a great blessing for a travel writer. You are at home when you are not at home. You are harder to pin down when they ask you where you come from. Say London or Manchester and people nod in recognition even if they have never been there. But say Wales. Say it in the French-speaking world, 'Pays de Galles!' and people will pause and look at you again. Pays de Galles? Portugal? Where?

That's all you need. There's the gap, right there. That second of consideration, or reconsideration, in there is where it all changes. Now you can have an exchange. Sometimes I draw a map. Sometimes I say, 'It's all mountains and sheep and rugby and rain!' and people laugh. From the Andes to Algiers, people laugh. In Morocco I say, 'We are the Berbers of Britain!' and Berbers, the Azamigh people, are delighted by the unexpected alliance. When you walk into places where they hate you the second you open your mouth – like the rugby bar in Tsumeb, Namibia, Jesus – for being a Brit, for being a Pom, for being

'Fucking English' you can say, quite challengingly, if the situation warrants, 'Oh, you don't like them, the English? You've got history with them, have you? And how far does that go back? Because they conquered Wales in 1283 (you ignorant git).'

It's all crap of course, historical nationalism, racism, prejudice, imperialism, colonialism, evil crap, and the real point of travel writing is to attack and destroy the powers of evil crap. You are not just trying to bring back some of the particular, idiosyncratic human truths which make us all from the same place, of the same family, one people. You are also – you, if you are anything like me, whom no civil service would ever appoint a diplomat (I applied to a Foreign Office Open Day, when I was a student, and did not even make that grade) – are an ambassador. An ambassador of eccentricity, of gossip and dancing and questions. One of my students at Manchester, a superb young man who goes dancing as a blonde femme bimbo, as it happens, who has terrific talent for describing people and place and who took to being taught by a straight white cis middle class git like me with great generosity, asked, 'But isn't travel writing just going around the world othering people?'

It was my favourite question of the year. I think travel writing is more like going around the world – which is also the next town, or the suburb you've never explored of the one you live in – othering yourself and everyone democratically, delightedly. We are all other, aren't we? Don't we find our respect for each other, our understanding of *each other* like that? I think that is more or less where I start.

Travel writers tend to be comfortably self-othering. Just look at the ambassadors Britain has writing for us now: Kapka Kassabova was born and raised in Bulgaria. Michelle Jana Chan was born in London and feels 'half Guyanese, half Czech'. Sophy Roberts, who grew up in Scotland, seems most at home in

Siberia, western Tanzania, anywhere far from Dorset. These are among our stars, and the new generation is rising: read Nathan Munday's *Seven Days: A Pyrenean Adventure.* We found ourselves in a pub in Porthmadog once. We talked about dancing and writing; just being there with him, listening to him and chatting, was as pure an experience of travel writing as were three of those days on the top of that bloody beer truck in the Congo. (It is not really about where you go so much as how you go, and who you meet there.) These people stand in a line which goes through Jan Morris and A.A. Gill and Michael Jacobs, through Norman Lewis, Bruce Chatwin and Freya Stark, through Gertrude Bell and Rebecca West all the way back to the person who sat down each night with a pen and paper and recorded what he saw that day on the *Golden Hind*, as Sir Francis Drake sailed it around the world.

If I could have one wish for the future of our trade, it would be this. Somewhere in a corner of Wales today, in some small town in the rain, someone reads this piece and looks out of the window. Or perhaps they think about their daughter or son or niece or a student or a friend, and sends it to them. That person reads it, and looks out of the window, at the low mulling brows of the near hills, and perceiving that that road there, winding up into mist, also winds down on the other side to the sea or a station on an airport, and from there to Newport, to Marseille, to Tangier, to Istanbul, Cape Town, Novosibirsk, hears and accepts its call.

All I need is my passport, a notebook and a pen, this person thinks, *you* think, and maybe not today, maybe not tomorrow, but before too long you take that road. You commission yourself to find out what these places are like, and who lives there, and what breakfast and work and love there are like, and then you write it down.

If you are reading this, wondering if you are that person, allow me one last pitch. Although many of the greats are not and were not men, white and lucky, a lot of the travel sections in the bookshops are by us. I worked with Barbara Keys this summer, a professor of American history. She is writing the first biography of Kissinger by a woman, and it is going to be massive if I am any judge, which I am (knowing great writing when I read it is the one skill I can prove I possess). Anyway, we were beavering thrillingly away when I had the strangest flash of understanding: one of those fabulous flashes when you realise you must have been an idiot not to have known it all along. The old world, the old normal, was mostly made and written by lucky white men with certain accents, men of a certain kind. If you are not one of these, then now, *right now*, you get to make it and write it all new. So, how's that for a job opportunity? Does that sound worth doing or what? What do you say? Look! The road is just there, calling you. Take it, I beg you. Take it now.

THE MORTAR OF WISHFUL THINKING

Liz Hyder

I'm an imposter.

There, I've said it. I was not born in Wales, nor do I live or work there now. I have no claim, no right to be in this anthology. And yet... just over the border in South Shropshire where I've lived for a decade and more, Wales calls to me, whispering in the woods, blowing in the winds from the west over the valleys and hills until it rattles my windows at night. For you see, like the Snow Queen's splinter, a piece of Wales lives in my heart. It always has done, ever since I was a child when I first fell in love with it. With its stories. With its landscapes. With its beautiful language. With its mysteries and histories that hide in plain sight...

I can't remember now exactly how old I was when we first set off for North Wales from our home in North-East London, the car boot of my dad's old orange Honda packed with homemade cakes, spare dungarees, anoraks, and wellies. But I remember us arriving. I remember the cemetery set high up on the left of the little leafy lane, looking down upon us newly arrived holidaymakers. I remember the seven gates we passed as we turned off right, making our way down a seemingly endless track with its succession of seemingly endless gates, each one first opened by our little hands before being locked safely behind us. I remember the cromlech, the ancient stone burial tomb that looked as if it had been made by giants, that we passed on our way to the imposing grey stone house we were to stay in. I don't remember ever having seen one before. Thousands of years old, my mum said. Thousands...

The house smelled of damp and stories, rising from the landscape as if it had erupted out of the ground somehow, gathering stones and holding them together with the mortar of wishful thinking. The taps in the kitchen creaked when you turned them, running brackish brown water until it became clear. There was a list of emergency numbers for all the things that could go wrong. Electricity, gas, water, hospital, doctors. And yet I don't recall the house having a landline and this was long before the days of mobile phones. The twin bedroom I shared with my brother upstairs had metal bedsteads with mattresses so old they swallowed you, the sides rising up as if you were sinking into well-kneaded dough. And there was a mystery too. A door in what should have led to a back room, but instead opened into a strange cavernous space, a huge empty whitewashed hall with a fireplace big enough to stand up in. It was unused, and no wonder! None of us liked it in there. It felt chilly in more ways than one. So, the door stayed firmly shut except for the odd dare to go in and stand in the fireplace, warm hand on cold stone.

There was even a pony in the field opposite, a real velvety chestnut one. The stuff of my girlish dreams – until you smelled his horrible breath. We nicknamed him Reeky. We ran whooping through fields of gorse, my brother and sister and I, clambered over stone walls in places I am sure we had no right to be. We were explorers, we were wild. The fields and lanes belonged to us. The sea on the horizon belonged to us. And all the while, the cromlech just out of sight but never out of mind. Ancient land, ancient stories. If you held your tongue out, you could almost taste them.

But the best was yet to come. A dark night, after tea (for supper surely only existed in the pages of books where people toasted muffins on fires with long forks), we sat in the sitting room, an atmospheric place with sofas as ancient and creaking as the mattresses upstairs. One wall was filled entirely with shelves of old books. So many books, their spines so bent through repeat readings that the titles had faded, and you had to squint (I had bad eyesight even then) to decipher what tome you might be holding. But there was something else too. A folder. A large black heavy folder. And inside were stories. Dozens of stories. Real life stories. Cuttings from newspapers of strange things that had happened in the area over the years. People who'd gone missing in lakes, ships that had nearly vanished at sea. Stories from people who'd survived, from witnesses. Black type, headlines and paragraphs, page numbers on yellowed newspaper cuttings that were doing their best to curl at the edges where they lay imprisoned in A4 plastic document folders. In the two weeks we were there, those stories seeped into me as I read and re-read them, eyes wide with disbelief and wonder. There are two that stay with me still. The person swimming in a remote lake who struggled suddenly, disappearing underneath the surface. An off-duty policeman who witnessed this, diving in to help before the same too happened to him. Both strong swimmers, both vanished in the blink of an eye. The dredging of the lake later revealed nothing, not even their clothes, not a trace left... There was a cutting too about a ship, some kind of trawler that rode the waves, experienced sailors one and all, when a mysterious, powerful force dragged it downward in a rough sea. Engines on full throttle, they pulled out, managed to escape only to find, when they returned safely to port, that there were sucker marks the size of dinner plates on the timbers of the hull.

The black folder held within it the weird, the frightening, the mysterious and the impossible. Here be monsters, indeed. The red dragon on the Welsh flag we saw everywhere suddenly seemed quite plausible for this was surely a place where magic might happen, where *anything* could happen. Where the crow that watched us from the rowan tree might cast a spell. Where the quiet lake backed by sheer quarry walls could be transformed into a hiding place for a sea-serpent, the buzzards circling overheard into vultures, and the cromlech we passed every time we left the house in the car, well, why couldn't giants have built it after all?

And then there was the magic in the language around us too, in the unfamiliar words I saw everywhere – araf, ysgol, ysbyty. Place names that sounded like incantations, the waves of Welsh I heard around us in the shops sounding uncannily like powerful spells to my English ears. We learnt to say good morning and thank you, to count to five. The words tasted delicious, and I recited them to myself as we played amongst the dunes of Harlech, the old castle looking on from high above. We ventured down the old slate mine at Llanfair, just up the road, and all around us were stories. Everyone we met seemed to be a story-teller, tales of memories of the past, of the gossip of the now. I remember once, in a sweet shop, I came across a packet of sweets I'd never seen before. As an afficionado of confectionery, this was impossible. I knew all the sweets; I'd tried them all. It was a source of particular pride that my brother and I had tried every single one of the sugary options available at Hatch Lane in Chingford. I touched the red shiny packet longingly, enquired for more details and was told by the person behind the counter that this particular sweet shop sometimes trialled new sweets for one of the big sweet manufacturers. To this day I have no idea if this was utter bollocks made up on the spot or not but still, I counted out my pennies and bought them. I'm still rather fond of Skittles now, truth be told. And I love that all these years later, I still don't know what the truth of it might have been. For Wales had by then already become lodged firmly in my mind as a magical place filled with dragons and ruined castles, mysteries and magic, and joy of joys, first in line for new ranges of chewy sweets.

Can you blame me for falling in love? I had no idea at the time, but it was the start of a long love affair. I read Jenny Nimmo's beautiful and haunting books, soaked up the Chronicles of Prydain by Lloyd Alexander, delved into the weird and wonderful world of the Mabinogion. I read adventures set on Welsh steam trains (and cannot for the life of me find my copies or the name of the author) and decided that more than anything, even more than being a tomboy, I'd really like to be Welsh.

We returned, my family and I, not to the strange house with the seven gates and cromlech, but to different places in North Wales over the summers that followed. To Llyn Crafnant above Trefriw where I climbed around the edges of the lake, drank ginger beer from stone bottles sealed with corks from the little café and lost my favourite toy boat as it headed off to the other side of the lake, never to be seen again. We went to the Llyn Peninsula where it was even wilder than us three children were. And yet, although I remember the dippers in the stream by Llyn Crafnant, the wildness of the peninsula with its stormy skies, nowhere else has lingered in my memory so long, haunted my dreams as much as that strange stone house with its folder of stories...

And then, in truth, I forgot all about Wales. I fell in love with theatre, became utterly absorbed by it. I joined the National Youth Theatre at sixteen, spent my summers not in Wales but on the Holloway Road making props and A-frames, painting backdrops and crewing shows. I went to Bristol, to university, my heart then already leaning away from theatre, towards film and television. I returned to London, landed a job at the BBC. My days were spent working on promoting TV and radio shows, my evenings often in watching those same broadcasts being recorded. I loved it. And then, one day, I didn't. So I left. I dabbled in theatre PR where my path crossed with Kaite O'Reilly. Her exquisite play, Woman of Flowers, prompted me to dig out my old, half-forgotten copy of The Mabinogion. I worked with Riot Communications for the Welsh Books Council and discovered a whole library of Welsh writers new to me a voyage of discovery. I read page-turning books by the likes of Juliet Greenwood and Myrrha Stanford-Smith, admired Jim Perrin's passion for all things mountainous, gorged on Carol Rumens' beautiful poems, ate my way through Gilli Davies' recipes, and became a huge fan of Richard Gwyn's visceral writing. Without me even realising it, Wales had snuck back into my life. And then, in 2010, I moved to Ludlow, a market-town in the Marches, the borderland between Wales and England and once, many moons ago, the administrative capital of Wales.

I carried on writing during this time, on and off, as I pretty much always did. Little stories here and there, poems and children's books, screenplays and short films, but nothing seemed to stick. And then, one year, I went on holiday to North Wales, back to Harlech, to those same sand dunes I'd played upon years ago. I walked in the Rhinogs, looked out towards fairy-tale Portmeirion and the little island in the estuary. One rainy day I headed underground to the Llanfair Slate Caverns, the same moss-covered, dark and rusting mine I'd been to all those years earlier. It was to spark the idea for Bearmouth, my debut young adult novel. The Slate Caverns are an intriguing place, damp and cavernous, and pleasingly low-tech. You're handed a hard-hat and a large torch and told to mind your head when you enter. I spent hours wandering around, listening to the trickle of damp on the mossy walls, exploring each different space in turn. Over a century ago, boys worked down there from just twelve years of age, their right nostril slit on their first day, to test them, to see if they were 'man enough' to work down there. There was a stretcher too, shaped like a wooden coffin without the lid. And strangest of all, there was a figure in the rocks, high up, that the workers would doff their caps to as they came and went. It felt like a cult somehow. When I emerged from the mine, brain a-whirl with ideas, the first inklings of what would become Bearmouth were already lodged firmly in my imagination. Without realising it, I had found the key I'd been looking for, the key to unlocking a new level of creativity. It was, in truth, simply to write as myself, to tell the stories I wanted to tell, not to chase someone else's dream but to write my own. That little black folder all those years ago, brimful of stories, had finally called me back. And now that it had, I kept returning, I couldn't help myself.

I wandered the Kerry Ridgeway, the old drovers' road from Bishops Castle that runs high up along the border, hedgerows holding the countryside together like seams in a dress. I saw black skies filled with stardust and the Milky Way at Rhayader, walked the edges of the strange dark reservoirs of the Elan Valley and wondered what mysteries might lay beneath their still surfaces. I went to Ceredigion and walked the coastal path, picked ripe blackberries laced with sea-salt air, saw dolphins careening in the waves. I stepped into the Judge's Lodging in Presteigne with its original gas lighting still aflame, felt the oxygen sucked out of the room as the shadows flickered in the basement, and garnered a new understanding for Victorian ghost stories. I went to Pembrokeshire, to the candy-coloured townhouses of Tenby, to the creepy St. James' church and perfect tiny castle at Manorbier. I roamed inland to the Preseli hills, stood under ancient cromlechs, pondered the meaning of stone circles. I saw porpoises, baby seals, red foxes, and black rabbits. And all of it felt like electricity, stories charging through the air, whispers in the breeze. I listened out for them, ears pricked like a tuning fork, hoping to hear the right note, the hum of inspiration. And I did hear it. I always do. It fed into stories already told, feeds still into ones yet to come, distant ones on the horizon like far-off clouds that will one day edge closer to making it onto a page.

Wales is not the only place I find inspiration, of course, but it is somewhere I find to be *consistently* inspiring, whether through landscape and language or its own incredible creative output and innovation. I love it. I always will. And partly because of that, I feel defensive about it too. I feel Wales has been hugely under-appreciated by the wider United Kingdom, even taken for granted, for a very long time. Twenty years ago, when you'd tell English people you were holidaying in Wales, it generally led to jokes about sheep, falling into tired stereotypes in a way that saying you were heading to Ireland or the Highlands never would. And yet, I think in the past decade, heightened further by the pandemic, we've seen a seismic shift. The hordes of welcome – and indeed less welcome – tourists that have descended on even the most remote parts of the country during the Covid years has meant a rediscovery. I've noticed now that if I say I'm off to Cardigan or Cardiff, to North Wales or Pembrokeshire, the reaction has already shifted. The success of TV shows like Keeping Faith/Un Bore Marcher and Hinterland/Y Gwyll have undoubtedly played a part in this – not just in terms of showcasing Welsh storytelling and performing talent but also in broadcasting the Welsh language directly into the living rooms of people who might never have heard it before. There seems to be a wider appreciation of Welsh products too, of the craftsmanship of Welsh tapestry, of Welsh designers, of Welsh food and drink. New storytellers like the fantastic children's writer Lesley Parr are breaking through, and Wales is now onto its second Children's Laureate. The brilliant Firefly Press and others are punching well above their weight, and Wales Arts Review is still, deservedly, as strong as ever, reaching out to a wide global audience to celebrate, question and debate. Hay Festival, that high-dose of intellectual adrenaline, a live culture-shot of ideas and exchanges, will continue despite recent turmoil and I sincerely hope will continue to support Welsh writers even more than it has done over the previous three decades. Russell T Davies, undoubtedly one of our greatest living television writers, continues to go from strength to strength, championing his home country in some shape or form in pretty much everything that he does, and Welsh musical talents like Cate le Bon and Gwenno continue to push themselves creatively, producing fantastically distinctive new music. Wales is suddenly cool and trendy, a happening place. Which, to those of us who've loved it for a long time, is no surprise. It always has been!

And yet, there are issues with this 'new discovery' of Wales. House prices and rents along both its rugged and beautiful coastline and further inland have gone through the roof. Incomers keen to try a new life outside of cities have made even more places unaffordable to locals. It's happening in the Marches too where I live and yes, I too was once an incomer to Shropshire. Like all things, I think it's a question of balance, of new blood and ideas, of those newcomers being willing to fit in, to make an effort, to contribute and, in Wales, to at least attempt to learn some of the language. The working at home revolution which has happened in, let's be honest, mainly middle-class jobs, will undoubtedly have a long-term impact across all four nations. Then there's the environment too, what form new subsidies might take for Wales' farmers, the need to rewild and how that might be managed, the impact of far greater levels of tourism than ever before. But Wales is nothing if not resilient, fiercely so. Recently, in St David's, I came across Grain, a pop-up that saw the brilliant Bluestones Brewery team up with the established pizza place in Newport. Both small independent businesses, both ambitious and innovative, pushing at the boundaries, experimental in both their drinks and food, working together to create a brand-new outlet that is every bit as inspiring as you might hope. I heard too, first-hand from the remarkable writer Rebecca F John about her new publishing house, Aderyn, specialising in historical and speculative fiction, her ambition to share these new stories with wider audiences. Two very different examples of innovation in two very different areas, but both ideas that came about during lockdown. I hope that all these new tourists who have 'discovered' Wales over the past few years will be intrigued enough to find out more, to read the writers who live and work there, discover stories and voices that are new to them, tales from the likes of Caryl Lewis and Gary Raymond, from Jenny Valentine, Jackie Morris, and Eloise Williams. I hope too that they will continue to tune into TV stories by Welsh writers and listen in to the next generation of talented musicians.

Whatever the future might hold for Wales though, it's not just the Welsh that will champion and defend it, that will stand their ground and support it, it's those of us from outside who will join in too, those of us who love it for a myriad of reasons, those of us spread all over the globe.

I know there are always places that get under one's skin, that resonate and chime on a level that is somehow profound. But

Wales will always have a special place in my heart. Even now, whenever I cross the border and I see that distinctive 'Croeso i Gymru' sign, I still feel that same flicker of excitement I felt all those years ago when we headed for the first time into the country where the impossible felt possible, where dragons really might roam free, to that mysterious stone house with its black folder of stories just waiting to be discovered...

I know now that I will never be Welsh, I will always be an imposter, a visitor, a tourist who fell in love with a whole country and loves it still, but I've made my peace with that. For Wales has given me so much in return for my adoration, wildlife and walks, books and music, TV, theatre, and art and, above all, the courage to write the stories I want to tell. That little splinter, that tiny piece of Wales in my heart, it will always be with me now, come what may.

So, thank you Wales. Thank you for the inspiration. Diolch o galon.

WHEN I WAS TWENTY-THREE, IT WAS A VERY GOOD YEAR

Craig Austin

In the match-hot Summer of 1994, Rudolph Giuliani is only a handful of months into his first term as Mayor of New York. As a Republican candidate seeking election in a historically Democratic city, Giuliani runs a vigorous anti-crime campaign that promises 'civic clean-up' and, most visibly, an eradication of Times Square's panhandlers and strip joints. Giuliani may now be viewed as a hateful hair-melting weasel jumping through flaming fascist hoops at the mere click of Trump's tiny fingers, but in the early part of the 1990s he was broadly welcomed across the majority of the city's electorate as the only candidate capable of summoning a rain that would *'wash all the scum off the streets'*.

'He's what the city's been crying out for', we are informed, by a stocky man of undeniably Italian heritage who is painstakingly kneading and stretching vast swathes of dough across the floured marble counter of a dollar-a-slice pizza joint on Washington Street, Hoboken. We are in Frank's town, only a short trip across the Hudson River and a 10-minute PATH train journey into the notorious fleshpots of the West Village. The PATH train smells good. It smells alien, exotic even. A uniquely American aroma that – much like the absence of mobile phones – acts as a daily reminder that we are a long way from home. Nothing in Wales, nothing in London, smells like the PATH train. Just as there's no place back home that serves breakfast quite like the Malibu Diner. A joint whose extensive menu I routinely scour in the hope of finding an egg cream. A thing of wonder that I first became aware of via the pages of Louise Fitzhugh's 'Harriet the Spy'; a book that first ignited an 8-year old's lifelong obsession with urban Americana. I feel sure that the smallest sip will be enough to formally seal the deal, to bring it all back home.

His narrow eyes divide their time between a wall-mounted TV and the culinary task at hand, as news reports alternate between the recent murders of Nicole Brown Simpson and the Colombian footballer, Andrés Escobar. The infamous Simpson Bronco chase having taken place on the same day that the opening ceremony of the 1994 World Cup was marked by Diana Ross missing a pantomime penalty at Chicago's Soldier Field. Itself, only a matter of days before Escobar would be gunned down in a Medellin car park, reportedly as retaliation for having scored an own goal that contributed to the team's early elimination from the tournament.

The pizza is good. Far too good to be sold at such suspiciously bargain-basement prices, and it is not until sometime after that it dawns on us that this dollar-a-slice, dollar-a-beer operation is nothing less than a money-laundering operation; situated as it is only a short stroll from The Bagnoli Club. A half-lit, blinds-drawn establishment where, if you peer closely enough through the slats, you can just about make out tables of portly middle-aged gentlemen playing cards in their underwear. Less than a year later, Vesuvio Pizza will have closed down abruptly and without fanfare, its employees scattered to the outer reaches of Weehawken and New Brunswick; joining others from lower Manhattan who by then will have begun to feel the heat of

Giuliani's anti-shakedown shakedown. But for now, the charade plays out in ways that satiate our dry throats, hungry stomachs and increasingly empty wallets. After all, who are we, a ragtag group of South Wales innocents of barely legal State drinking age, to question the societal scaffolding of *'The birthplace of baseball and Frank Sinatra'*?

It's barely been a week since I first stood in the sweltering city street outside the Port Authority Terminal, inadvertently holding up a narrow section of rush-hour traffic as I argued with a red-faced cab driver who was flat-out refusing to take my crisp $50 note in payment for our ride from JFK. He had pointed out, understandably in the circumstances, that a note that clean and crisp could not possibly have been issued in 1978, the date that now appeared to time-stamp a worryingly large proportion of my pristine holiday money. Facing imminent and inevitable defeat, we quickly bundle together a collection of fives, tens and singles in order to abate the wrath of a driver who utters a plethora of Eastern European insults under his breath. In doing so, I swiftly come to regret taking up the offer of a dubious friend-of-a friend to exchange my meagre Home Office wages at what seemed to be an alarmingly generous 'private' rate. The coming days will entail the artificial ageing of these notes via a protracted process of rolling, folding and crumpling, in advance of them being stealthily redistributed across a series of low-value purchases along stretches of the Jersey Shore. Newport, as ever, has taught me well.

The Civil Service is not often celebrated as a gateway to ambition, but it has presented me with the gift of social mobility in a way that the habitually clichéd springboards of working-class escapology never did. I am not tough enough to be a boxer, not skilled enough to be a footballer, insufficiently special to make a meaningful go of rock 'n'roll, and not – in my twenty-something's mind's eye – enough of a dick to join the army. Instead, my unlikely launchpad into London proves to be the Newport Passport Office. A job that once afforded me the freedom to take an entire workforce out on strike in support of the ambulance workers at the tender age of 19 and suffer no formal reprimand for being partly complicit in letting off a nightclub smoke machine in the Trade Union office. It is a job that also presents me with the opportunity of a staff transfer to a sprawling brutalist office block on the edge of St. James's Park. A building at the geographic heart of the city that I'd first fallen in love with at the age of 10. A hot summer's day during which I bought the first Duran Duran album from the big HMV on Oxford Street and was astonished to encounter Trafalgar Square street-vendors selling cans of Coke at the, then, shockingly exorbitant price of 50p.

Credit cards, though this view remains a somewhat unpopular view, offer me social mobility too. And with it an opportunity to snub my nose at the parsimonious *'don't buy what you can't afford'* ethos that was – evidently, unsuccessfully – drilled into me by relatives and authority figures from Pillgwenlly to Pontypool. I first get one at the age of 20, and swiftly jettison any notion of paying off the balance, *sans* interest, at the end of each month, when I realise the incredible purchase power that this suddenly affords me. I use it to cover the cost of a meal for five at the Golden Tandoori on Clarence Place and treat the individual cash contributions I receive in part-payment as free money. The same card pays for me to travel down to London on increasingly frequent excursions; to buy bowling shirts from Lloyd Johnson, creepers from Kensington Market, and jeans that I have read about in the pages of The Face.

In keeping with my strident belief that people who are 'good with money' suffer from a chronic lack of imagination, the same card also buys me a bucket-shop return ticket to John F. Kennedy airport with Air India. A hastily arranged, barely funded venture forged in the white heat of late-night pub bravado and the giddy possibility of it all. It will be the first time that I will ever have boarded a plane. It gives me a taste, the intensity of which rivals the one that Shaun Ryder acquired in Barbados. Once aboard, we will watch *Cool Runnings* on a pull-down screen and smoke duty-free cigarettes at the back of the cabin – the last year that this will be permitted other than on flights to and from Japan. We will also drain an entire box of wine, inflate its empty inner bag, and toss it around the compressed cabin like a beach ball. Like dicks. The kind of behaviour that would now result in an emergency landing in Newfoundland and the barrel of a Homeland Security gun being pointed squarely at our puny pale chests. It is true that I could have saved up for this ticket, this trip, and only embarked upon it when it could be funded via solvency. Though that day may never have come. It certainly wouldn't have come before I was 35, and what good would have come of that in real terms? Like any giddy thrill, New York deserves to be enjoyed when you are both cocksure and toe-curlingly naïve in equal measures.

I have experienced Times Square when it was a magnet for hookers and blow, and in later years when its sleazy demi-monde glamour had been scrubbed spotlessly clean by the busy cartoon gloves of Mickey Mouse, and I know which one I prefer. By the age of 35, your primary traits and core beliefs are hardwired, baked in. At the age of 23, they remain sufficiently soft enough to be moulded. You can stand outside that same Port Authority bus terminal in baking city heat and inhale deeply on the Camel Light that L, another former citizen of Newport, has just handed you. L slowly exhales, turns towards me, and grins.

'It's all changed now, hasn't it?'

A seemingly throwaway line, yet one so perfectly cinematic that it sparks an exhilarating unspoken moment of recognition between us. A silent acknowledgement that we may finally be about to become active participants in life, rather than mere observers. A life heady with urban exotica, the kind only previously experienced through the yellowed pages of secondhand books and the grainy tape of VHS cassettes.

The proprietor of Vesuvio Pizza overhears us discussing the Primal Scream show that will take place later that day at The Limelight on 6th Avenue and W 20th St. The Limelight has already entered the after-dark pantheon of Gotham legend and its very name conjures up the possibility of gaining adjacency to metropolitan magic. A prospect almost unthinkable to me only 18 months previously, on the Wednesday nights that I'd walk through the entrance to *Cinderella's* at the bottom of Stow Hill and hand over three of your shiny Welsh pounds. Primal Scream is going through a truly baffling period that seeks to underline the band's socialist credentials and commitment to racial equality by plastering the confederate flag across their record sleeves and attendant tour publicity. Imagery that is all set to stink up 6th Avenue almost as much as I had done days previously, when naively referring to it as 'The Avenue of the Americas' in conversation with a scornful taxi driver from Yonkers.

'You wanna see that show tonight?' the owner asks without looking up, his thick crown of grey hair partly obscured by a paper hat that acts as a token nod to Garden State food hygiene regs.

'My buddy owns that place' – *because of course he does.*

'Maybe. We're down to our last few dollars though.'

'I didn't ask you that'.

'Well yeah, then. We wanna go'.

'No problem', he says, continuing to go about the business of dough-kneading, sauce-spreading and ambiguously promising.

I crumple my nose, uncomfortable with the absence of certainty that surrounds this intangible carrot of nightlife opportunity that has been dangled in front of us. An awkward silence hangs in the air as we exchange puzzled glances and watch the same guy expertly prise open yet another catering can of pizza sauce. Moments later, he hands us each a molten slice of the latest batch along with a flurry of paper napkins.

'No, it's fine' he says, waving away our crumpled dollar bills. 'It's on the house. You're all good Europeans'.

On-the-house beers are distributed too, along with another napkin that is performatively handed to me in a manner befitting of the grand gesture. On it, in blue biro, are scrawled the words: *Steve. These guys are my personal friends.*

I can't help laughing – a bad move, it would quickly transpire – at the improbability of it all. A solid gold gift, shop-soiled by ambiguity and central-casting cliché.

'What do we do with this?'

'What do you fuggin' think you do with it? Wipe your ass?'

The kneading continues, this time sound-tracked by a series of displeased grunts.

'Thanks', one of us offers, if only to break the jarring silence.

'That's more fuggin' like it. You're welcome. Don't forget to tell your buddy how lucky he is'.

I offer up a chastised 'thanks', while imagining a laughing Manhattan doorman scrunching up this delicate sliver of paper in his massive New York City fist and directing us back to the bumpkin-loaded bridges and tunnels from which we came.

Directly after Primal Scream's show, The Limelight will revert to its usual club-night offering. One of its attendees will almost certainly be Michael Alig, the self-proclaimed leader of the self-celebrating 'Club Kids', and, latterly, a murderer. We might be lucky enough to pick up one of the many $100 bills that Alig often tosses onto the crowded dancefloor simply to revel in the resultant human scramble. Maybe he'll urinate upon us from the balcony, or even directly into our drinks; yet more of his loveable foibles. Or maybe he'll invite one or two of us back to his apartment and murder us while high on crack. Maybe he'll then dismember us and carefully place our limbs in a garbage bag within a duffle bag, before tossing our severed remains into the Hudson River. Consigning us to an eternal half-life of suburban ennui, floating back and forth between New York and New Jersey. The cruellest of fates for a young man such as I, one who aspires to be a broken hero tearing up the highway on a last-chance power drive. It's just a shame I can't drive.

Ultimately, the fickle hand of fate decides that we remain defiantly un-murdered. And all the while, a handwritten golden ticket sits folded in the back pocket of my jeans, nagging away at me. My selective memory is not what it was, but I do recall at least two versions of how this scenario plays out. In the first, an initially perplexed doorman expresses amusement at the tentatively tendered napkin before reading the biro scrawl and calling over another guy in a headset. Swiftly, we are ushered into The Limelight's fabled doorway and directed towards a circular booth in the balcony. A carton of cigarettes is placed on its table, and we are provided with waitress-service until the early hours. The drinks are free, and no one looks down upon us for being so severely under-dressed. The Primal Scream show is a sideshow now, a tired-looking Bobby Gillespie phoning in his 'Villefranche Jagger' tribute act in front of a neon flag that celebrates segregation and white supremacy. On the way home, we begin to gleefully collate the multitude of anecdotes that no one in Newport or Streatham will believe to be true.

In the second, we sit slumped across the bar of Kelly's on Washington Street as the third bucket of Rolling Rock is dutifully placed before our shiny sunburnt faces. I retrieve the napkin from my pocket and use it to pat dry my sweaty forehead. We laugh about what a ridiculous notion it was anyway, about how terrible Primal Scream are, and how we wouldn't have wanted our otherwise blissful trip to end in unnecessary public ignominy. Yet what we complicitly fail to acknowledge is the burning sense of what-might-have-been that eats away at our indolent small-town timidity. The Stones' 'Midnight Rambler' comes on the jukebox. It sits well with the beer and instils a sense of raucous communion in those present. The bartender shuffles her way along the line of bottles in time with the music, smashing her palms down on the counter-top at an appropriate break in proceedings.

'Talkin' 'bout The Boston Strangler!', she yells, in a sandpaper voice sponsored by Philip Morris Inc.

I smile and take a long slug of cold beer, the pissy fizz filling up my stupid country-mouse face. At the age of 23, and temporarily New York-adjacent, I'm pretty sure I know the meaning of life. It doesn't help me a bit.

ITALIANS IN THE RAIN

David Llewellyn

"Tuscany looks weirdly like Port Talbot."

I tweeted this in May 2019, from a plane which had just landed at Florence's Aeroporto Amerigo Vespucci. The view from my window was one not of the Duomo and the Palazzo Vecchio but of rolling green hills overlooking the city's modern urban sprawl. Add a cloudy sky, steelworks and the M4 and you could be 900 miles away.

It reminded me of the line attributed to the English journalist Rene Cuttforth, who described the Welsh as "Italians in the rain". I don't know the exact context in which it was said, but I've always fancied it was in reference to our sanguine nature, matriarchal working-class families, and the vaguely Mediterranean look so many of us have, but I believe it goes much deeper than that.

There's the language, for a start. Though I grew up in a predominantly Anglophone eastern valley I recall a Welsh-speaking geography teacher telling us that Cymraeg had retained more Latin than its Germanic nearest neighbour. She didn't go into much detail, but thinking about it now, I realise it was staring us in the face. The name of my hometown, Pontypool (from Pont-Y-Pwll) described an historic bridge over a flood plain, and on that trip to Florence I crossed the Ponte Vecchio. When describing a window they say "finestre", we say "ffenestr". When calling someone "darling" we say "cariad", they say "caro".

All this goes back to the Roman conquest of Britain, and the Brythonic language that evolved from a hybrid of Vulgar Latin and the local tongue, dominating much of the western side of Britain till the arrival of those pesky Anglo Saxons. That Welsh not only survived but evolved over the following centuries remains a miracle.

In flying from Cardiff – via a cross-terminal dash at Schiphol – to Florence we were following in the footsteps of those who travelled to pre-Risorgimento Italy by horse and by boat. In the 18th century, before the Napoleonic Wars rendered much of the Continent off limits, the Grand Tour was a rite of passage for young men of means.

One of them was Sir Watkin Williams-Wynn, 4th Baronet, heir to the vast Wynnstay estates of North Wales. In 1768, aged 19, he travelled to Italy with his companions Thomas Apperley and Captain Edward Hamilton, and like many of their contemporaries they had a group portrait painted by the renowned artist Pompeo Battoni.

In this painting they are portrayed as men of learning and culture; Williams-Wynn holding his own crayon copy of a Raphael fresco, Apperley drawing the Baronet's attention to a passage from *La Divina Commedia,* and Captain Hamilton dressed in his regimental finery and holding a flute. All this, against a backdrop of Doric columns and classical statuary.

On returning to Wales, and perhaps inspired by his time abroad, Sir Watkin became a patron of the arts. The Batoni portrait was followed by one of Watkin and his wife Henrietta as newlyweds, painted by Joshua Reynolds. The young baronet and his bride are pictured against a scene of neo-classical grandeur, an elegant balustrade and an arched doorway that is supported only aesthetically by its decorative Ionian pilasters.

This is Roccoco cultural appropriation, an imported Arcadia, and if the scene painted by Batoni was a tad theatrical, the feeling here is one of a stage set, and Sir Watkin and his wife the players. That sense is only heightened by the knowledge that Henrietta died just three months into their marriage, and that the painting was completed after her death.

Richard Wilson was one of the artists who later enjoyed the patronage of Sir Watkin Williams-Wynn. Born in the village of Penegoes he lived and worked in Italy from 1720 to 1727, and though he began as a portrait painter he was inspired by an encounter with the Venetian artist Francesco Zuccarelli to produce Arcadian peasant scenes and landscapes, often for patrons from Great Britain and Ireland on Grand Tours of their own. The growing popularity of such paintings would have a profound effect on British art in the late 18th and early 19th century, inspiring artists such as Constable and Turner.

An apprentice of Wilson's, Thomas Jones (1742-1802) would follow in his master's footsteps, and his travels around Italy mark a turning point in his style, the earlier mythical scenes and imaginary landscapes giving way to naturalistic depictions of what he'd seen with his own eyes. Today, he is perhaps best known for the oil sketches he made while visiting Naples in the 1780s. These simple, realistic studies of brick walls, with laundry often hanging in windows, feel surprisingly modern, more like the cityscapes of Edward Hopper than the bucolic fantasia and high drama of his early work.

The most well-known surviving portrait we have of Jones is the one on display in the National Museum of Wales, painted by the Italian portraitist Giuseppe Marchi while he was visiting the younger artist at his family home in Pencerrig. In it, Jones is depicted as the young country squire, fresh faced and blue eyed, against a suitably Romantic brooding grey sky.

A later Welsh artist went to Italy and remained there for the rest of his long life. Born in Merthyr in 1802, Penry Williams was the son of a house painter, and showed a precocious talent for draughtsmanship, making two paintings of the Merthyr Riots when just thirteen years old. Sponsored by the Welsh industrialist John Josiah Guest he left Merthyr to study at the Royal Academy in London, and in his 1825 painting of the Dowlais Steelworks he created what may be one of the earliest industrial landscapes in British art.

By 1827 he had settled in Rome, and began painting landscapes and scenes of peasant life. There he met a fellow Welshman, the sculptor John Gibson, and the two men lived together until Gibson's death in 1866.

Gibson's career was a product of the late 18th and early 19th century fascination with all things classical. In Britain the nobility and burgeoning upper middle classes were decorating their estates with simulacra of the ancient world; their not-so-ancient temples overlooking languid lakes, the terraces punctuated by Venuses and Adonises with a full complement of limbs.

Gibson made his fair share of these, most famously the 'Tinted Venus' now in the collection of Liverpool's Walker Gallery. They show a greater affinity for the female form than some earlier sculptors – Michelangelo's Night and Dawn from the Medici tombs springing effortlessly to mind – but they remain cold, academic studies in feminine beauty.

It's in his depictions of men that we see another gaze at work, and his choice of subject matter is suggestive. His mentor, the Italian sculptor Antonio Canova, encouraged him to use live models, even when depicting classical subjects, and so whether it's Narcissus gazing longingly at his reflection or a sleeping shepherd boy, perhaps one of the love-struck shepherds of Virgil's *Eclogues*, his sculptures of men and boys are sensual and lifelike.

In these pieces I'm reminded of Donatello's David, another sculpture that drew on classical influences. This groundbreaking bronze, the first attempt at a free-standing nude since the days of antiquity, depicts a slim, boyish character with one hand on his hip, one foot resting with his toes entangled provocatively in Goliath's hair.

That stance is known in art terms as *contrapposto,* counterpose; the human figure resting with the torso turned slightly so that the shoulders and hips are unaligned. There were often practical reasons for this in marble sculpture, a way of distributing the weight so that neither ankle would break, but you'll notice it too in Botticelli's Venus and in ancient statuary. With its rediscovery during the Italian Renaissance this stance quickly became associated with classical beauty, making Donatello's David the subject of controversy and speculation about Donatello's virtue – or lack thereof – during the prudish years of the Counter Reformation and beyond.

We see *contrapposto* again in a painting by Gibson's companion, Penry Williams. *The Fisher Boys,* painted at some point in the mid-19th century, depicts two young men in Phrygian-style caps and white smocks, leaning together against the prow of their boat and gazing out to sea. It's an example of *Rückenfigur*, a common motif in Romantic art, the subjects with their back to us, as in Friedrich's *The Wanderer Above the Sea of Fog,* and it's strikingly different from Williams's other scenes of peasant life. There's an intimacy between the boys, one resting his elbow on the other's arm, their hips almost touching. It feels like a moment observed with longing, and I'm reminded of Dirk Bogarde's von Aschenbach gazing wistfully at the silhouetted boy on the beach in Visconti's *Death in Venice.*

These early modern cultural exchanges between Wales and Italy were never a one-way street. Long before Wilson, Jones,

Gibson and Williams set off on their travels, the Florentine sculptor Torrigiano was banished from Tuscany; punishment, it's said, for giving his fellow student Michelangelo a broken nose. After time in Rome and a stint as a mercenary he was invited to England by Henry VIII, to create a tomb for his late father, scion of the Tudors of Penmynydd, and England's first king of Welsh descent.

Henry is said to have been dissatisfied with the quality of English craftsmen, but Torrigiano created dazzlingly lifelike effigies of Henry VII and Elizabeth of York, lying on a podium decorated with a host of *putti*, making it Britain's earliest example of Renaissance sculpture.

Though art continued to bring Wales and Italy together, in the 19th and 20th centuries it was often music that formed a cultural bridge between the two. The comedian and actor Paul Whitehouse, born in the Rhondda to opera-singing mum and opera-loving dad, once remarked that Italy and Wales were the two countries where working class people enjoyed opera. I don't know if that still holds true, but it was certainly the case in my own family, where great opera singers and great singing were revered, and at a time when I was still working summer holidays in my father's garage my mum took me to watch the WNO perform *Madam Butterfly* at Cardiff's New Theatre.

Born in Madrid in 1843, the Italian soprano Adelina Patti led a peripatetic existence, her family emigrating to the US and a new life in New York City when she was still a child. In a career spanning over forty years, she worked with Verdi and Rossini, and toured South America and Russia, becoming friends with Tchaikovsky along the way.

At the height of her fame Patti could demand $5,000 in gold per performance, and had a parrot trained to squawk "CASH!" whenever her promoter entered the room. When she finally retired it was not to the spa towns of Switzerland or the French Riviera, but to her estate at Craig-Y-Nos Castle in the Swansea Valley. There she had built her own theatre and funded a rail extension bringing the Neath and Brecon railway to her doorstep. She spent her later years giving small performances for friends in her theatre and making gramophone recordings, some of which have survived.

Adelina Patti died at Craig-Y-Nos in 1919 but in accordance with her will was buried in Paris' Père Lachaise cemetery, to be closer to her father's remains and the memorial to Rossini. She had already gifted the city of Swansea with the winter garden from her estate, and it was later rebuilt on the seafront and named the Patti Pavilion in her honour.

It was during those years that greater numbers of her fellow countrymen and women crossed the continent and made Wales their home. Famously, many of them set up shop with cafes and ice cream parlours, until no valleys town was complete without a Mario's, a Marenghi's, a Belli's or any of the countless Italian names which became a familiar sight on every high street. An aunt, working as a nurse in London in the '50s and '60s was amused when English friends raved about the latest thing... cappuccino! Back home in the valleys they had been drinking "frothy coffee" for decades.

The first and second generations of Italians in Wales would make their own mark on the cultural scene. The artist Ernest Zobole, a founding member of the 56 Group, was the son of Italian immigrants who had settled in Ystrad in 1910, his father a mine worker and his mother a shopkeeper. Over a century after Penry Williams painted a steelworks and left for Italy, an Italian artist and his peers began painting the industrial landscapes of the Rhondda Valleys.

Born Vittorio, the actor Victor Spinetti was one of the second generation of Welsh Italians, his Welsh-born father and Welsh mother proprietors of a valleys chip shop. After training at what was then simply the Welsh College of Music and Drama he performed with the Joan Littlewood Theatre Workshop, winning a Tony Award for his performance in the Broadway production of *Oh, What a Lovely War!*

Following an uncredited role in the 1964 film *Becket* he became a close friend of Richard Burton, and would later join him and Elizabeth Taylor in the cast of Franco Zeffirelli's *The Taming of the Shrew.*

Their time in Rome is well documented in Burton's diaries, but unlike earlier grand tourists such as Ruskin and Goethe, or his contemporary Jan Morris, the Welsh movie star was not the most enthusiastic of visitors.

Wednesday 23rd March 1966 – *"I tried to read (Luigi) Barzini's The Italians but found it intolerably prolix and self-congratulatory. I'll try it again and make another desperate attempt to like The Italians and the Italians."*

Thursday 21st April 1966 – *"I'm not sure I like Zefferelli. He's a coward and devious with it."*

By November Burton and Taylor were back at their Swiss home and planning a trip to Venice when the region was hit by terrible storms, with Northern Italy bearing the worst of it.

Monday 7th November 1966 – *"Florence and Venice have been severely flooded. There is great fear, not only for the people but for great works of art. In Florence 6 million precious books are under the deluge."*

For Florence, it was the city's worst flooding since the 16th century. Thirty-three lives were lost, five thousand people made homeless, and countless books and artworks destroyed. Born and raised in Florence, Franco Zeffirelli led campaigns to raise funds to aid restoration and repair, and made a film, *Per Firenze* (For Florence) highlighting the city's plight. Its narrator, who else?

Wednesday 17th November 1966 – *"At 2:30 I met Sheila Pickles and the Italian TV man re the documentary on Florence... I will try to do the narration in Italian for the Italians and in English for the UK and USA."*

The Basilica of Santa Croce was one of those worst affected, a torrent of mud and heating oil causing structural damage and the irreplaceable loss of some of its most precious treasures. The repairs and restoration work took decades, and in places is still ongoing.

Back in 2019 it's the first place we visit once we've checked into our hotel, my mother-in-law complaining that her room hasn't a view. No, really.

It's a brisk walk across a surprisingly small city, though every corner you turn introduces you to another landmark. In the Piazza Santa Croce we're frowned at by Dante, who died in exile 80 miles away, and doesn't look too pleased about it. We receive a similarly terse greeting from the woman who checks our Firenzecards, barking at us in Italian for reasons unknown. Does she think that we're Italian? Have we already passed for locals?

It's worth the hassle. Stepping into the church for the first time is breath-taking; it's impossible to take everything in at once. Walking around, dumbstruck, we pass Giotto frescoes depicting the life of St Francis, twenty-two spectacular medieval stained glass windows and a *Who's Who* of memorials and tombs. There's Galileo, and Machiavelli, and Rossini, the latter's remains having been moved here from Père Lachaise in 1887. On one wall there hangs Donatello's exquisite relief of the Annunciation. Turn around and you are facing the tomb of Leon Battista Alberti, whose treatise *De Pictura* (On Painting) was one of the foundational texts of Renaissance art.

Standing beneath the Cappella dei Pazzi's blue glazed terracotta ceiling, I realise that the so-called "Stendhal Syndrome", that feeling of being physically and mentally overwhelmed by Florence's beauty, is very real. We step out into the first cloister, and though the forecasts have predicted rain the clouds begin to part, the sun shines and a host of sparrows is chirruping in the eaves. Everything about this city is wonderful, and for a moment we just stand there, my partner, my mother-in-law and I, basking in it.

Welsh people in the sun.

BREAKING INTO PRISONS: Welsh Poetry in the World

Jonathan Edwards

The Italian prison guard with the steely look and the three days' growth of beard was holding a mobile phone up to my face, while the eyes of his elder colleague flicked back and forth from the screen to my face, from my face to the screen. On the screen was a picture of my face, from a recent website post about my poetry, and what these guards were trying to determine was if I was who I said I was – a Welsh poet arriving at the gates of Genoa Prison in order to give a poetry reading. I'd gone and left my passport at the hotel, so now a BBC news page featuring a photo my father had taken in the garden in Crosskeys, placed next to the text of a poem I'd written while sitting on the sofa in my living room, was all that stood between me and entry to a maximum-security Italian prison. The guard's eyes flicked from the screen to my face, my face to the screen, and I remembered that the poem on the website was about a nun travelling at high speed on a bicycle, over the cobbles of an Italian street. I wondered if there was anything seditious in such writing, anything that could be considered a significant threat to security. Then the prison guard broke into a huge grin, and jabbed me in the ribs, in the universal bloke language for *Hey, you're alright!* A few minutes later, I was reading poems about growing up in South Wales – the hills and the terraces, the schools and the trees, the dive-bombing herons, the factory chimneys – to a roomful of Italian prisoners.

There is much in this story which resonates in terms of being a writer in Wales. Like lots of writers, I spent most of my twenties trying to break in, not poring over blueprints of bank vaults or plans for tunnels, but scribbling drafts and tinkering with stanzas. And, when you've got somewhere as a writer, the joyful process of gadding from one festival to another, from reading to workshop, youth hostel to village hall, can sometimes feel a little like an endless parade of trying to prove that you are who you claim to be, that you match the photo or the website description of yourself, that you can somehow make sense of the words you spent years writing or which, rather, somehow appeared there, in front of you, on a page and caused you, once in a while, to punch the air. Writing will always in some ways resemble a prison because it involves sitting here, in a room on your own, looking at the wall, and some days not doing much more than that. But of course, out of those conditions comes the greatest freedom – that of the imagination. As one of the most famous residents of a prison, Norman Stanley Fletcher, puts it, *Dreams is freedom.*

To begin, though, with real-world prisons. In 2018, I was very lucky to be part of two literary festivals held in prisons, running workshops with prisoners. *Morning and afternoon workshops with poet Jonathan Edwards,* said the festival programme. *Born and bred in South Wales, his book* My Family and Other Superheroes *includes Evel Knievel, Sophia Loren, Ian Rush, Marty McFly, and a recalcitrant hippo.* That day – not unusually in this world – I felt a bit like a recalcitrant hippo myself. I'd never been inside a prison before and had no idea what to expect. The festival organisers assured me that everything would be great but also that I might consider sitting near the panic button in the room in case of any issues. I gave exactly the same workshops in that environment as I've given to pensioners and schoolchildren, published poets and folks who've just wandered in, at Eton and Aldeburgh, in London and Ledbury: I get people to write poems about people. Just as, in any good poetry workshop, one quickly forgets who is the poet in the room and who are the students, so in this instance, within ten minutes, the divisions of poet and prisoner were gone: because of the act of reading and writing poetry, we were all humans.

It helped, of course, that the prison was close to Wales. Many of the prisoners were from the valleys, talked like I talk, loved Dylan Thomas, came from two villages over from me, wrote poems about characters like those I know – in some cases, wrote poems about characters I *am*. Some prisoners wrote deeply moving work about horrible fathers. Some wrote love poems to their girlfriends, funny poems about how they missed going down the pub. All, all wanted and wanted to read their poems. At the end of the day, I left with a mug created by the prisoners in ceramics class, with a wobbly rendition of my name on it. It's in pride of place on the mantelpiece in this room I'm writing in, now. But, even more, I left the prison that day with a sense of the most enormously rewarding time, of hours well spent, what poetry can do.

If poetry can offer imaginative escape, it has also given me physical movement, travel, new space. In 2015, I visited the Kolkata Book Fair as part of a British Council project. One day, I was teaching Year Seven the finer points of comma use in a South Wales secondary school. The next day, I was stumbling off a plane in India, riding through the streets of Kolkata in taxis with other Welsh and Indian poets, reading at book festivals, meeting publishers, writing a sestina-in-collaboration. In the city's heady alleys and markets, we made a poetry film, discussing our impressions of the city.

The greatest gift that opportunities like this give writers is connection with writers from other parts of the world, poetry friendships, the opportunity to collaborate. When lockdown hit, in early 2020, one of the first things I did was to resume a poetry collaboration with one of the Indian poets I'd worked with as part of the British Council project. In 2016, we'd walked round London, beginning collaborative poems in each of the city's great railway stations. Now, we resumed those collaborations, dug out our dozing notebooks from that time, sent drafts and redrafts of lines back and forth across cyberspace, needing to feel connected across distance at the very time when travel was impossible. We wrote through our memories, through time and through place, exploring the special connections that poetry can create. We tried to describe the experience of strolling round London train stations at a time when to do so seemed as alien as journeying to the moon. Even if you're stuck in Crosskeys, poetry allows travel – although it's not possible of course to be *stuck* somewhere as gorgeous as this.

Other opportunities for travel emerged through the kindness of the Versopolis project, a European co-operation of poetry festivals, which I'd been connected with by the folks at the Ledbury Poetry Festival, after winning their poetry competition. As well as enabling me to travel to Genoa and experience the things outlined at the start of this article, I also visited Gdansk, and my poems were translated into Polish. One aspect of my writing is that it often refers to historical or pop culture events, and often does so in ways which have a slightly problematic relationship to truth. One of my poems has Ryan Giggs playing in a match for Wales six months before he'd made his actual international debut. No one has ever noticed this about the poem, however many times I've read it in Wales. But the man translating my poem into Polish did notice, and there followed a really interesting conversation about the relationship between factual and imagined truth, as well as one about some intricacies of the history of the Welsh national football team. A translation of another of my favourite poems, 'The Hippo,' revealed that the Polish for 'hippo peepshow' is 'hipciowy peep-show,' a fact which made me feel that the poem had been written purely so that translated phrase could exist in the world.

While the reception of English-language writing from Wales outside the UK has in my experience been invariably generous, one question I have about poetry is the extent to which such writing is fairly valued in the UK, and whether a writer from Carmarthen or Colwyn Bay, for example, can achieve the same success, in relation to their talent and effort, that can be achieved by someone from the Midlands or Manchester. As someone committed to the development of writing in Wales, who wants things to be better for the writers who come after me, one question I have is whether a glass ceiling for Welsh writers operates, where there's a more open sky for poets from other parts of the UK.

I once had the experience of a filmmaker from London coming to my village to make a film about my work. We talked in detail about this area of the South Wales Valleys, the rich history, the gorgeous people, the industry, and I read a number of poems in a number of suitably photogenic locations which were filmed from a number of angles. I wasn't shown the film in advance and, when it was shown, in a London club, it consisted almost entirely of shots of washing lines, run-down buildings and torn advertising hoardings. None of the poems had made the final cut. I live in one of the most beautiful places on earth, with breath-taking, sweeping mountains and views of a valley. It's very difficult to set a camera up anywhere here and not record something that's stunning. There was much laughter in the London room in response to the film's trotting out of stereotypes of Welsh life. Afterwards, one of Wales' leading writers, who was also there, asked an interesting question. Would it be considered acceptable to present any group of people other than Welsh people in such a comic way?

One thing I've wondered about is the extent to which this problem affects the access of Welsh writers to the big UK institutions of poetry: the significant book publishers, literary journals and awards. Once, at a London awards ceremony, I found myself as the only Welsh writer among a large number of poets shortlisted for the awards. This was in a year when there were a number of notable collections published by writers from Wales, even by some of the big London publishers. As poet after poet came to the mike to read their work, I couldn't help wondering: did the quality of the work mean that the right writers had been chosen? Or were there writers from Wales who deserved to be there every bit as much as those selected?

It's worth looking through the big canon-making institutions in the UK and asking what the representation of writing from Wales is like. Do the most significant UK publishers of poetry celebrate writing from Wales? Do the most significant UK awards celebrate writing from Wales? Are there people of influence, at editor and judge level in these institutions, who are committed to writing from Wales? Look through the contents pages of significant UK literary periodicals from outside of Wales, and can it be said that poetry from Wales is given fair coverage?

Such questions and isolated examples need to be set of course in the wider context of the overall very warm and welcoming support of poetry from Wales around the UK, and the significant poetry organisations outside of Wales which go out of their way to generate opportunities for Welsh writers. Moreover, if there are questions to be asked about the reception of our poetry in the UK, we also have to look at whether the institutions within Wales are always serving the writers, readers and culture of Wales in the best possible ways.

One thing that is certainly true is that the writer development and support programmes in Wales are absolutely the equal of those in England. Literature Wales' mentoring programmes have much in common with the Jerwood/Arvon programme, and do an exceptional job. The experience of working with a published writer on the developing manuscript of a collection, working the poems through several guided drafts and developing a relationship with that writer, can be transformative, taking a writer with potential to the position of being publishable. It can also have a huge benefit in terms of connecting the emerging poet to a supportive community of writers, and is no less a gift of an experience for the mentor than it is for the mentee. Moreover, the opportunities that Literature Wales gives to writers for freelance work, especially in this time of the pandemic, make being a writer in Wales viable, and the work of the organisation is one of the very best things about being a writer in Wales.

The Jerwood/Arvon mentorship programme has supported a range of lauded writers, including Niall Campbell, Richard Scott, Rachel Long, Romalyn Ante, Liz Berry, Ella Frears and Maitreyabandhu. How easy is it, I wonder, to construct a list of English-language poets from Wales who've come through our mentoring programmes, whose work has been equally deservedly lauded in the last ten years? Of course, as well as the way in which writing from Wales is received in the rest of the UK, there are issues such as funding levels and population density which make this comparison unfair. But I am absolutely of the opinion that our exceptional writer development programmes are resulting in exceptional work, so it's worth looking at what other aspects of writing in Wales can be improved.

One thing that inevitably has to be looked at is the nature of publishing in Wales, and on that basis, I would like this article to make one modest suggestion for how things for writers in Wales could be improved: that the bodies who fund publishing in Wales engage with writers as a way of quality-assessing that funding. It seems to me to be absolutely essential that any body giving public money to a publisher in Wales needs to be going to writers – and to readers, of course – and asking them whether they are happy with how things are. Perhaps such systems already exist but, as a writer who's been working actively in Wales for nearly a decade, I have to say I've never been made aware of them. I feel sure that writers with Welsh publishers are very happy with all of the things publishers have to deliver: how writers' work is edited and marketed; the provision of royalty statements, contracts and the financial management of writers' work; and the extent to which Welsh publishers are staffed and run by deeply engaged, passionate and transparently-appointed representatives of the diverse range of our writing communities. But unless someone is going to writers and asking them about these things, writers without agents – as poets in Wales invariably are – can feel voiceless, powerless and alone in terms of how they are treated by publishers, wary of putting their heads above the parapet for fear of how that might impact their careers. This is dangerous, because the relationship between publisher and writer has a key role in determining the decisions a writer makes in a career, including whether the writer even continues. Ultimately, of course, the impact here is on the cultural life of Wales. If publishers or the bodies that fund them actively and openly seek feedback from writers, which is inevitably going to improve what they deliver, that could be so brilliant for how things go in Wales.

I raise all these issues and ask all these questions, of course, from a position of significant privilege and fortune in terms of how my own poetry has been supported and received by all these organisations, inside and outside Wales, I'm referring to – indeed, as someone whose work has been over-celebrated – and out of the most enormous gratitude for this. I also know that any barriers to the real writer can be really as useful as applause, are only motivators to write harder and better, to soar over them. When I think of being a Welsh poet in the world, I think of the greatest moments of my life, on the streets of Kolkata and Gdansk, London and Genoa, and say an enormous *Thank you* for them. To be a poet in Wales is to be blessed, with the greatest writer support systems and the greatest subject matter – the beauty of our country, history and people – which can be accessed just by turning your head.

I also ask my questions, though, out of a knowledge of the depth of talent and hard work of writers in Wales, and a desire for every Welsh writer, now and in the future, to have the applause they deserve. The English-language literary culture of Wales is dominated by the shadow of Dylan Thomas' premature death, and is as such in part a history of the books that weren't written, the books we have lost. It's so important that we all get everything right, look for every opportunity to be better. For the Welsh writers who come next, I want things to be even fairer. I don't want one Welsh writer who should keep going to give up: I want every Welsh writer standing outside an Italian prison as a guard checks their photo on his phone. Or rather, I want every Welsh writer doing whatever the hell it is they dream of.

If I started this article with the image of standing outside a prison, I'd like to conclude with an image I'll borrow from *The Great Escape*. It's night, and Steve McQueen is standing over there in the trees, twitching a bit of rope to let the escaping prisoners know when the guard isn't looking, and they can emerge from the tunnel that the whole prison community have spent the last few months, have staked their lives, to build. The rope twitches and a head emerges, mole-like from the ground. As it does the lights come up, and the night is gone. There's no need to worry, though, because the prison camp, the guards, the watch towers, have all gone too. If you look across the grass, you can see now that there isn't just one hole, but a hundred, a thousand, heads emerging from every one. Look again and you'll see that every person lifting themselves from a hole is holding a pen, and they're stepping forward now, sitting at a desk to write a poem, or else standing to read. Every one of them is Welsh. In front of them is a clear view of the entire world, all its readers waiting for those pens to move, for those mouths to open. Just imagine that. Just imagine how bloody brilliant that would be.

IMPACT OF THE BLACK LIVES MATTER MOVEMENT IN WALES

Charlotte Williams

In October of 2020 the First Minister, Mark Drakeford, went on record as saying, '*Welsh history is Black history and Black history is Welsh history*'.[1] He was responding to a longstanding but accelerated call for more attention to what we might call Black histories in public education, including within the national school curriculum. Now, I am not an academic historian, but it was clear to me that what he was actually suggesting was so much more than an interrogation of historiography. Because, whilst the 'Black history' debates speak directly to matters of integrating understanding of the contributions of Black people to Wales over time, they also demand attention to those long standing and ongoing debates about national identity, the nature of Welshness and the aspirations of this young democracy toward inclusiveness.

These matters are as much about racial inequality today as they are about that of yesterday; indeed, the reclaiming of lost, omitted or disguised histories is seen as crucial to contemporary developments on race equality. This is because race equality goes well beyond public policy to ask questions about the very identity of society itself. It evokes debates about nation and national belonging, about histories, culture and development. Who we are? Who we would like to be? This holding up a mirror to Welshness, the nature of Welsh identity, is not lost on politicians and policy makers who must square the oxymoron between an appeal to an ethnically based distinctive national identity, as foregrounded in making the case for devolution, and the ambition to build more civic and inclusive representations of national identities.

In the twenty years of devolved government these issues have taken on a new social energy. That Wales is, and always has been, a multicultural society is now reported almost as a banal matter of fact. That many people could probably give a lay account of the links of the iron masters, the slate barons, the wool merchants and the missionaries to the trade in slaves, or speak to the appearance in their localities of Black people from the past – servants, students, gardeners, musicians and more, is indeed heartening. Neither would it any longer be of remark to hear a Black person proclaim their Welsh identity or claim a sense of place and belonging to a locality of Wales, speaking in English, Welsh or a heritage language. Yet, it remains rare to see that person in a decision-making or leadership role in Welsh affairs and even rarer still to hear them attest to not having encountered racisms as part of their lived experience. Such is the anomaly of any notion of progress on race equality, such is the anomaly of history.

Yet this term, *Black history,* has increasingly found a place within contemporary public policy. Indeed, recent events such as the Windrush scandal, the Brexit immigration debates and the Black Lives Matter campaign have mobilised this terminology, as have calls to decolonise education at school and higher education level. These calls are close to home with, for example, current efforts to embed Black histories as a mandatory element of the national curriculum or debates about Wales' public monuments. All this proceeds, I would suggest, without too much real care in defining what Black history means. If, for example, it loosely refers to the histories of the Black African and Caribbean diaspora then it omits recognition of swathes of other minority cultures pertinent to its ambition to highlight what is hidden.

That said, and definitional issues put aside, the arguments for the significance of increased attention to Black history are longstanding and well-rehearsed. Opening up these hidden or distorted histories can reveal recognition of the contributions of Black and minority ethnic peoples to the economic, social and cultural development of the nation; they can animate agency, heritage and belonging for black people today; tell us about change; and let's face it, their omission has become increasingly embarrassing and damaging to the credibility of the discipline of history itself. The Royal Historical Society 2018 Report *Race Ethnicity and Equality in UK History* acknowledges the need for '*substantial structural and cultural change within the discipline*'[2] and James Phillips writing in Llafur in 2020[3] referred to the need for a long overdue re-investigation of systemic racism in Welsh history.

I say again, I am not an academic historian, and I recognise the recent trend towards the democratisation of history may have both positive and negative impacts. If it means we are all users of history and can be involved in the how of knowledge building, then an important dimension of today's activism for racial equality has become this revealing of the past. On the other hand, this revealing of the past by anyone and everyone, with little or no critical exploration or even understanding of the context of the facts could potentially lead to a montage that discredits the very stories it seeks to promote and at worst serve to undermine the enterprise that is historiography.

Despite my personal fascination and curiosity in this seam of Welsh history my preoccupation has been with contemporary social policy responses to Black and minority ethnic peoples in Wales. What is of interest to me therefore is the way in which the notion of Black history connects with this particular contemporary moment in Welsh social policy making.

The landmark of the pandemic, itself history making, has provided a magnifying lens on a critical conjuncture in the race politics of the UK. If in this Covid-19 era we have been obliged to pause and reflect on big issues of our time, the spectacle of the murder of George Floyd by Minneapolis policeman Derek Chauvin triggered a global outcry on matters of racial inequality which consolidated under the banner of the Black Lives Matter (BLM) campaign. The campaign itself quickly extended from a protest about police injustice to a protest about wider institutional injustice and then the demand broadened to protest over the symbols of slavery and past colonial power, across the western world. From the statues of HM Stanley in the north to Thomas Picton in the South, Wales was going to make transparent its involvement in, and rewards from, the ugly trade. And more. The BLM campaign demonstrated very clearly the enduring link between historical legacies of colonialism and imperialism and racial inequality and injustices today.

This jolt to the national consciousness set in motion a number of politically driven initiatives in Wales aimed at shifting the agenda towards a more active anti-racist stance. A Ministerial sub-group would quickly demonstrate the disproportionate effects of the pandemic on Black and minority ethnic communities in terms of infection and mortality rates as well as social and economic impacts. It was glaringly apparent that because racial and ethnic minority groups tend to be overrepresented in precarious work and in certain sectors of the labour market, they were considerably more affected by lockdowns, more likely to have lost income and become unemployed and to be vulnerable in terms of their profile in the health and social care workforce. We learned that 44% of medical staff of the UK are from ethnic minorities but 95% of those who died were from ethnic minorities. This provided evidence of their vital contribution, without which the system in Wales would surely collapse. In response to the findings of the subgroup, which was chaired by Professor Emmanuel Ogbonna, the government commissioned a number of evidence reviews on racial inequalities across a sweep of social policy areas including education, health, housing, crime and justice, employment and a review of representation of minority groups in leadership to underpin its new Race Equality Plan. This would be complemented by a detailed review of Arts, Culture and heritage. The evidence glaringly attested to the compromised life chances of Black and minority ethnic peoples in Wales and their lack of representation in decision making positions in Wales over a considerable period of time.

As the statue of Edward Colston was toppled in Bristol, the Welsh government would conduct its own thoroughgoing audit of statues, monuments and street names with connections to the slave trade, (perhaps documenting a street near you) under the steer of Gaynor Legall, a prominent Black political leader. And in response to a mass petition on the absence of Black history in schools, the government convened a Ministerial working group, which I chaired, to consider how to enable and embed these lost or hidden perspectives into the heart of the new curriculum. In fact, the Black history Committee of Race Council Cymru had for some considerable years been advocating for just such a development without any inroad. An opportune moment had appeared.

This unprecedented ratcheting up of policy attention to racial inequalities on the part of the Welsh government and many of its associated institutions carried particular import in as much as it signaled a new trajectory in race policy in Wales which would stand in stark contrast to approaches prevalent across the wider UK. After 20 years of devolution and 20 years of a devolutionary settlement that had constitutionally embedded race equality from the outset, the government would acknowledge its failings and seek to steer a more proactive course towards an '*Anti-racist Wales by 2030*', acknowledging deep institutional racism and the problematic of implementation despite many good intentions. Things were stepping up. Wales would ostensibly shift from a historically largely laissez-faire approach towards an active, nationally responsible and interventionist plan on race equality. The key departure at this juncture being the considered and orchestrated investment of Black and minority ethnic actors in the design and shape of this policy future. A highly participatory and novel approach drew on the strengths of both top-down and bottom-up stakeholders to craft a refreshed plan; a plan which would be firmly embedded within the principles of the broader distinctive values underpinning Welsh social policy making.

This stance is not, however, without challenge. Years of lethargy and resistance to change characterise Welsh public policy and institutional life. In as much as we can hear the oft cited claim of Wales as a tolerant nation or a sanctuary of safety, we can also summon the spectre of heavy-handed policing, ongoing miscarriages of justice towards Black and minority ethnic people, vitriolic on social media and acknowledged and widespread institutional racism. Currently, three high-profile cases continue to raise grave questions over injustices perpetrated by the state; that of Moyied Bashir, Mohamud Hassan, and Siyanda Mngaza, all raising ongoing appeals. And then there's the recent case of Christopher Kapessa, aged 13, who the Crown Prosecution Service established was pushed into a river *'with two hands'* but decided that it would not be in the public interest to launch a prosecution. Within 24 hours of being pushed into the Afon Cynon, South Wales Police Force had concluded that this was a tragic accident rather than a tragic incident in which 'race' just might play a part.

Doubtless there are complex considerations in all of these cases and indeed policing falls outside the remit of the Welsh government, but collectively these instances continue to impact negatively on the Black communities of Wales and undermine trust in the institutional processes.

And then there are other major institutions in Wales that have accepted the levy of institutional racism. In an investigative review that they themselves commissioned, The Arts Council and the Museum of Wales were both recently pilloried in the press for their lack of diverse representation in the workforce and lethargy in relation to access and participation of minority ethnic groups. And in education in Wales, we might as well adopt a phrase once used by the Director General of the BBC, Greg Dyke when describing the organisation as 'hideously white'. As a pupil today you are very unlikely to have had the opportunity to be taught by a member of the Black community and are indeed unlikely to do so in your entire education, including at university, if you remain in Wales. Big questions are consistently raised about implementation and about representation. How could the strong values-led steer of central government be made salient and compelling to the broad governance of these affairs across Wales?

And then there is the wider public. If you look out and about at street level there is no doubting a strong sense of multicultural conviviality in Wales and an expressed national sentiment that speaks to a welcoming, tolerant and inclusive Wales. Black and other minority groups often give positive voice to things being different in Wales from elsewhere in the UK. The 2021 *Fear and Hope Wales* report that aims to gauge public attitudes shows that the vast majority of people across Wales celebrate diversity and community, and are open to difference and change. However, it also demonstrates that there is a sizeable proportion of the population who hold more hostile attitudes which contradict a view of Wales as welcoming, open and tolerant. The report highlights a number of potential pressures in the current context that might tip the balance against such conviviality, in particular the expected retrenchment of public services and increased austerity post-Covid, the ongoing manipulation of populist racist hostility on social media and the political crafting of an invidious divide between Black and white working class, as accelerated post-Brexit.

This complex multifaceted picture of race and Wales is exactly what the history of the matter tells us. Drop a pin at any point in history and you will find both progressive and regressive elements, empathy and antipathy. Such that we have to ask: do the claimed Welsh sensibilities of tolerance, empathy and internationalism drive or inhibit change for race equality?

My engagement with race studies in Wales started with reading Ken Little's classic 1947 study, *Negroes in Britain*. You'd pay quite a princely sum for an original copy of that book today and rightly so. Much as it has been criticised for its negative top-down social sciencey portrayal of the Butetown community of Cardiff, it remains an important document in the historiography of writings on migrant minorities in Wales for just that reason. It provided a rigorous sociological record of one of the oldest continuous settlements of a Black community in Europe, commenting on its multilingual, multi-ethnic, multi-faith demography and on indicators such as race relations, employment, housing, health and wellbeing, clearly evidencing disadvantage. It also revealed the policies of containment and the oppressive policy interventions of the time into the lives of residents within that highly stigmatised one square mile of Cardiff, a phenomenon Little's key critic the sociologist, St Claire Drake, himself a Black African-American observed was undergoing a process of redefinition: from a social condition *to a social problem*. As an aside, I can tell you this excellent case study of Black history in social policy never saw the light of day in my own degree days at Bangor University.

But we can go back even further in history. Neil Evans' writings on the 1919 Cardiff riots, highlight an anomalous situation of white working-class resentment of immigrant labour coexisting alongside this peaceable and highly miscegenetic community. As an academic historian, Neil has spent a very notable career addressing the historiography of writings on migrant minorities and his excavation of the tolerance thesis along a chronological timeline[4] argues that whilst this claim of Welsh exceptionalism has been an important and continuing thread historically he can make no case in support of the tolerance thesis, citing examples of both strongly anti-racist sentiment and action but at the same time arguing we should be wary of observing anything like a universalist anti-racist culture.

What Neil is drawing attention to here, is the unevenness between and within nation of any coherent stance on anti-racism arguing for the need to seek out a 'bottom-up' lived experience as well as a top-down politics of race in tracing policy development. Here the past speaks to the present. Race and racism find different articulations in different places at different times. It might be difficult in parts of Wales to convince a teacher, social worker or civil servant of the need to prioritise attention to race and racism if their service population doesn't seem to be suggesting such. Salience and engagement with the issues remains a huge barrier to progress. Moses Roper may well be the symbol of the remarkable abolitionist efforts in our history as might ultimately be many of those white young people who took the knee and stood side by side with Black protesters in the BLM campaign. But neither could proclaim or guarantee Wales as an anti-racist nation. The actions of government can lead, symbolise and aspire to anti-racism but it is we the people that make it happen, or not. And, as we all know, an anti-racist nation is not the same thing as a racially equal nation. Sadly, the evidence suggests we are far from being able to speak of a post-racial society and far from being able to draw on a coherent historical record that demonstrates any particularity on anti-racist thinking.

The fact is that race itself is a slippery phenomenon and race equality equally subject to the winds of change. It depends on what you are looking at, from what perspective and on how you are measuring success or otherwise. I'd like, as the historians and sociologists do, to refute the whole nonsense of the idea of race itself, to dispute both its biological and quasi-scientific origins as a way of ordering communities and evidence and indeed wish it away as having any utility even a social construct. The history of the matter tells us that the majority Welsh identity has itself been bruised by racisms as well as minority ethnic communities and that this is a pivotal point of alliance. Many Welsh nationalists of the 18th and 19th centuries would readily identify with the plight of their imperial subjects on just such racialised grounds, but hold back from questioning imperialism itself, an anomalous positioning in evidence even today.

The history of the matter also reveals Welsh people's role in empire building, missionary trails that followed the routes of the colonial expansion, deep lines of connection to the slave economy, settler colonialism and a coal power that fueled colonial expansion. In short, global connections and interactions which should easily place Wales in the World claiming its own responsibility in the sins and gains of the past and easily qualify the fact that Welsh history is Black history.

This Black history of Wales can, of course, be constructed from a number of perspectives. Bottom-up through the lives of individuals like John Ystumllyn, Nathaniel Wells or Dorothy Bonarjee; by pursuing commodities like iron, coal and wool; by looking at cultural transformations or indeed by tracking race as a theme in social and public policy. We can usefully summon this history in contemporary debates to place and locate the minority communities of Wales and to celebrate their contributions. But here is the rub.

Leaving aside those complex questions of ownership, authorship and representation in history making, those questions about how history is constructed, what knowledges are selected and told, my fear is that Black history is too often construed as just a number of fascinating little stories drawn from across Wales, a showcase of discrete artefacts and memorabilia resurrected within particular expressions of *cynefin* without context, connection or critical exploration. This is, of course, a very effective way of ensuring Black history remains marginal both in popular debate and within a historiography. Black history can all too easily be seen as an interesting add-on extra, compartmentalised or listed as part of a long list of specialised subjects or events rather than being embedded into the main narrative. A fact that has allowed Wales to dodge attention to addressing the role of local, regional and national connections to the history of empire and colonialism and cling to a safe set of stories that does not dislodge or unsettle the majority perceptions of white Wales. I concur with James Phillips when he says *'interpretations of the lives of ordinary people cannot be pieced together effectively if those uncomfortable aspects of the puzzle are shied away from'.*[3] In our lay hands, in particular, we are guilty of deploying such Black histories as a salve for contemporary yearnings for belonging amongst the Black community when more substantially we should address this as a matter of collective national identity.

Were we to consider Wales and the World as a meta-narrative and robustly explore a transnational historiography, this would take us beyond the problematic of specific content, beyond the selecting of what/who exactly counts as Black history, how much and where, to those big themes of empire, imperialism and colonialism and globalisation that bind these perspectives and that concern us all, not just people from Black communities. This process is underway. Research by Chris Evans on Welsh involvement in and financial gain from the slave trade is but one example. We know those slave ships that left Liverpool and Bristol needed a reservoir of labour and employment opportunities for sailors and ship's captains which were filled by Welsh crew. And we know that the mining of copper in Anglesey and its processing in Swansea serviced the operation of slavery in many ways. This is everyone's history not just Black people's history.

Perhaps the optimistic view is that in Wales we are less threatened by this questioning of the past in terms of national identity and not aligned to the defensive and protectionist little Britain visioning that is now the trope of Brexit-England. Resistance to such interrogation has been a noted feature of right-wing political leaning across the UK, the Brexit debates casting this questioning of Britain's past as unpatriotic, woke-driven loony leftism. In stark contrast, the current policy trajectory on race equality in Wales is clear evidence of an openness and willingness to reshape Welsh national identity within a new participatory democracy, to open up that dialogue and questioning as a matter of everyday citizenship. The questioning of public monuments, places, street names and nationally held artefacts associated with slavery has suggested a new transparency and has raised public awareness. The discipline of history is publicly ruminating and Welsh history is being actively revisited. We are questioning understandings of *cynefin* in the national curriculum and are preparing to work on a decolonising agenda within education aimed at equipping young people as ethical and informed citizens of Wales and the world. This refashioning of Welsh ways of life, its imagery and identity and interrogating Wales' imperial past has long been argued by Gwyn Alf Williams, and it is what will make these contemporary policies travel. But it will take broad collective endeavor to realise the government's ambitions in this respect, a deepened understanding of the import and use of this history; an understanding of why racial category emerged, why it exists, what sustains it and how it plays out in the lived experience of Welsh citizens today.

What is critical is that we don't leave the Black history debate suspended in the ether of interesting stories but work to connect it to the present context and seize what just might be a critical conjuncture in current affairs, an opportunity to move forward in a different way. From the social intimacies of inter-racial marriages, the ebbs and flows of multiple migrations, to the analysis of industrial and economic development, to today's transnational and digital connections, there is a need to build a more robust framework for locating this refreshed look at the past.

Rising to the radical agenda that the government has put

forward will mean, not reducing the change effort to a technical or managerialist activity of institutional procedure, or add-on tokenistic attention to putting a little black on whitestream agendas but actively promoting narratives rooted in a refashioned idea of Welsh ways of life, exploring histories that make connections and develop symmetry, and seeking out the potential allyship that was evident in our past. Addressing the solidarities of a strongly working-class tradition in Wales, and looking beyond host/minority, black/white thinking will be important. We can look to the past for examples of shared mobilisations, encourage and sponsor new groupings and alliances to form robust advocacy coalitions and forge new style relationships between policy actors, academia and the third sector. There are many great examples on the record of Welsh action for racial justice that provide a basis for empowering action in the present. And as academics we will need to take the challenge of interdisciplinary approaches to ethnicity studies and trans national studies in Wales more seriously.

There is a long way to go in building trust and confidence and making real the new vocabularies of power sharing and participation within this vision of an anti-racist Wales. But the seeds to successful change rely on a confidence in redrawing the past.

The pandemic era is far from over and its full impacts are not yet known, but what is already clear is that it has brought in its wake a critical moment of reflection on the aspiration for a more racially equal Wales at a time when a populist backlash suggest divisiveness, competition and individualism. This moment of reflection has demanded looking back into that history, taking stock of where we are now, as well as looking forward to what we, as a nation might craft by way of alternative futures. The First Minister's message is signaling clearly that we need to revisit and reimagine our past in order to regain a more racially equal future but also, I believe, he is suggesting that there is no such thing as Black history as distinct from our collective history. In this respect *Black history* takes on a new meaning and becomes more of a useful cypher for exploring racial inequality, an opportunity to re-examine and reorder a past in order to direct a future, to open out a strong rationale to underpin why we are addressing this today irrespective of the complexion and demography of our local area. Black history matters to us all. So, let's follow the First Minister's steer and embed Black history in a refreshed Welsh history that speaks to Wales in the world, then we can talk with confidence about Welsh history.

With thanks to Neil Evans and Dr. Marian Gwyn for their earlier review of this paper.

---

[1] https://twitter.com/fmwales/status/1311576846895665153?lang=en

[2] https://royalhistsoc.org/racereport/

[3] J. Phillips (2020) Respecting the Past, Responding to the Present: Confronting 'Race', Racism and Memorialisation through the 2020 Llafur Summer Series. Llafur Vol 12:4, pp. 95-107

[4] N. Evans, How White was my Valley? Immigrants and Minorities in Modern Wales. Llafur Vol 12:4, pp. 68-95

Dame Shirley Bassey, Angus McBean Photograph (MS Thr 581).

Vivien Leigh, Angus McBean Photograph (MS Thr 581).

Emlyn Williams, Angus McBean Photograph (MS Thr 581).

Sir Watkin Williams-Wynn, 4th Bt.,
Thomas Apperly and Captain Edward Hamilton
Artist: BATONI, Pompeo (1707-1787)

Thomas Jones (1742-1803)
Artist: MARCHI, Giuseppe (c.1735-1813)

The Fisher Boys
Artist: WILLIAMS, Penry (1802-1885)
© Amgueddfa Cymru / National Museum Wales

REBECCAITES, OR 'BECCAS.

Image from the Illustrated London News using the Welsh hat to identify “Rebecca” as a representitive of Wales https://welshhat.wordpress.com

Unnafred Shones, wife to Shon-ap-Morgan, with her son and heir Morgan-ap-Shones, satirical print
with permission of British Museum Images

The Wales Window in the Sixteenth Street Baptist Church, Birmingham, Alabama
© Virginia Jones Photography

'The Four Spirits' Public Memorial
Sculpture by Elizabeth MacQueen in Kelly Ingram Park, opposite the Sixteenth Street Baptist Church
© Cerith Mathias 2013

A plaque at the Sixteenth Street Baptist Church dedicated to the Wales Window and the four girls who perished in the bombing
© Cerith Mathias 2013

The Wales Window in the Sixteenth Street Baptist Church,
Birmingham, Alabama
© Virginia Jones Photography

THE MOMENT IS FOREVER: The Wales Window of Alabama

Cerith Mathias

Next year marks the 60th anniversary of the bombing of the Sixteenth Street Baptist Church in Birmingham, Alabama. A shocking act of racism that killed four young girls who were attending Sunday school. It was the deadliest moment of the US civil rights era, a tragedy that ushered in sweeping legislative changes that had been long called-for across the country.

Events that day also began deep connections between Wales, the church and the movement for racial equality following a national gesture of goodwill and compassion in the form of a stained-glass window known as the Wales Window, created by the artist John Petts. It forever linked two families on opposite sides of the Atlantic — the Petts family in Wales and the family of the Reverend John Cross, the church's Pastor in Alabama.

To grasp fully the significance of the change brought about by the actions of their fathers, Cerith Mathias spoke to the children of those changemakers John Cross and John Petts to ask about their memories of that time and what the Wales Window means all these years later.

The morning of Sunday, September 15th, 1963, began grey and overcast in Birmingham, Alabama. The days preceding it had been cloud-covered, filtering the city in a slate-toned light. The temperature was a little below average for the area at that time of year, with long shirt sleeves replacing the bare arms of a scorching Southern summer a little earlier than usual.

For 13 year old Barbara Cross, despite the weather the morning dawned with a sense of excitement. It was the beginning of the school year, her second as a resident of Birmingham. Her family had relocated to the city in June the previous year, when her father the Reverend John Cross had been called to pastor the Sixteenth Street Baptist Church, the oldest black church in the area. It was to be the first time he'd initiated Youth Sunday under his ministry, and she was eager to get to church and enjoy the proceedings with her friends.

Her mother had decided to stay at home that morning; she wasn't feeling well and with Barbara and her three siblings, Michael, Alma and Lynn on the brink of another school year, she had chores keeping her busy, so father and children made the twenty minute journey across town from the parsonage to the church. Autumn was Reverend John Cross' favourite time of year. A change of season, a punctuation point in the calendar often associated with new beginnings, a time to refocus.

That morning, the Sixteenth Street Baptist Church, a large, broad and solid looking structure that commands the corner of Birmingham's Sixteenth Street and Sixth Avenue North was filled with the chatter of children. After their Sunday school classes, which were held in the church's basement, the younger members of the congregation were to take part in the main morning service upstairs. With classes underway, Reverend Cross turned to the final preparations for his sermon, taken from Luke 23:34, in which Jesus on the cross asks God to forgive those crucifying him. As always there were church matters for him to tend to, including many administrative tasks. There had been a problem with the gas hot water heater in the kitchen area – something that would need to be fixed. A job for another day however; today his attention was focused on his congregation, on the children of the church on Youth Sunday.

In the church basement, Sunday school lessons were beginning to wind down. Barbara Cross' class had finished and fresh in her mind was that day's lesson – 'A Love that Forgives' – where along with her classmates she had learned about brotherly love and the act of forgiveness. Forgiveness was to be the overarching theme of worship that day, one that would be continued in Reverend Cross' sermon.

Many of the children were milling around in the basement before heading upstairs for the morning service, one group of boys deep in conversation about football and the church band of which they were all members. Barbara Cross was still in the basement too; her teacher, Mrs. DeMann, had given her a task to finish before she could join the service upstairs, she was to write down the names of those who would be moving up to the next age level in Sunday school. A good, respectful student, Barbara set about the task at hand, declining a request from her friend Addie Mae Collins that she join her and three classmates, Carole Robertson, Cynthia Wesley and Denise McNair in the girls' bathroom after class. Promising Addie that she'd be along as soon as the assignment was finished, Barbara handed over her wallet for safekeeping, telling her friend that she'd collect it from her in just a moment.

Upstairs, her father had left his study. John Cross made his way to the Sixteenth Street side of the building to sit in on the women's bible study class, their lesson that morning also about forgiveness. The time was a little before 10.20am. As Reverend Cross listened to the women's discussion, a telephone rang in the church's office. In her role as Sunday school secretary, 15 year old Carolyn Maull answered.

'Three minutes' said a male voice before hanging up.

Carolyn replaced the receiver and made to leave the office. She took around fifteen steps. Downstairs, the boys' animated conversation was still in full swing. Barbara Cross had just added a fifth name to her list of students. A great roar tore through the church, a noise unlike anything the children had ever heard before. At first, the Reverend Cross thought the faulty water tank in the kitchen had finally given way, but soon realised that the fumes filling the air weren't gas, they were powder. The building shook violently and in the basement everything went dark.

When the bomb exploded it was 10.22am.

Hours earlier, under the cover of darkness, a small splinter group of the racist white supremacist organisation the Ku Klux Klan, had carried out something they had previously been overheard boasting about. The group, all local to Birmingham, had planted a stack of dynamite under the church steps and set a timer for the blast to coincide exactly with that Sunday's worship.

On the other side of the Atlantic, in the small Welsh coastal village of Llansteffan the weather was brighter. A sunny September day greeted the artist John Petts, as he prepared to spend his Sunday with the usual division of family and work, a split between kitchen conversations and hours spent in his studio, a converted cow-shed in the garden of the family home, Cambrian House in the heart of the village. A home life the acclaimed stained glass artist shared with his wife, the poet Kusha Petts and their three children, David, Catrin and Michael.

Owing to the time difference, morning in Alabama was afternoon in Wales, and at the time the Cross family were settling in to church proceedings, John Petts was already stationed in his studio. After a typical Sunday morning of answering correspondence and dealing with paperwork, he had left Kusha sitting in the garden enjoying the September sunshine while he continued work on a window that he'd been crafting for three months. As he worked, his radio burbled in the background, tuned as it often was to the BBC's Home Service.

Back in Birmingham, Reverend John Cross had quickly grasped the situation unfolding in his church. Calling on his congregation to evacuate the building, to 'get out!' He ran downstairs, crisscrossing the basement, going from one room to another to make sure the children were leaving safely. When he finally reached the pavement outside, he stood in clouds of smoke, dust and debris; some of his congregation were injured, others frantically searched for family members and friends. His daughter Barbara had been struck in the head by a light fixture, her younger sister Lynn, aged just 4, had been taken to hospital. The church itself had been badly damaged, the sanctity of promised sanctuary wounded. The stone steps had been destroyed, windows smashed, the twisted fragments of brick and glass spilling out on to the street. The face of Jesus in the church's main stained glass window was blown clean out, his watchful gaze seemingly vanished.

Needing to calm the amassing crowd, Reverend John Cross began pacing the pavement.

'Please go home,' he urged, tears streaming his cheeks. 'The Lord is our shepherd, and we shall not want.'

People were still unaccounted for. Stepping back into the church through a gaping hole that had been slashed into the east wall, Reverend Cross and others began to dig through the rubble. There, where only a short time before the girls bathroom stood, they discovered four bodies. Under the wreckage lay 14-year-olds Addie Mae Collins, Carole Robertson and Cynthia Wesley and 11 year old Denise McNair, huddled together, John Cross thought, as if they were hugging.

In Wales, as the afternoon sunshine outside his Llansteffan garden studio began to melt into early evening, John Petts' concentration had been abruptly broken by a news bulletin on the radio. News of the atrocity unfolding in Alabama had travelled. He was horrified firstly by the loss of life; after all his daughter Catrin was the same age as three of the girls who had perished. At the same time, as an artist, details of the church's smashed windows also caught his attention.

'My word, what can we do about this,' he thought, his mind not able to pass over the information he'd just heard. He hurried from his studio to tell Kusha of the news, an idea already nagging at him that somehow they ought to do something in response, a 'gesture of fellowship and goodwill... surely that's better than just tut-tutting and protesting and saying, "how dreadful," and then passing on to a happier part of the news.'

The thought would give him no peace, sending him back and forth between studio and wife, wife and studio, the details of the racist bombing swirling around his mind. Kusha Petts, equally appalled by the news, yet knowing her husband's nature issued him with the prompt he needed. "Now look," she told him, "Either do something about it or shut up."

It was the jolt Petts required. Sunday though it was, he headed for the large black Bakelite telephone in the kitchen and dialled the number of his friend David Cole, the Editor of The Western Mail. Cole suggested that they run a fundraising campaign in the newspaper to replace the large stained glass window in the Sixteenth Street Baptist Church with a window of Petts' design. No one would be allowed to donate more than half a crown each, to ensure that the gesture would truly be given 'as a gift from the people of Wales.' Two days later on Tuesday September 17th, the Western Mail launched the campaign with the headline 'Alabama: Chance for Wales to

Show the Way.' Photographs were printed in the newspaper of children giving their pocket money to the appeal and donations arrived from all over Wales. Within weeks the target of £500 had been surpassed with the fund closing at £900, and Cole quickly found himself making preparations for John Petts to visit Alabama to discuss the replacement window with Reverend John Cross.

The campaign had been a success. However, one problem remained. Constrained by the segregationist Jim Crow laws which were practiced statewide in Alabama, as a white man, John Petts' presence in a black neighbourhood in Birmingham, working with a black church would not only be met with disapproval by the state's devoutly pro-segregationist Governor, George Wallace, but it could also be mortally dangerous for both himself and Reverend John Cross. Knowing this, both men decided to bridge the man-made divide, the legitimacy of which neither chose to recognise.

'The people of Wales offer to recreate and erect a stained glass window to replace one shattered in the bombing of your church,' read the initial telegram sent by David Cole and John Petts to the Reverend John Cross. 'They do this as a gesture of comfort and support.'

The reply: Wales was 'the only country to offer such direct and material assistance.'

*

In Birmingham, the months prior to September the 15th had been tumultuous. As one of the most racially divided cities in the US, a situation enforced both legally and culturally, racially motivated bombings were not extraordinary at that time. Nearly fifty unsolved incidents had taken place from the late 1940s through to the mid-1960s, leading to the city's macabre nickname 'Bombingham.'

Reverend John Cross had agreed to Dr King's request that the Sixteenth Street Baptist Church be used as a meeting place for the civil rights movement. Becoming the beating heart of the movement's campaign to be 'Free in '63', the streets directly outside the church were where Dr Martin Luther King Jr's calls for non-violent protest met with water cannons, baton wielding police officers and the snarling, snapping jaws of police dogs. As the movement's hub in the city, the church also became the organising centre of the children's crusade, a drive that in May 1963 produced the Birmingham Accord — an agreement to de-segregate schools, lunch counters, drinking fountains and public bathrooms in the city.

Dr King proclaimed that change was coming to 'the most thoroughly segregated city in the United States,' and that 'the walls of segregation will crumble in Birmingham, and they will crumble soon.'

Just a fortnight before the Sixteenth Street bombing, on August 28th King made his 'I Have a Dream' speech at the Lincoln Memorial in front of over two-hundred-thousand people who had marched on Washington. Meanwhile, a menacing tension crackled through Birmingham's streets.

The unremarkable, overcast weather in the days before Sunday, September 15th provide a deceivingly bland backdrop for events that month. September 4th had seen the integration of the first three of the city's schools. White supremacist rhetoric spat back biliously at the move, Governor George Wallace sent state troopers to Birmingham in an attempt to derail the process and the ten days that followed were filled with violent anti-de-segregation protests. Rioting ensued and the home of civil rights attorney Arthur Shores, an ardent advocate of integrating the city's schools was bombed for the second time in fifteen days. Suspected Klansmen toting confederate flags planted themselves at two of the newly desegregated schools' gates. On September 10th, President John F. Kennedy federalised the Alabama National Guard to enforce integration, a deployment of federal authority not seen since the aftermath of the Civil War. Speaking to The New York Times, state Governor George Wallace stood firm in his prejudice telling a reporter that in order to halt integration, 'What this country needs is a few first class funerals.'

A week later, a group of white supremacists enacted Wallace's rhetoric by planting a bomb at the Sixteenth Street Baptist Church. The bomb would senselessly snuff out the lives of Addie Mae Collins, Carole Robertson, Cynthia Wesley and Denise McNair and injure twenty two others. The resulting chaotic unrest immediately afterwards also claimed the lives of two teenage boys: 16 year old Johnny Robinson who was shot in the back by police officers and 13 year old Virgil Ware who was shot while riding through a residential suburb on the handlebars of his brother's bike. The bombers, members of a splinter group of the Ku Klux Klan known as the Cahaba boys, were already suspected of other racist attacks in the city. Despite being identified in the investigation that followed the bombing, it would take another forty years before they were brought to justice. The Reverend John Cross and his daughter Barbara would testify at each of the three trials that were to come.

Events in Birmingham were condemned the world over. The death of the four girls shocked those with the power to bring about meaningful change to act. That Sunday altered forever the course of the civil rights movement, and became according to many, a catalyst for the Civil Rights Act of 1964 and the Voting Rights Act of 1965. A day never to be forgotten, commemorated by a stained glass window designed and made in a small Welsh village and installed to convey the brighter days that its creator hoped the Southern sun would reflect through its panes.

Indeed, Petts' window would stand as more than a gesture of support. Its bold design became a symbol of the civil rights movement itself, a statement that change was not coming, but that it was already here. The window told those supporting the segregationist status quo that things were going to be different from now on in. Petts' window would be the first ever depiction of a black Jesus in stained glass form in the United States.

John Petts sailed to America in March 1964, spending a week with Reverend Cross and the church's building committee. His arrival and the purpose of his visit was kept from the press for fear any publicity would result in racist backlash. He was accompanied everywhere by a bodyguard, and for safety the Reverend Cross sent his wife Julia along with Barbara and her siblings to stay with relatives for the duration of Petts' time in Birmingham. Petts and Cross had much in common. Reverend Cross was a people person who loved to talk, his wife often joking with him, 'Cross you've preached too long', while it was said that John Petts had the gift of the gab and was a phenomenal talker, his presence in a room never going unnoticed. Both Johns had also served in the Second World War. Petts, a conscientious objector who abhorred violence of any kind, was reluctant to talk about much of his wartime experience which had placed him at one point near the Nazi concentration camp Bergen-Belsen. Cross had spent time in France and Japan and had suffered the humiliating racist abuse of his fellow American soldiers throughout his service. Both men were witness to the ugly behaviour of humankind. The window, for both was to convey another way of being. 'What this window is fighting about,' Petts said 'is what man does to man.'

Upon Petts' return home to Wales, the importance of the commission weighed heavily upon him, and the artist struggled to settle on a design, one that would speak to 'the problem of what we do to each other during the short time we have the gift of living on the earth.'

Both Petts' sons, David Felix-Dexter and Michael Petts, remember that time in their lives vividly. The level of activity in their family home increased significantly while their father worked on the window.

Michael, who was 7 in 1963, remembers 'a level of angst' in the house. 'Both of my parents were disturbed by this event. And I can remember a lot of to-ing and fro-ing going on and this heightened state of alarm and disturbance.'

David, who was 16 in 1963 recalls the significance his father immediately placed on the window.

'This one had a completely different atmosphere and energy and momentum attached to it, the energy was quite remarkable,' he says. 'Our little coastal village in Wales was linked to a major international story. At that time, the death of children by violence was significantly other, it was a major piece of international news.'

David remembers clearly the moment his father, after much agonising, struck upon the design for what would become known as the Wales Window.

'He drew a hand, and such was the power in that drawing and the atmosphere and the energy of it, that he had to come up into the kitchen, into the house to tell us about it.' David says 'He wasn't quite shaking, but he was in a form of shock because something had happened that took him right out of himself. The bar was raised in this drawing that he'd done.'

Inspired by a verse from Matthew 25:40 that presents the message of brotherly love: 'Truly, I say to you, as you did it to one of the least of these my brothers, you did it to me'. Petts' window would depict a black Jesus 'a suffering figure in a crucified gesture, with one hand flung wide in protest, the other in acceptance.' Above his head, a rainbow constructed of tiny pieces of blue, purple and pink glass to represent racial unity, underneath the crucified figure the words 'You Do it to Me' in large black lettering. Below that, spelled out on tiles of red glass, 'Given by the People of Wales.'

David was to model for the torso of Jesus, asked by his father to twist and turn in different directions, the contortions representing the bodies of civil rights protestors under attack by the painful jets of police water cannons on Birmingham's streets.

'If you look at the window,' David says 'the figure is tilted to the left. So, I had to stretch in that position so John could look at what was happening with my breast bone and muscles.'

The head of the figure was modelled for by a photographer friend of John Petts, a man named Bill Paterson, who travelled to Llansteffan from London to stay with the family. The artist was also to take inspiration from his visits to Cardiff's docklands, then known as Tiger Bay and its multi-racial Rainbow Club, where he sketched the movement of the children there at play.

Both sons agree however that the most vital figure in Petts' process at that time was their mother, Kusha.

'Without my mum, it wouldn't have happened.' Michael says. 'She gave him that push by telling him to do something.'

'She had a sensibility and an awareness that he didn't have,' David recalls. 'Kusha was always quietly assisting someone who just lost a partner or a child or a parent. Or she was in attendance to a number of people who were dying. It was something she did, to participate, to share. And that's where they connected, he (Petts) had that too and that participation, that sharing is the background of this window.'

'For me the window says that there's no time for hate. We will reach out in love no matter what happens,' says Barbara Cross. The arrival of the gift from Wales she remembers fondly as 'a beacon of light' in a time of darkness, its unveiling taking place on June 6th, 1965 — the day of Barbara's 15th birthday.

'He was ahead of his time,' she says of John Petts, 'the way it's saying "stop the violence, stop the murders." The window speaks volumes about forgiveness.'

Forgiveness is a practice that has shaped Barbara Cross' life since that dark day almost sixty years ago.

'It's symbolic that our lesson that day in church was "A Love that Forgives." Because I hate what they did to us, but I can separate the deed from the person that did it. I wasn't taught to hate,' she says.

The dark shadow left by the bombing is unlikely ever to recede fully from Barbara's life; she still feels its presence to this day.

'If I hear loud noises, it bothers me, because I remember that sound. I'll never forget it,' she says. 'I get emotional, but I must be able to share this history through my tears.'

For a long time, she didn't like discussing the bombing in public. She says her nerves had suffered terribly and she shook for years afterwards.

'We were expected to go to church and to go to school like everything was normal,' she says of the weeks immediately following the bombing. 'I didn't have any counselling until I was an adult.'

Thinking of the classroom task given to her by her Sunday school teacher that day and the wallet that she never collected from her friend, she takes a deep breath.

'That writing assignment saved my life.'

Her father, the Reverend John Cross also bore the burden of that day until his death in 2007. In the later stages of his life, Barbara had been his caregiver.

Delayed justice for the victims took its toll on John Cross, during the three trials held many years after the bombing. He blamed himself for allowing Dr King and the civil rights movement to make his church the centre of its activities in Birmingham. Barbara says in his older years he would cry often.

'I think he had nightmares,' she says. 'But I told my dad, "You were courageous because if it wasn't your church, it would have been Dr King's Church or anybody's church. You knew that Dr King was trying to make a difference." I was so glad I had a chance to tell him that before he died.'

The events of September 15th, 1963, are seared into America's history, forever branding a moment of deep shame on its timeline.

'I like to think they are angels of change,' Barbara Cross says of her four classmates, none of whom lived beyond the age of 14. 'Sometimes it takes tragedy to bring on transformation. When people realise the hatred.' For the connection forged that day between her community and the people of Wales, she is thankful.

'We live in this huge world. And when you can bridge the gap between different nationalities or races, I think that's beautiful. It shows love in action.'

A rekindling of that love and of Wales' artistic relationship with Birmingham is currently underway. A partnership between the Sixteenth Street Baptist Church and Wales' youth organisation, the Urdd was established in 2019 and a virtual choir made up of young people from Birmingham and Wales was formed during 2020's Coronavirus lockdown, their online performance providing some much needed positivity during a difficult time the world over. This year, the Urdd choir will visit Alabama, performing at the University and visiting the Sixteenth Street Baptist Church and the current Pastor, the Reverend Arthur Price. The visit will be reciprocated, with Wales planning to host the Birmingham choir at the Urdd Eisteddfod in Denbigh. Connections between Aberystwyth University and the University of Alabama in Birmingham have also been strengthened, with a study exchange programme now in place. Links between two nations brought about by an artistic response to a very human tragedy.

'The messaging behind the Wales Window is timeless really,' says Michael Petts. 'It's still totally relevant. It's very powerful, really straightforward and no-nonsense. It might be fifty plus years old, but it's just as relevant now, if not more so.'

As an artist, John Petts was acutely aware of his work's legacy.

'There are cathedrals with stained glass windows which were put in in the fourteen hundreds. And the fact that he was part of that tradition meant that he was absolutely fastidious about doing a really good job,' Michael Petts says. 'He made sure that absolutely everything was done properly because it was going to last hundreds of years. So he was fully aware of, I would say constantly aware of the legacy that he was leaving.'

When John Petts passed away in 1991, the then Pastor of the Sixteenth Street Baptist Church, the Reverend Chris Hamlin sent a note of condolence to Kusha Petts. She responded in characteristically thoughtful manner with a poem she'd titled 'Day by Day,' words intended to comfort in a time of grief. She wrote:

> 'The Moment is Forever
> as it flies
> Future, Past and Present
> being one.'

As world events continue to demonstrate, John Petts' Wales Window, now a much-loved symbol of hope and change was never intended as a final statement, an end to the conversation about how we treat our fellow human beings. Petts was painfully aware that progress is not a linear force marching ever forward towards an endlessly bright future. His experiences had taught him that civil liberties and rights are hard-won and to be closely guarded and that kindness does not always prevail.

'For me the window is about doing the right thing and not being afraid of the consequences of that,' Michael Petts says. 'It's a message about vigilance. Never be complacent about the human condition and the absolute atrocities that can and do happen through negligence towards each other.'

This piece is based on first hand interviews with Barbara Cross, Michael Petts and David Felix-Dexter. Additional information was provided by: Dale Long, Jim Lowe and Ann Jimmerson, who are members of the group Kids in Birmingham 1963, Reverend Chris Hamlin, along with original recordings of interviews with John Petts held by The Imperial War Museum and original recordings of interviews with Reverend John Cross held by the Birmingham Civil Rights Institute Oral History Collection.

WHAT ARE WELSH WOMEN MADE OF?
From Lady Venedotia to Nessa

Rhian E. Jones

What are Welsh women made of? Several confident answers to this question have been given over the past few centuries – usually by men. From the Mabinogion to Curnow Vosper's paintings of a red-shawled Sian Owen, Welsh women before the twentieth century tended to be portrayed within culture by others rather than representing themselves. In 2003 the Welsh Assembly became the world's first legislature to achieve equal gender representation, and between 2006 and 2007 had a majority of female legislators, but the prominence of actual women – rather than female cultural archetypes – as representatives of the Welsh nation is still a relatively new phenomenon.

It is perhaps ironic that one of the best-known 'female' figures of 19th century Wales is Rebecca, the symbolic leader of the riots that swept 1840s Carmarthenshire and beyond. 'She' was of course not a woman but a quasi-mythological character, who was embodied by various male actors in the course of their protests. I will argue, however, that images of Rebecca within political and popular discourse of the time acted as a bridge between pre-existing symbolic or stereotypical ideas about women based in Welsh society and culture, and early nineteenth-century images that sought to portray Welsh women in accordance with a prevailing cultural ideal of romantic sentiment developed by middle-class artistic circles. The gulf between these idealised portrayals and the lived reality for Welsh women was made apparent over the course of the nineteenth and early twentieth centuries, including through the use of Rebecca's image.

Since that time, Welsh women have come to actively represent themselves and others in literature, film, music and politics. Of the parallel traditions that depict Welsh women as on the one hand passive, quaint and regressive and on the other empowered, disruptive and radical, contemporary Welsh women have chosen to represent themselves in terms of the latter over the former. The departure from and disruption of stereotypes by women in Wales, particularly within popular culture, is shown in eclectic and active ways that mirror the social, cultural and political changes that Wales has undergone. A more pluralistic, complex and diverse popular conception of Welsh women is liberatory, allowing women to slip the coils of social convention and cultural stereotypes and to represent themselves on their own terms.

UNNAFRED SHONES TO MRS FITZHERBERT

In the early nineteenth century, awareness of Wales as a distinct entity increased among both the Welsh themselves and external observers. Nineteenth-century Wales' myriad of economic, political and cultural changes proved decisive in the forging of a modern Welsh identity, with the Welsh appearing as sophisticated historical actors rather than passive observers of change. Matthew Cragoe has noted the growth of a particular Welsh politics, at the core of which was the recognition of Wales as a self-conscious and separate nation.[1] Visual imagery, particularly the satirical prints and cartoons which accompanied the rise of a popular press in Wales, played an important role within this process.

Pre-nineteenth century images of Wales in the English popular press were frequently abusive, derisory or condescending. In particular, the 'Poor Taff' stereotype became prominent in satirical literature and prints from the seventeenth century. This image of Wales and the Welsh, invariably expressed as a male figure, was characterised by chronic poverty and a paradoxical pride in and concern with ancient lineage. A 1740s woodcut published by the London-based publisher of street literature William Dicey, subsequently widely reproduced, illustrates the progress to London of 'Shon-ap-morgan, Shentleman of Wales', showing him riding a goat in lieu of a horse or carriage, weighed down by leeks, toasted cheese and scrolls detailing his family tree.

Poor Taff's female counterparts are few; the companion woodcut to 'Shon-ap-Morgan' depicts his wife, 'Unnafred Shones', also riding a goat to London, complete with a leek in her hat, but derives most of its satirical impact from the accompanying inventory of her husband's goods, which is written in a comic Welsh-English dialect. The predominant image of Wales remained that of the poverty-stricken, hot-tempered and garrulous Welshman up until the era of the Napoleonic Wars. At this point, formerly hostile caricatures of both Wales and Scotland underwent transition as the focus on a united defence of Britain, based on its constituent countries' common bonds of Protestantism and opposition to Catholic France, took precedence in popular culture. This loosening of the grip of older images, along with the flourishing of pictorial satire in the years 1760-1820 and the emergence of complementary stereotypes of the three nations, notably John Bull, supplied a fertile ground for the growth of alternative portraits of Wales.

The presentation of Wales as a female figure specifically is uncommon before the nineteenth century, particularly outside

Wales itself. An early instance appeared in 1785 when the Welsh cartoonist Thomas Pennant illustrated the legal controversy over the publication of a pro-democratic treatise by William Shipley, Dean of St Asaph's in Denbighshire. Pennant depicted Wales as an elderly and deranged 'Mother Cambria', possessed by a demonic Shipley.[2]

The 1780s also saw a plethora of visual attacks on the character and behaviour of the Prince of Wales. Despite his tenuous connection with the country itself, prints involving him drew on a long tradition of Welsh satirical iconography. They were frequently augmented by portrayals of his mistress, Mrs Fitzherbert, whose innuendo-ridden depictions were amplified by her characterisation as a sexually permissive and coarse Welshwoman. The 1786 print *Taffy and hur Wife, Shentleman of Wales* showed the couple riding a goat, Poor Taff's traditional mode of transport, with Mrs Fitzherbert, her hat displaying the three plumes of the Prince of Wales' heraldic crest, sitting astride the animal with her skirt hitched around her knees. The caption observed that 'The Welch women all ride cross-legged and bare-backed.' The ways in which femininity figured in such representations drew on popular notions of the lowered standards of Welsh sexual morality which would prove significant in later state investigations of Welsh life, notably the 'Blue Books', and the response to them of the Welsh themselves.

In the early nineteenth century, these less than flattering depictions gave way under the upsurge of Romantic interest in idealised popular culture, costume and customs among the Celtic nations. Travelogues of journeys through Wales, which had previously mocked or lamented the country's inhospitable landscape and incomprehensible natives, began instead to eulogise the untouched and dramatic nature of the Welsh scenery and the quaint appearance, behaviour and living conditions of its inhabitants. Within Wales itself, the early nineteenth century saw the promotion by a literary and artistic elite of reinvented images of the Welsh ancient past and present. Devices such as Iolo Morgannwg's revival of the Gorsedd of Bards, and the design and promotion of standardised Welsh national costume by the Welsh heiress and arts patron Augusta Hall, Lady Llanover, formed a mutually beneficial relationship with the emerging Welsh tourist industry.

Hall's prize-winning essay for the 1834 Eisteddfod on *Advantages resulting from the Preservation of the Welsh language and National Costume of Wales* was instrumental in the promotion throughout the 1830s of the idea of a national dress, and in the shift of the dominant symbolic image of Wales from male to female. This shift formed part of a wider cultural consolidation of symbolic representations of 'the nation' as female, drawing on ideas that accepted the feminine body as a vessel for allegorical representation, such as Delacroix's painting *Liberty Leading the People*. Within Wales, this enforced an intriguing dichotomy whereby the rapidly industrialising modern Wales centred on real-life images of male miners and ironworkers, whereas the female body remained associated with nostalgic ideas of rural Wales.

The outfits in Hall's 1834 *Book of Welsh Costumes* were based on the more archaic elements of female rural and occupational dress, and tailored to incorporate the local manufactures of specific regions. Hall's basic costume involved a flannel petticoat, apron and shawl, with a tall hat of black felt or velvet. While not necessarily representative, authentic or popular, versions of the dress were adopted and promoted by Hall's landowning and artistic circle, foisted upon their female servants and exhibited at balls, dinners and Eisteddfods.[3]

The boom in mass tourism occasioned by the expansion of the railway network into Wales throughout the 1830s and 40s reinforced the idea of particular costume as a conscious expression of authentic Welshness, as artists and publishers mass-produced lithographs and prints showing 'typical' Welsh scenes which invariably included women in Welsh dress, along with widely recognised visual symbols: the mountainous landscape, the harp, the leek, the spinning-wheel, the market-day or Eisteddfod scene. This image was by default female, and by further specifications was elderly and rural. In her survey of the influence of the *Book of Welsh Costume*, Christine Stevens states that by the 1840s 'all of the elements of what was to become national dress were already instantly recognisable as [the accoutrements of] an elderly Welsh woman.'[4]

This incarnation of national dress as a manifestation of national identity persisted into the twentieth century in forms such as Curnow Vosper's *A Market Day in Old Wales*, drawing on and catering to a particular idea of Wales despite bearing a decreasing resemblance to contemporary rural dress and lifestyle. Prys Morgan observes how this image of Welsh womanhood became 'very soon accepted as the symbol par excellence of the Welsh, a kind of Welsh Marianne or John Bull'.[5] Unlike the latter two figures, however, this image lacked any implication of antagonism or belligerence, and was defined instead by its cosy, quaint and unthreatening qualities.

REBECCA TO DAME VENEDOTIA

When considering depictions of nineteenth century Wales, it is remarkable how little trace has been left in visual imagery within or outside it by the social and political protest which gained the country so much attention, including the Rebecca riots, the

Merthyr Rising and Welsh Chartism. This relative absence is particularly surprising given the striking use of costume, iconography and symbolism by participants. One exception to this rule of relative absence came at the height of Rebeccaism in June 1843, when the *Illustrated London News* carried an artist's impression of "Rebecca Rioters, or 'Beccas". This illustration showed Rebecca participants in the stereotypical tall black hats promoted by Lady Llanover, despite the absence of such headgear from press and trial reports of the real-life riots.

A few years later, several striking visual images were produced in the course of the widespread and angry defensive reaction to the criticisms levelled by the Education Commission in the notorious 'Blue Books', the work of English commissioners, which attacked the country's levels of morality, religiosity, sobriety and cleanliness as well as education.[6] Of these, the most interesting for our purposes is Hugh Hughes' 1848 cartoon, entitled *Dame Venodotia Sousing the Spies*. This image shows Wales in the form of an elderly woman, Dame Venodotia, complete with shawl and tall black hat, avenging the slurs of the Education Commission by ducking the English commissioners in Cardigan Bay.[7]

Hughes' cartoon suggests a fascinating variety of influences. Certain aspects of it imply consistency with older ways of presenting Wales: the naming of Dame Venodotia – an ancient name for north Wales – retains elements of the preoccupation with ancient lineage for which the Welsh were stereotyped. However, the origin of Venodotia in Arthurian legend, as one of several ancient British kingdoms alongside Albania (Scotland), Cornwall, and Demetia (South Wales) suggests that Hughes' etymology may have been chosen as an attempt to assert parity for Wales with other regions of Britain.[8] Moreover, the decision to represent the kingdom of north rather than south Wales further suggests a perception of the more isolated rural north as the reserve of 'real' Wales empowered to act in defence of itself, in contrast to a south weakened or compromised by industrialisation and Anglicisation.

But Dame Venodotia also demonstrates the influence of newer ideas and shifts in perceptions of how Wales should be represented. The term Dame, while obviously redolent of contemporary pantomime, potentially heightening the image's comic effect, also implies a degree of matriarchal respectability which stands in contrast to previous stereotypes of the sexual morals of Welsh women, present for instance in portrayals of Mrs Fitzherbert. In view of the outcry over the Education Commission's claims in this area, Hughes' choice of this term and of this female archetype looks like a deliberate response to them, asserting the propriety and respectability of Welsh women while simultaneously depicting their symbolic vengeance on those suggesting otherwise.

In a separate image of 1848, Hughes again referenced Arthurian legend in his portrayal of the historian and biographer Jane Williams, whose pamphlet *Artegall, or Remarks on the Report of the Commissioners of Inquiry into the State of Education in Wales* had been published in March of that year. Hughes depicted Williams as Artegall, an Arthurian knight of justice, chastising the commissioners in the guise of errant schoolboys. In Hughes' image, the comically small scale of the commissioners relative to the imposing and brawny Dame Venodotia, and the disempowered absurdity of their fate, indicates an inversion of natural socio-economic and sexual hierarchies as well as of the relation of England to Wales.

The cementing of symbolic Welsh identity as a woman in national dress has been heavily criticised by the historian Deidre Beddoe for the implicit passivity of the images thereby produced. She notes how the donning of national dress objectified the wearer through its ornamental and impractical nature, rendering her fit only for the passive demonstration of nationhood despite the costume's basis in occupational dress.[9] However, the symbolic representations of Wales produced in the wake of the Education Commission debate and discussed above are images of powerful and active femininity. I suggest that in order to produce a 'Welsh Marianne' able to act with agency and authority, artists and cartoonists not only enlisted the objectified images of women in national dress but blended them with older concepts which associated feminine signifiers with licensed use of the unruly, mocking and subversive.

Such associations had received a recent and highly visible profile in reports of Rebeccaite activities. Press descriptions which emphasised participants' heavy use of visual imagery, and the focus on their leader as an abstract female figurehead, deeply implanted the image of Rebecca in public consciousness. Although few imaginative attempts were made to visually depict Rebecca herself, those that did drew upon dominant contemporary images of Wales: the depiction of Rebeccaites in the *Illustrated London News* shows them as recognisably male but wearing shawls and tall black hats. The illustration thereby drew on the most high-profile symbols of Welsh national identity in order to identify its subject, adding a larger dimension to Rebecca's public image by suggesting her as a representative of Wales rather than specifically of its south-western tenant farmers.

Subsequent images such as Dame Venodotia therefore reflect the merging of the female symbol of Wales with the tradition of active and empowered femininity expressed by Rebecca. The image of Rebecca prevalent in contemporary press reports and popular consciousness, as a dispenser of popular justice and opponent of unjust authority, provided a symbol of female agency more conducive to popular acceptance and support than the passive and objectified fashion plates produced by Lady Llanover. Such images enabled a response to criticisms of Wales and the Welsh in which the female figure as a symbol of Wales was combined with the concept of empowered female agency which had gained currency in contemporary public consciousness as a result of Rebecca's exploits, to render such images less passive and more popular.

The image of Dame Venodotia as protector of Wales and avenger of injustice directly recalled older symbolic uses of the feminine, but, by channelling these through the collective identity symbolised by Welsh national costume, it allowed them to be expressed on behalf of Wales as a nation, rebuffing criticisms and redressing wrongs while empowered by the weight of collective popular authority. The resultant images were informed by traditional associations of the feminine with subversion and popular justice, but, by also appropriating the symbolic trappings of Welsh national identity, these associations could be mobilised to represent Wales as a whole and to defend it. The concept of a Welsh feminine figure as disruptive and subversive rather than passive and antiquated would have significant implications, offering Welsh women an alternative concept to draw on in their own presentation.

MEGAN LLOYD GEORGE TO NESSA

In contrast to the passive objectification which Deidre Beddoe identified in Welsh women's national dress, the twentieth century saw Welsh women become more prominent as creatives, activists and producers, not simply as images produced by others. Well into the twentieth century, however, mainstream images of Wales still tended to be those of men, whether industrial workers, rugby players, slate quarry workers, bombastic politicians and trade union leaders, or male voice choirs. The most prominent cultural role for women was the 'mam', a beloved but often sentimental stereotype which says little about women's material status or power. Contemporary Welsh women, however, have managed to transcend the historical dichotomies of passive quaintness and disrespectable disruption, and to blend both into new forms of representation which have also become accepted as images of Wales itself.

Megan Lloyd George's election in 1929 as the first Welsh woman MP, followed in 1950 by Eirene White and Dorothy Rees, did not immediately lead to significant political representation – indeed, until the end of the 1990s, Wales had only four women in Parliament, all of them Labour MPs. It has been argued that this was a function of the cultural politics of areas dominated by heavy industry, with even women, who made up the core of local voluntary teams, holding relatively conservative views about who should represent them nationally.[10] However, rather than being a uniquely Welsh issue, this reflected the obstacles to women's political chances more generally; at UK General Elections from 1918 until 1983, less than 5% of Conservative and less than 8% of Labour candidates were women. The Assembly and Senedd, meanwhile, managed a far more impressive level of representation, gaining global attention in 2003 when the Assembly became the first legislature to achieve equal gender representation. It is important to note, however, that this was a function of active engineering by Labour such as all-women shortlists and the 'twinning' of constituencies – actions which did not pass without controversy.

Historical developments from the 1970s onward have altered both political and cultural ideas about women in Wales. The shift from manual labour and heavy industry to a service-based economy, exemplified by Max Boyce's immortal line "The pit-head baths is a supermarket now", was also a shift in the gendered nature of work in Wales. The search for a post-industrial Welsh identity has therefore involved a reconsideration of gender roles and dynamics in both overt and subtle ways. The involvement of Valleys women in the anti-nuclear struggles of the early 1980s saw many join the women's peace camp at Greenham Common – and end up imprisoned for direct action – while the men of their communities cooperated to take up domestic and family care in their absence.

The far-reaching economic and social disruption of deindustrialisation, despite its devastating effects, enabled women to take a prominent place as supporters and campaigners in the 1984-5 miners' strike, both organising community support groups and directly articulating political demands through speaking tours and benefit gigs. Involvement in this activism sparked the political careers of women like Sian James, as portrayed in the 2014 film *Pride* – one of several recent creative revisitings of the strike which paid attention to the progressive alliances formed between mining communities and social movements for racial and sexual equality against the socially reactionary onslaught of Thatcherism.

Leanne Wood's leadership of Plaid Cymru from 2012 to 2018 marked an important disruption of traditional divisions. As a Valleys girl, her decision to learn and speak Welsh offered a way of bridging anglophone and Welsh-speaking communities, and her outspokenness on social justice, republicanism and anti-fascism was attuned to the concerns of working-class socialist Wales as well as the priorities of Welsh nationalism. The inroads made by Plaid into Labour's Valleys heartlands have not been sustained however, and in May 2021's round of elections Wood lost her Senedd seat to Labour. While the latter upset can be attributed to the historically high support expressed for Welsh Labour in May 2021, it's interesting to consider whether Wood's ousting as leader of Plaid indicated the persistence of tendencies resistant to her unapologetically militant politics, which may have counted against her more significantly than her gender.

Meanwhile, beyond the arena of formal politics, Welsh women were taking more prominent and active roles in twentieth-century popular culture. The stereotype of Welsh music as confined to male voice choirs and the occasional female harpist was disrupted by the success of women folk, rock and pop artists within Wales and beyond. Initially this could include the retention of historical representation as a way to present Welsh women, such as the depiction of Mary Hopkin in Welsh national dress in 1969 by the Welsh pop magazine *Asbri*, which also referenced her success in chapel singing competitions. These traditional frames of reference, which could implicitly position women in traditionally passive and ornamental roles, began to lose their grip in the 1970s and 80s as a number of Welsh groups – including Young Marble Giants, Datblygu and Melys – contained female members who were accepted on their own musical and aesthetic terms.

The later 1990s in Wales was marked by a widespread efflorescence of pop culture, alongside the putative political 'new era' for the country ushered in by the founding of the Welsh Assembly. This included a surge of Welsh bands onto the UK stage, a movement in which women were prominent – perhaps none more so than Catatonia's Cerys Matthews. The band's sophomore album *International Velvet*, released in the run-up to devolution, was a departure from their previous melodic but timid indie, and proved a crossover hit, Cerys' vocals accommodating both the lush delicacy of folk and the brash bombast of rock. Significantly enough, the title track's sardonic refrain of 'every day when I wake up I thank the Lord I'm Welsh' became co-opted into the irony-free cheerleading of a 'New Welsh Cool'. Cerys' attitude and aesthetic, however, was a neat fit not only with the devolution era but with the wider swaggering hedonism of Britpop's imperial phase. Her 90s reign as a rock 'n' roll adventurer – heroically hard-drinking, happily plain-speaking, and joyfully unrestrained – upended the 'passive Welsh woman' stereotype, and allowed an image of active and opinionated Welsh womanhood to be integrated into the national pantheon.

A few years later, Cardiff choirgirl Charlotte Church's switch from delicate 'Voice of an Angel' to politically opinionated bad girl saw her upend her own stereotype, breaking free of passive presentations to assert her own identity, which drew on several less respectable tropes of Welshness for women, from pint-drinking to espousing radical socialism. Both she and Catatonia, along with other exponents of 'Cool Cymru', were supporters of Welsh devolution, lending their voices both rhetorically and musically to the cause. In 1999, a concert held in Cardiff Bay to mark the opening of the Assembly featured both Church and legendary Welsh singer Shirley Bassey. The daughter of a Nigerian seaman from Cardiff's Tiger Bay, who balanced factory-work with club-singing before pursuing fame in London, Bassey is deeply rooted in often overlooked historical legacies that indicate how nuanced Wales is. But, as illustrated by her appearance at the 1999 Rugby World Cup opening ceremony in a sequinned dress fashioned from the Welsh flag, she is now also a straightforward symbol of the nation itself.

Bassey's beloved position in popular culture – easily matching the status of other unequivocally Welsh entertainers like Tom Jones or Max Boyce – and her obvious embodiment of

Welshness, provide a way of disputing reactionary insistences that Welsh = white. This issue came to prominence in recent debates over the national census, when calls were made to include the specific categories of Black Welsh and Asian Welsh. But the racial and ethnic heterogeneity of Wales goes back centuries: Tiger Bay was one of the country's first multiracial localities and Cardiff has the UK's oldest Somali community, while the city, along with Swansea and the Valleys, was also home to thriving Jewish communities.

Butetown was the birthplace not only of Bassey but of Wales' first black headteacher Betty Campbell and of Gaynor Legall, Wales' first black female city councillor, all women who have contributed to the cultural shaping of contemporary Wales. Today, women from Shavanah Taj, Wales TUC's first BME General Secretary, to Merthyr musician Kizzy Crawford, have further established the racial nuances of Welsh identity. Support for Black Lives Matter by activists like Cardiff's Bianca Ali, along with recent climate change protests all over Wales, have demonstrated that the greater interconnectedness of global issues has resulted in a Welsh political identity that is intersectional and internationalist.

Perhaps the most recent and visible presentation of Welsh life, and Welsh womanhood, on a UK stage has been *Gavin and Stacey*. Although not immune to criticism for playing on one-dimensional and sentimental presentations, the sitcom has also attained the status of national treasure. Co-writer Ruth Jones' character Nessa is an iconic creation; whereas Joanna Page's sweetly domestic Stacey is a more familiar Welsh female archetype. Nessa draws on the cartoony misrule of 'Rebecca' and the upfront hedonism of Cerys Matthews, drolly embodying the kind of self-possessed sexuality that was historically mocked or scorned in Welsh women. Nessa is also literally stamped with her national identity via the Welsh dragon tattoo on her upper arm. As simplistic or sentimental as both characters may be, this duality indicates the room for manoeuvre in contemporary images of Welsh women.

The later twentieth century has seen the emergence of a culturally empowered assertive Welsh femininity that contrasts with the quaint touristy picture of a historically passive Welsh woman, but draws on the parallel representations of radical 'disruptive' Welsh womanhood shown from Rebecca to Dame Venedotia. Within the past fifty years, Welsh women themselves have been instrumental in challenging, refining and sometimes turning upside-down the ways in which they have been presented within popular culture and media. The frequent presentation of Wales itself through female symbols or stereotypes has meant that ideas about the country have gained in nuance and detail alongside these changes. As Welsh women – and men – continue to respond to historical change in a way that asserts their agency and heterogeneity, the next fifty years will undoubtedly go on to produce further images that reflect this.

The extent to which cultural 'leaders' such as Cerys Matthews, Charlotte Church, Shirley Bassey and Ruth Jones are indicative of a wider change in the status of women in Welsh socio-economic terms is debateable. Cultural representation is undoubtedly powerful, but material conditions are more powerful still. The declaration in 2018 that the Welsh government is a feminist government, for instance, must be measured against the country's still inexcusably high levels of child and women's poverty. As the socio-economic circumstances of Welsh women retain a hold on their capacity to represent themselves, it is imperative to address these issues if a true depiction of the multiplicity and heterogeneity of

Welsh women, and what this says about contemporary Wales, is to be possible.

[1] Cragoe, Culture, Politics and National Identity, p.16, p.38

[2] Lord, Words with Pictures, p.79

[3] Lord, Words with Pictures, pp.130-35; Stevens, 'Welsh Costume', pp.7-9

[4] Stevens, 'Welsh Costume', p.5

[5] Morgan, 'Keeping the Legends Alive', in Curtis (ed.), Wales: The Imagined Nation, p.33

[6] Ieuan Gwynedd Jones, Mid-Victorian Wales (Cardiff, 1992), pp.103-165; Cragoe, Culture, Politics, and National Identity, p.40

[7] Hugh Hughes, Dame Venodotia Sousing the Spies, reprinted in Lord, Words with Pictures, p.144

[8] Thomas Bulfinch, The Age of Chivalry (New York, 1913), ch.3

[9] Beddoe, 'Images of Welsh Women', in Curtis, Wales: the Imagined Nation, p.233

[10] Blaxland S., (2020) "Welsh Women MPs: Exploring Their Absence", Open Library of Humanities 6(2). p.26. doi: https://doi.org/10.16995/olh.548

HOME TO YOU:
Transience and Cate Le Bon's Discography

Caragh Medlicott

When I was twenty-one, I found myself stranded along the M4 motorway, somewhere between Cardiff and Birmingham. Not *literally* stranded, you understand, but metaphorically – ideologically. I was nearing the end of my English Literature degree at Cardiff University, the foreboding shimmer of 'real life' like a mirage on the horizon, and I'd started to experience a kind of transience. Where once my native Birmingham was 'home' and Cardiff was merely 'uni' – at some point along the road, without my conscious knowledge, both had taken on home status. Which took precedence, then: the place I'd grown up, or the place I'd become an adult? Graduation was upon me, and I felt my allegiance split between two nations.

I knew, of course, that home was more than a physical place. The conceptual nature of home is one finely spun into the fabric of storytelling and popular culture, from Dorothy clicking her ruby slippers to 'home is where the heart is' fridge magnets. You don't need to have *seen* the blue skies of Alabama to feel something evoked in Lynyrd Skynyrd's iconic opening riff. Home can be a person; a memory. The word 'Hiraeth' has long been appropriated by Word of the Week slots and sentimental wall art designs for this very reason. Its proliferation is such precisely because it amalgamates the feelings of both nostalgia and homesickness, a bittersweet mix of pleasure and pain.

In the summer of 2016, my friends and I escaped to the black mountains for Greenman festival – a sort of unspoken farewell celebration. It was here that I first encountered Cate Le Bon. Good live music is so often soul nourishing, but the really special occasions border on something numinous. The oozing golden light of dusk, the sinuous mountains bristled with trees in the distance, the heads of the audience raised like goosebumps along an arm... and then there was the music. Roaming guitar melodies swinging to and fro, swelling choral arrangements, the sax parping, the drums rattling – and the voice. Staccato but also ethereal, like a Welsh Nico. The psychedelic lyrics – 'can't be forever in your summer land / feeling like geometry' – beckoned the audience towards a surrealist realm, the sun mellowing into a red strip along the horizon. I remember thinking that the whole set had an uncanny quality, but not in an unpleasant way – more like the trickle of a shiver down your spine, the delicious chill of a ghost story. Cate Le Bon, real name Cate Timothy, conjured something that evening. Crunch time came, and I decided to remain in Wales.

When Le Bon first rose to prominence – supporting Super Furry Animals' Gruff Rhys on his solo tour in 2007, and then releasing her debut album, *Me Oh My,* under his label in 2009 – reviewers were quick to draw out the dark fairytale imagery infusing her work, the lyrics with a folkloric type of strangeness. Some critics seemed to confuse these themes with an aesthetic choice, viewing Le Bon's Welshness, bilingualism, and rural Carmarthenshire roots not as mere facts of identity but whimsical notions which added to her overall image. Certainly, Le Bon has dipped numerous toes in the silvery waters of psych-folk in the past, but the warm shaggy jangles of her earlier records have built into more intricate and ornate arrangements in recent years (which, not coincidentally, aligns with Le Bon's growing number of major producer credits). From her very first record to the considerable critical acclaim of her 2019 album *Reward,* she has resisted the straight story arcs commonly associated with the folk tradition, opting instead for inscrutable poetic reflections.

Returning home from Greenman in 2016, this inscrutability became a point of fascination for me. Not only did I submerge myself in the music, I also found myself gravitating more and more towards Le Bon herself. Cate Timothy the person; Cate Le Bon the character. I read and watched interviews, scrolled Wikipedia. From the chic French bob to the cool, laconic persona – it seemed hard to draw a line between what was genuine, what was designed, and what was imposed externally. When it came to her nationality, in particular, it seemed there was a buzz of static separating the Welsh woman proud of her identity and the tokenism of music journalists who – as Shaun Curran put it in *The Independent* – viewed Le Bon as the latest member in an ensemble of "Welsh oddball experimentalists". This idea, that Le Bon's Welshness was inextricably intertwined with her own eccentricity, interested me. In my experience, national identity was a slippery subject. Growing up Catholic and Irish descent, I'd never really felt English *or* Irish. At best I felt culturally (while not devoutly) Catholic. I was a small part of an eclectic and considerable Birmingham-Irish community. Now that I was formally homed in Cardiff, not residing merely as a student, that sense of identity felt more scattered than ever before. Yet there was something in Le Bon's music which smelled to me like liberation – songs at once rooted in Welshness and transcendent of it.

Indeed, Le Bon's oeuvre establishes her as an artist not only comfortable with the liminal space of oblique lyrics and dreamlike soundscapes, but a natural inhabitant of it. This recurrent thread runs, in various forms, throughout her entire discography; the idea of the idiosyncratic made homely. Reviewing *Crab Day* for *Pitchfork,* critic Laura Snaps compared Le Bon's fourth album to "[an] old house whose creepy anachronisms become a strange comfort". And it's there in her earlier work, too. The avant-pop concoctions of her second album, *CYRK,* employ fizzing guitar riffs and circular lyrics in a way that becomes enveloping. This use of repetition ripples throughout Le Bon's music, rendering her frequent penchant for strangeness into something both familiar and not, a kind of sonic *jamais vu*. The pleasant dream you can't quite remember.

A sense of place and home subsist as ambient ideas which occasionally bob to the surface. Her pensive and obscure lyrics are moored to the idea of home, not as something actual, but as a symbolic space for both selfhood and connection with another. On 'The Man I Wanted', Le Bon sings:

> What I hoped for most,
> Was to be his greatest host,
> He'd make my hands his home.

It's a deceptively calm song – it's fuzzy guitar strums thick and intense like the sky before a downpour. Still, though the idea of a transient home-space is present on *Me Oh My* and *CYRK,* it is nominal compared to the shift which followed, both conceptually and literally, on her third album *Mug Museum*.

In 2013, Le Bon swapped a rainy Cardiff for the sunshine-soaked, star-studded streets of LA. Despite the change of location, the move stateside didn't pivot Le Bon's introspection and commercialise it into something plastic and shiny. *Mug*

Museum actually follows in the wake of Le Bon's maternal grandmother's passing, connecting it intimately with her roots and personal history. In an interview with *The Gentle Woman,* Le Bon insists that the album is "not a record about grief". Instead, *Mug Museum* draws its title and central concept from the themes of memory and sentimentalism. How something as simple as a collection of mugs, might – to one person – encapsulate a small history of being; nostalgia and memory metamorphosising the everyday item into something exceptional.

Once again, I saw fragments of my own life mirrored in this experience. Le Bon moved away from Cardiff in 2013 – the same year I moved *to* Cardiff for university. A few weeks into my first term, my own maternal grandmother passed away. I wasn't familiar with Le Bon's music at this point, and how I wish I had been, but in retrospect I can see how I too became sentimental about physical objects during this period of grief and transition. I kept my old favourite books by my bedside, sometimes opened them up just to press my nose to the pages. When friends came round, I stuffed my childhood teddy bear in the wardrobe, at once embarrassed and possessive. In spite of my sensitivity, this period also coincided with some of the most formative days of my life. I'd never lived anywhere but Birmingham before, and I'd shared a room with my younger sister until the day I moved out; to be alone in a new city, in charge of my own life, I felt almost dizzy with independence.

That sanguine feeling of both homesickness and hopefulness comes through on *Mug Museum,* too. It's an album with more bite than the two that came before, imbued with frenetic energy; the background organ silhouetted with spare sixties guitar, horn toots and occasional punky thrashing off in the distance. Its off-kilter mannerisms are paired with lyrical reflections which, truly, are less morbid than her previous two albums. 'I forget the details but know the warmth' Le Bon sings on the album's titular closing track, bare-bones piano punctuated with the creaking of a stall. It characterises this nostalgia as something heartening, a warmth which might seep into the continuous present of our lives, regardless of circumstance or physical location.

The bittersweet nature of memory, something both cherished and moth-eaten by time, is dominant throughout *Mug Museum.* Le Bon's lyrics call to mind the literary preoccupation of author Kazuo Ishiguro, a writer whose novels have often contemplated the function of memory as a sort of neurological cutting room – a place where past events are both edited and disposed of entirely. Yet, while Ishiguro seems to view memory as a distorter, a thing which moves us further away from the truth of reality, Le Bon tends towards a more optimistic outlook. 'Aunty Rita in my life / Making tracks for me to find' are the opening lines of 'Sister', the chorus refrain 'I won't die / I'm a sister'. In the same way that homeliness is a transient concept to Le Bon, so, too, is personal identity. The edges of selfhood blurring with the traits acquired, both genetically and socially, from family members – like fingerprints dried in clay.

To me, there is a profound solace in this idea. We're often told that deceased loved ones live on in our hearts, in our memories – but few people point out that a part of them is also *literally* imprinted within us. Whether that be in the twirling strands of our DNA, in our mannerisms, or simply in our way of viewing the world. It's an idea which holds implications not only for grief, but for our identities more broadly. Attending Catholic school in Birmingham, there was often an odd competitivity amongst the student population surrounding who was, and wasn't, "Irish" enough. Friends with two Irish parents might accuse others of appropriation – of being "plastic paddies". It set in motion an odd sensitivity in me, as if having English and Irish heritage was an inherent conflict which demanded I pick a side. Uncovering an affiliation with Wales in adulthood could have complicated things further – yet what Le Bon proposes isn't anything so crass as genetics by percentages or a tribal type of possessiveness. Instead, *Mug Museum* renders home as a place at once nuanced and specific. It seems to say that to *feel* at home doesn't have to coincide with *being* home. The tension between the physical and the non-physical is also referenced in the album title – a name which took on greater meaning following the album's completion.

To commemorate the release of *Mug Museum,* Le Bon hand-pottered one hundred mugs. It was a pursuit taken, she tells *The Gentle Woman,* with the aim of soothing a restless mind post-recording. The project first began when she enrolled on a six-week course at the Ball Clay Studio in LA – hardly the typical outlet for most of the city's resident music artists – where she intended to create gifts for those who worked on the album, and later, following their accumulation, send them as extras to anyone who pre-ordered *Mug Museum.* As a therapeutic undertaking, it not only gives insight into the process of Le Bon's craft (that is, one approached with intensity and care), but the way her identity was received in America. "The guy that ran the place could hardly understand a word I said because of my accent, so we had to get by on smiles", she explained. Symbolically, Le Bon's pottery can also be read as an act inspired by homesickness, making something new in pursuit of a tangible connection with both an old place and the new one; a way of not only bringing home with you, but recreating it. Far from flattening her quirks and more avant-garde sensibilities, Le Bon's LA existence seemed, if anything, to spotlight both her Welsh identity and unique, personal perspective.

Speaking to *Wales Online* in 2016, Le Bon offered a telling depiction of her "frugal" life there, saying: "Me and Huw [Evans] would just sit talking to each other in Welsh all day [...] It was this wonderful little bubble we were living in, despite the big city surroundings". And while her identity was often tokenised by Americans eager to share tales of their distant Welsh heritage, the retention of Le Bon's selfhood was such that, despite a considerable stint stateside, her style only flourished further – yet still organically – on her fourth record, *Crab Day*.

What is perhaps most notable about *Crab Day* is its composition. Rendered musically first and foremost, by the time Le Bon sat down to write the lyrics, she had already established vocal harmonies without picking the words to go with them. Given this context, it's not surprising that *Crab Day* debuts a new-edged primitivity. One that feels, oxymoronically, controlled. With the introduction of zipping marimba, strings of jittery rhythm sections, not to mention room enough for sax and her characteristic post-punk guitar shimmied into jaunty refrains, it's both everything but the kitchen sink and an exercise in expertly honed arrangements. It's this very ability, to simulate the naturalism of a jungle with materials akin to the botanical gardens, which has made Le Bon a producer of choice for not only many of Wales' indie mainstays, but also Deerhunter on their 2019 record *Why hasn't everything already disappeared?*

The tension between control and surplus isn't *Crab Day's* only exercise in irony. Its denser arrangements could, at times, be taken for something more serious – ditching the nods of rustic twee cast over *Mug Museum* – yet lyrically, it opts for eccentric abstraction. Its playfulness manifesting often as joviality, with occasional gestures towards darker waters. Where her third album tethered Le Bon to family, to home in the immaterial shape of shared identity, *Crab Day* ostensibly cuts that line altogether by destabilising meaning and forgoing any clear root of thematic inspiration. The LP's eponymous song, 'Crab Day', commemorates an invented holiday made up after Le Bon's young niece took issue with the absurdity of April Fool's Day. The lyrics are quirky and irreverent, with even the more sophisticated images – 'Words like glassy beading' – undercut by the nonsense idea driving it forward:

> Swim across to greet me on Crab Day,
> Spend a lovely dream on Crab Day.

The plethora of inanimate and unusual things Le Bon compares herself to on this record – geometry, a motion picture film, a dog, a tenpin ball – are not merely bizarre in a quaint and wonderland-esque manner, but also offer a sense of dislocation. Nowhere is this more astutely felt than on 'I was born on the wrong day', a song Le Bon wrote when her mother, after unearthing Le Bon's birth certificate, realised they had got her birthday out by one day. She sings:

> I was born on the wrong day,
> I met my mother and adjust the windows.

Conceptually, it plays with the idea of potentiality, of the way a life might bifurcate in accordance with the rituals and beliefs we uphold. The central lyric may be read in a multitude of ways, but perhaps its most obvious interpretation suggests that experience is more important than objective reality. Hence, Le Bon was "born" on the wrong day, not just celebrating the wrong date.

Le Bon's own spectrality, the transience of both her selfhood and influence, is recurrent throughout *Crab Day*. Behind the baroque pulsating of these tracks is a querying uncertainty. On 'Find Me', Le Bon sounds playful, chipper, a teeter-totter xylophone providing a creepy undertone. Lyrically, the chorus hones both this sense of fun and ephemerality:

> Well, I might be somewhere in the house
> Somewhere in the house
> I might be, might be
> Sighing in your tomb
> Sighing in your tomb
> Find me

It's the uncanniness of such songs, ones which seem to at once set your foot tapping and your head scratching, which conjure the liminality of dreams. It is certainly a deliberate and well-exercised decision on Le Bon's part – one elevated by the vocals intoned throughout. Amidst even the most experimental sonic backdrops and haunting melodic refrains, Le Bon's singing is at once a through line of familiarity and a thing of haunting transcendence. Unlike many of today's indie and pop artists, Le Bon has never assimilated even the tiniest twang of an American accent in her singing voice, which to this day remains consistently and formidably Welsh. It is her voice and accent which so often acts as an anchor when swimming in Le Bon's most surrealist dreamscapes. After all, we have all experienced the displacement of dreams – of a home which is not home, of imaginary places both familiar and not. Le Bon seems to enjoy channelling this transcendence, while her voice ensures we never stray too far from the shore of her own selfhood. Still, on *Crab Day,* especially, to overly scrutinise lyrics is to overthink Le Bon's tendency towards onomatopoeic tactility – yet what we can glean in the recurrence of her own characterisation as an intangible, flickering being, is that she finds something esoteric in her own individual experience. It's an idea that Le Bon seems to both revel in and be frustrated by – the limitations of her own emotional subjectivity. This very thing might just be the crux of Le Bon's returning, again and again, to home as a space of both comfort and displacement. The interiority of Le Bon's emotional landscape finds both relief in her connection with others (as on *Mug Museum*), while sometimes alienating her altogether (as on *Crab Day*).

In the years which followed, home continued to be a *literally* transient notion to Le Bon when she left America and headed, instead, to the isolated mountains of the Lake District in Cumbria. As scene changes go, this one is pretty seismic. Growing up, I actually spent some of my earliest summers in Cumbria in my Great Aunt's tiny old cottage nestled out in the wilderness. For one week a year we would pack up the car and drive over for a holiday. Quaint and lovely as it may have been, I often quietly dreaded these trips. From the winding country roads to the old, creaking cottage which never quite seemed to settle, I found the whole place unnerving. I was used to and fond of the city where you could quite easily convince yourself that, even in the darkest of night, someone somewhere was buzzing about – getting on with things. By comparison, the Lake District felt eerily silent and isolated. If the shift from Birmingham to Cumbria felt significant, I cannot imagine how stark the contrast must have been eloping from LA. So, why do it? A tortured soul escaping to the remote countryside for peace of mind and artistic introspection is practically a cornerstone of the creative cultural narrative (not to mention the fact that Le Bon's choice of location connects her with the 'lake poets' of the Romantic era). Yet, Le Bon – living alone – wasn't there only to make music, but also to make furniture. She enrolled on a woodwork class, spending her days perfecting the art of chair-making while using her evenings to play piano late into the wee hours. And yet, the resulting album, *Reward,* sonically gives away little of its bucolic roots; it's not acoustic or even especially earthy, instead its cool and opulent arrangements are lit by diaphanous electronic melodies, oblong soft-rock diversions, solitary siren-like vocals. For all the prettified and lavish flourishes which spiral out from *Reward's* centre, its heart is one of flinty melancholy. As critic Sam Sodomsky aptly notes, "like Greek filmmaker Yorgos Lanthimos, Le Bon takes pleasure in blending horror and fairytale, elegance and absurdity". And this same poetic juxtaposition exists within Le Bon herself, both drawn to the physical craft of woodwork and the spiritual act of experimental music-making. It's true that her carpentry work, her pottery, is not consumed by a wider audience in the same way that her albums are, but its importance to her seems paramount both in and of itself and in its connection to her music making. Surely *Reward* would not sound the same had Le Bon spent the time solely focusing on writing her next album. It seems clear that working cross-discipline is a source of inspiration for Le Bon, the sparks from one artistic pursuit jumping across boundaries to alight ideas in another.

As if to prove a point, opening track 'Miami' assures the listener that there'll be no pastoral detours to follow. Synth swells in and out like cloud-veiled moonlight, there are parps of her trademark horn, and Le Bon sings: 'I take some time / I have some thoughts' – it's a gentle introduction to the inception of her solitude and the meditations which will follow. Though the album was conceived in Cumbria, it was recorded in California, with musical contributions from Red Hot Chili Peppers' Josh Klinghoffer and Warpaint's Stella Mozgawa – with a vocal cameo from Kurt Vile. In production terms, *Reward* builds on the sonic sweeps of controlled precision and free-wheeling jam sessions that first debuted on *Crab Day*. At times, these experimental diversions can feel amorphous; the music unravelling in a pattern of cascading instruments, the effect loose yet styled – like an undone braid.

Lyrically, *Reward* retains much of its predecessor's abstraction, yet there is a feeling, here, of greater meaning packed beneath the surface. Its first single, 'Daylight Matters', nestles a sense of quiet loss amongst its soft-rock melody and chiming electric guitar. Its first verse recalls:

> A day in the life
> Arranging the chairs
> and I'm never gonna live it again'

It seems to encapsulate both a literal place and a moment in time, Le Bon once again mingling past locations with memory, lamenting the impossibility to get back to either. Other songs like 'Sad Nudes' – needling with broken piano chords – speak more immediately to the solitude of Le Bon's setting; the song's deadpan repetition of 'sad nudes' seems to conjure both vulnerability and a desire for connection.

Nowhere, though, is Le Bon's taste for evanescence more prominent than on *Reward's* third track 'Home to You'. Here, home is no more a stable concept than love or pleasure – it is something which is both universally understood, and experienced subjectively by each person. Its lyrics are impenetrable:

> Home to you
> Is a neighbourhood in the night kitchen
> Home to you
> Is atrocity in the town

Though Le Bon's words purposefully resist specificity, they conjure ideas of both community and fragility – the collaborative nature of home, something made up of people, not just bricks. The music video for 'Home to You' was created in collaboration with the residents of a neighbourhood in Košice, eastern Slovakia – directed by filmmaker Phil Collins and co-produced by Kino Úsmev – it offers a moving depiction of both isolation and connection. The visual stories presented communicate these ideas with watchful emotion; kitchen porters sharing a moment of affability on a cigarette break – construction workers walking home with shoulders brushing. Amidst the dilapidated grounds of a high-rise building, friends kick a ball around. Paired with the song, the video strengthens the key message of 'Home to You' – that of home as not only a literal place, but also the warmth of an adopted family. If home is transient to Le Bon, it's because the people who complete it may also come and go.

For me, listening to Le Bon has been about more than just great music. In the transience of her world, both actual and the ones imagined on her albums, I have found an emotional education. One which proves that home, that nationality, need not be anything so simple or static as just a place or a country. I have learned that I can feel Irish, I can feel English, and I can feel Welsh. On some days I might feel without borders at all. Even my name bears the marks of split identity. My first name, Caragh, is Irish. While Medlicott, my surname – fittingly enough – has its roots along the Welsh/English border. My identity is not an isolated thing, but something criss-crossed and interconnected with my loved ones and the experiences that have shaped me. It is Le Bon's insistence on a connection with many, peripatetic homes which beats at the centre of this concept.

Had I been familiar with Le Bon's music nearing the end of my university career, I might have realised sooner that home is not a finite resource – but something we both make and can bring with us. Wales has now been my home for nearly a decade. My affinity for it, for its culture, for its community, and for the friends I have made and the experiences I have enjoyed make it a permanent piece of my identity – just as my childhood in Birmingham remains another fixed, non-conflicting part of me. Throughout her work, Le Bon has proven herself to be a consummate creator and musical auteur; the soul of her music is like a great and expansive loch – its beautiful glass surface only occasionally stirred by the aphotic depths beneath.

There is an old Welsh tradition in folklore known as Tŷ unnos (one-night house), its rules state that a person who can build a house in one night may be allowed to keep and own it. It seems as fitting a symbol as any for Cate Le Bon's own geographical restlessness – while she may have laid down new roots, constructed homes in place after place, her oeuvre proves that ultimately home is transcendent because it's something that we bring with us. Like the spun silver of a spider's web, home begins with self-creation, and may be transported and remade again and again. Its value lies not in its permanence, but in the magic of its transience.

BUILDING A FEMINIST WALES:
Is it Time for Culture to Lead Politics?

Emma Schofield

When it comes to questions of female leadership within politics, recent events have shone a spotlight on the issue on an international platform. As the world found itself in the midst of a global pandemic in early 2020, gender representation became a fascinating, if under-explored, element of government responses to the crisis. Nations which initially performed strongest in their bid to control the pandemic included New Zealand, South Korea and Taiwan, all nations which were overseen by a female political leader. In each of these countries, both infection levels and death rates compared favourably to many male-led nations, including the UK and the USA, where hypermasculine leaderships appeared to falter under the pressure of the pandemic. While it is still too early to say whether this trend will continue as the pandemic develops, or indeed to assess the full extent of how gender may have influenced political and social decisions made in response to the Covid-19 virus, the experience has already prompted discussion surrounding the potential benefits of strong female leadership within government.

Early research published by the Centre for Economic Policy Research and the World Economic Forum has indicated that COVID-outcomes are systematically better in countries led by women and, to some extent, this may be explained by the proactive and coordinated policy responses adopted by them.[1] Findings published in the British Medical Journal's blog support these assertions, arguing that 'Taiwan's effective pandemic control measures were complimented by effective social care', including free access to testing, daily compensation for people in quarantine and the provision of care packages to support citizens.[2] Yet, as ever in matters relating to gender in politics, caution is needed to avoid reducing pandemic responses to an act of gender stereotyping. Two academics from Kings College London recently drew on the topic to call for a more nuanced discussion of gender in leadership, pointing out that some countries with a male-led government, such as Algeria and Grenada, have introduced policies designed to directly protect women during the pandemic. Clare Wenham and Asha Herten-Crabb argue that 'though women's executive leadership deserves to be celebrated, providing important role models and necessary alternatives to the rise in hyper-masculinised "strongman" politics, focusing on individual women's success can paint a false picture of the state of gender equality.'[3] Wenham and Herten-Crabb go on to assert that 'policies that support women's livelihoods, their paid and unpaid labour, their ability to house and feed themselves and their families, will do more for women's political participation in the coming years than the media's disproportionate emphasis on individual women's leadership during this crisis', drawing attention to the importance of feminist government, as well as female leadership in improving the lives of women within a country.

Yet questions regarding the fundamental principles, and potential benefits, of female-led politics pre-date the Covid-19 pandemic. In 2018, when the Welsh Government declared its vision to create a feminist government for Wales, things were far from clear cut. Announcing the plans as part of a speech to mark International Women's Day that year, then First Minister Carwyn Jones set out his ambitions for Wales to 'become a world leader in women's rights and gender equality' through the establishment of a feminist government.[4] Unsurprisingly, the questions came thick and fast. How would this vision be achieved? What changes would be involved? How long would it take to achieve? What would a feminist government for Wales even look like?

While the concept of a feminist government might not have been one with which everyone was familiar, Wales was not the first nation to use the term. Sweden already boasts what it proudly terms a feminist government, defining the concept as a commitment 'to building a society in which girls and boys, women and men have the same power to shape society and their own lives, and live their lives to their full potential'.[5] The Swedish strategy is based on a number of principles, including three key actions which the government has taken towards ensuring equality. Firstly, the establishment of a national government agency for gender equality policy; secondly, the implementation of a ten-year policy to end violence against women; and thirdly, a modernised parental leave insurance system, designed to encourage gender-equal parenting. While progress has at times been slow, there are indications that this approach is gradually contributing to improvements in the lives of women across Sweden. With Wales keen to replicate some of the primary features of the Swedish system, now seems like an ideal time to consider how the transition to a feminist government for Wales is really progressing and what more needs to be done to position Wales as a world-leader for gender equality in politics.

In order to explore each of these questions in more detail, we perhaps first need to take a step back and look more broadly at the position of women in Wales. Unsurprisingly, the picture is both varied and complex. When it comes to the cultural landscape Wales has always boasted a strong female voice; there is a lengthy canon of Welsh women writers, musicians and artists and even though they have not always achieved the recognition they so richly deserve, they have often flourished, albeit against the odds. In politics, however, the picture has always looked somewhat different. Wales' first female MP came in 1929 when Lady Megan Lloyd George was elected as the representative for Anglesey for the Liberal party, going on to become a key campaigner for Welsh Government and a strong advocate for the introduction of a Secretary of State for Wales. Ironically, although the role of Secretary of State was eventually introduced in 1964, it is a post which has only once, in over half a century, been held by a female MP. Conservative MP Cheryl Gillan held the role for just two years, from 2010 – 2012, before being replaced against her wishes during a cabinet reshuffle.[6] For a short while it seemed as if devolution may have brought the dawn of a new era to politics in Wales. There was, in 2003, a brief moment of utopia when the National Assembly comprised an equal number of elected male and female Assembly Members, making it the first legislature in the world to achieve a gender balance among its elected members. Indeed, there was even a year when, following a by-election in 2006, the gender balance in the National Assembly tipped in favour of women, with no less than 31 of the 60 seats being held by women. Yet a closer look at these figures reveals a more complex situation. It is broadly acknowledged that the gender balance in the Assembly was achieved through the somewhat controversial use of all-women shortlists and a complex 'twinning' system designed to enforce equal representation across neighbouring constituencies, particularly within the Labour party. It is also worth noting that in spite of this milestone, many of the most senior roles within the Assembly still eluded female Members.[7] In 2006, for example, many of the highest-ranking roles, including those of First Minister, Minister for Health and Social Services, Presiding Officer and Deputy Presiding Officer, were all held by male Assembly Members. Notwithstanding the lack of women in senior ministerial roles, it is easy to underestimate the magnitude of this achievement, an outcome which positioned Wales as a leader in gender parity in politics on an international platform. Unfortunately, the promise and excitement held in this brief moment of parity did not last long.

By the time of the Welsh Assembly election in 2007, a mere four years on, the numbers had shifted and the equality balance which had marked Wales out as a world-leader for gender equality in politics, was no longer there. While the numbers of female Assembly Members initially remained encouraging, those numbers have declined over the proceeding years; following the results of the last Senedd elections in May 2021 women held just 43% of seats in the Senedd Chamber. Although this figure is still a higher proportion than the equivalent statistic in the Westminster government, which currently sits at 34%, it is still some way off the lofty heights achieved by the second Senedd. Moreover, a closer look at the representation of women in local councils across Wales shows that, in the Autumn of 2021, just six of Wales' twenty-two councils have a female leader, while only four of those councils boast a gender-equal cabinet. Unsurprisingly, the reasons for this lack of women at both a national and local level are not straightforward. Pressures with regard to childcare and family responsibility have long acted as a barrier to women in politics, as has the struggle to enter a sphere which has, traditionally, been a predominantly male space. Such issues are not exclusive to national levels, but also exist within local government. Testimonies given to the Expert Group on Diversity in Local Government for a report in 2013, highlighted similar issues, including the difficulty of standing as a female councillor in areas historically dominated by male representatives. In the report, county councillor Karen Elizabeth Pearson described how there are 'many barriers faced by rural women, particularly within politics, as this has been the Bastille of men for many years and as a result women are not always taken seriously or given the opportunities afforded to men'.[8] Eight years on from this report, it is clear that the measures suggested by the Group, which included cross-party strategies to widen participation, have not worked as hoped.

Writing for *Wales Arts Review* back in 2018 I argued that equality in Wales was in everyone's interests and yet, reflecting on that argument, it's hard not to feel as if progress along that rocky path has faltered somewhat. The vision described by the Welsh Government in 2018 was predicated on the principle that 'a gender equal Wales means an equal sharing of power, resources and influence for all women, men and non-binary people. This is a vision where the government aims to create the conditions for equality of outcome for all'.[9] Three years on and there clearly remains much work to be done to achieve this goal, not only to ensure gender parity within government structures in Wales, but to establish an environment in which political decisions are made in the best interests of all citizens.

In spite of no longer holding the mantle of a gender-equal legislature, it's important to note that there are still a number of positive signs within the gender balance in the Senedd. Since the birth of Welsh devolution, the proportion of elected female representatives has remained one of the highest percentages in the world when compared to other, similar legislative bodies.

As noted above, there has been some considerable fluctuation at each fresh set of elections; yet in spite of this fluctuation, 26 out of 60 seats in the Senedd are currently held by women. This is, however, only one facet of the complicated task of establishing a feminist government for Wales. Working to promote and maintain this balance is important and having an equal government for Wales is, without doubt, something to strive for, but what matters most are the decisions which are being made at ground level and the level of female representation across all levels of government in Wales. Laura McAllister, Professor at the Wales Governance Centre at Cardiff University, blogged in 2018 about the fact that 'in Wales – like virtually everywhere else – around 80% of all powerful, decision-making roles are held by men' and this fact continues to be an indisputable obstacle on the course towards gender equality.[10] As McAllister points out, this figure has to change if these roles are to become genuinely representative of the women who make up 52% of our population in Wales. When it comes to leadership roles within Welsh politics and governance, women are still far too notable by their absence.

Ultimately what is needed to achieve this vision of a feminist government in Wales is not only a cultural shift to ensure that female leadership becomes an ordinary and accepted part of the political landscape at all levels within Wales, but a commitment to policies which are fair and equitable to all. It is in this respect that politics has most to learn from the cultural world in Wales. Real support for women and a genuine desire to eradicate inequality and discrimination against women has to start at a young age and be consistent across all sectors. The progression towards a truly feminist Wales can only occur with a united effort across all areas of our political, cultural and education systems. A closer study of these three sectors shows a considerable variation in how women are represented. A glance at the current Welsh literary world shows a world in which women continue to take a front seat in leadership. At the time of writing the roles of Chief Executive of Literature Wales, Managing Director of Welsh National Opera, the Director of University Wales Press and the President of Pen Cymru are all held by women. Four of the top jobs in the Welsh literary world, heading up four of the largest and most influential arts organisations in the country and all four positions are presently occupied by women. Moreover, they're not alone; women hold an array of positions in publishing, music, drama and arts companies across Wales. Whatever barriers appear to exist to female leadership in Welsh politics, these appear not to be replicated to the same extent within the world of arts and culture.

In education, as in culture, female leadership is also in the ascendency. In 2021 there were four female University Vice Chancellors in Wales, accounting for exactly 50% of the country's eight Universities. Although figures suggest that women are still less prominent than their male counterparts in leadership roles within Higher Education in the UK as a whole, the value of having women in the most visible and high-profile leadership positions in half of Wales' universities should not be underestimated. In this area, Wales again has an opportunity to stand out as a lead player on an international platform. 2021 research by the European University Association suggests that just under a third of the top leadership roles in European Universities are held by women, a figure which is still significantly lower than that in Wales.[11] When it comes to schools, the picture in Wales is a little more complicated, but still predominantly positive when it comes to gender balance. School Workforce Census results from late 2019 revealed that 75.2% of all teachers in Wales were female, with 66% of headships in the primary sector held by women, although female headships are still less prominent within secondary education where women accounted for only 37.2% of heads.[12] Nonetheless, it is clear that women remain highly visible in both classroom and leadership roles in schools across Wales.

Seeing these positions in Welsh culture and education occupied by women is, of course, fantastic and should be celebrated, but it should also prompt us to consider why the same level of equality in leadership cannot be seen more consistently across politics in Wales. The question we must ask is one of how we can translate the examples of female leadership we see in the arts and education systems in Wales to promote equality at all levels from an early age. In direct contrast, while female politicians currently occupy nine of the fourteen cabinet positions within the Welsh Government, a number of significant key roles in the Senedd have, to date, never been held by a woman. The role of First Minister has yet to be occupied by a female Member of Senedd, while other key cabinet roles, including General Counsel for Wales, have never been held by a female Member. In addition, a number of other roles, such as Minister for the Economy of Wales, have only had one female postholder. If we genuinely want future generations of women to aspire to these roles it is vital to enable them to believe that to hold those positions is not only possible, but also feasible. Having women within as wide a range of leadership roles as possible would go far when it comes to inspiring the next generation of Welsh politicians and policy makers.

Encouraging young women to believe that a future in politics is a viable option for them also involves making the political environment as accessible as possible, another area where serious change is necessary. In order to achieve a situation where more women feel able to enter Welsh politics, at all levels, means taking seriously the responsibility to create a fair and equitable working environment for women. The Welsh Government's plan to create a feminist Wales, touches on the need to address financial and familial situations for women in Wales. Yet when it comes to economic and domestic circumstances for women in Wales, there is an urgent need for further change. Here again the effects of the Covid-19 pandemic can be felt, contributing to the worsening of economic circumstances for women living and working within Wales. 2021 figures show that a staggering 80% of savings made from welfare and tax changes in Wales over the past year are estimated to have come from women's pockets, while indicators suggest that the gender pay gap in Wales has actually widened since the start of the pandemic, increasing to around £1.90 per hour.[13] This revelation, accompanied by the fact that it has been widely acknowledged that women have borne the brunt of financial, employment and social hardships created by the Covid-19 pandemic, pose a significant obstacle to the creation of a feminist Wales. If we return to Wenham and Herten-Crabb's assertion that 'policies that support women's livelihoods, their paid and unpaid labour, their ability to house and feed themselves and their families' are key to ensuring that politics really makes a difference to the lives of women, it is clear that Wales still has some way to go. While such serious gender disparity still exists economically within Wales, it is impossible to imagine a point where true equality can be achieved.

What is also clear, is that having women in leadership roles is not the only solution when it comes to ensuring gender parity within politics. Even nations with strong female leadership are still struggling to balance the situation from an economic perspective; New Zealand has a strong female leader in the form of Prime Minister Jacinda Ardern, but still suffers with a gender pay gap of around 9%. The harsh reality is then that female leadership alone, is not enough to create a fair and equal society for Wales. Returning to the Swedish model of a feminist government reminds us that a government with this aim can only be judged to be successful when it has created a society which is equal and safe for all women. Moreover, one in which girls and boys, women and men have the same power to shape society and their own lives, and to live those lives to their full potential. In that respect, there is evidently still so much further for Wales to go.

While Sweden has established an agency for the creation and scrutiny of gender policy in the country, no equivalent body currently exists within the Welsh government. Like a number of other commentators and activists, I have previously called for the creation of a Women's Ambassador role, made up of not just one woman, but a team of women from throughout education, arts and politics to assess and promote equality across policy and economic decisions made by the Welsh Government. Such roles would not necessarily require significant power, but could act in an advisory capacity, scrutinising proposed policies and advocating for women's rights. Such a team would, undoubtedly, need both a Welsh Government receptive to this guidance and cross party support to be fully successful, but could be a much-needed step forward in the way in which we monitor progress towards the promotion and support for women's rights in Wales. A similar model is already in place in Scotland, where a Women's Enterprise group has been tasked with championing the progression of women in business. The creation of such a model for politics, culture and education in Wales would go a long way towards ensuring a more cohesive and progressive approach to how gender equality is addressed within government.

In addition to establishing a dedicated policy centre for

gender equality in the country, the Swedish Government has also implemented a detailed long-term strategy to tackle violence against women, including sexual crimes and human trafficking. The Welsh Government has repeatedly committed to address these areas in the time since it first announced its plans for a feminist government, but figures in Wales present a worrying picture. Recent research suggests that around 35,000 incidents of domestic violence in Wales went unprosecuted in 2019, the majority of these perpetrated against women. This number means that prosecution of abusers only occurs in around 12% of all reported domestic abuse cases in Wales. Here again the effects of the Covid-19 pandemic are also significant, with calls to the Wales national helpline *Live Fear Free*, rising by around 49% during the first lockdown. In addition, the helpline reported that call times had trebled, with those making contact to the helpline often reporting more frequent abuse with shorter escalation periods. It is, however, worth noting that the issue is not exclusive to Wales. In Sweden, as in much of the rest of the world, reports of domestic violence increased exponentially with the rise of the Covid-19 pandemic and associated lockdowns. Nevertheless, with lives at risk daily in Wales, it is vital that this trend is halted and further safe spaces for escape and recovery be provided for victims of domestic abuse in Wales.

The obvious stumbling block when it comes to tackling issues of violence against women is that discussion often follows a familiar pattern: one woman speaks out about her experiences of discrimination, inequality or harassment; more come forward, each with their own story to tell. At this point everyone agrees that the discrimination, inequality and harassment are unacceptable, in some cases celebrities come forward to support the cause; politicians make impassioned speeches about how the situation must change. In almost all cases, the discussion is endless, but the progress limited. Yet ultimately, it's not good enough that in 2022 we're still having these conversations and it's not good enough that society is still facing the same problems that we've been trying to combat for so long. In order for the Welsh Government to achieve its own stated aim of improving the safety of women and girls across Wales, real changes need to be made. These changes need to be made both systemically, enabling further prosecutions to be made so that offenders are brought to justice, but also culturally, embedding a change in attitude which promotes the prevention of violence against women, rather than just the punishment of perpetrators.

Of course, the creation of a safer Wales for women also relies heavily on identifying ways to improve the health and wellbeing of women in Wales, another of the Welsh Government's stated aims for the creation of feminist government for the country. Here also the Swedish model proves an interesting point of comparison. Sweden currently holds one of the most generous parental leave provisions in the world, a staple of its work towards a feminist government. Schemes in Sweden allow parents to take a total of eighteen months off work following the birth of their child, the majority of which is covered by almost 80% of their normal, full salary. Nonetheless, in spite of the generosity and accessibility of this policy, women in Sweden still tend to be responsible for three quarters of all paid parental leave, undertaking the majority of caring responsibilities. If Wales is serious about addressing the issue of parental leave and the balance of care, cultural changes are vital to ensuring that these areas of responsibility are no longer regarded as falling primarily within the remit of women. Here again, the introduction of a form of cross-party, cohesive advocatory body for women's rights could have a significant impact on how this issue is addressed, not only within politics, but also through education systems and the remodelling of our societal approach to parenting.

I use the term societal approach, because, whether we like it or not, issues relating to caring responsibilities and women's health are a problem which is facing everyone, not just women. It affects us all, whether directly through our own experiences or through events which have had an impact on women we know and love. Change must come, but it must be both fundamental and bold. Outlining an historic change in the law which will enable UK cabinet ministers to take up to six months paid maternity leave, Boris Johnson asserted that 'the choice between taking leave to recover from childbirth and care for a new-born child or resigning from office is not acceptable in modern times.'[14] Very few people would argue with this statement, but the problem is that this is the exact dilemma facing countless women across the UK in 2021, both within politics and in other professions, and Wales is not exempt from this issue. Examples are prescient even within the Welsh Government; ahead of the 2021 Senedd elections MS Bethan Sayed, the Plaid Cymru member who once held the mantle of Wales' youngest member of the then National Assembly, announced that she would not be standing for re-election as she felt that the role was incompatible with that of mother to her young son. In a statement, Sayed spoke honestly about how she felt her decision was one which 'could have been different if we had a better set up here in Wales. Perhaps if there had been a job share opportunity – something that's been discussed for several years – I may have felt more able and comfortable juggling my work as a politician and being a new mother'.[15] The issue highlighted by Sayed points to flaws in both the workload and legislature in place within the Senedd, with the long and unsociable work hours and the hectic legislative schedule acting as barriers to Members who need to balance their career with the demands of raising a family. Opportunities are ripe for Wales to make a real difference to women who wish to access politics while also raising families by addressing these issues, a move which would also send a strong signal about the Welsh Government's commitment to the creation of a feminist society within Wales.

Unsurprisingly, issues with juggling parental responsibility and career progress and earning potential, such as those outlined by Bethan Sayed, have also been adversely affected by the Covid-19 pandemic. In addition to undertaking the primary responsibility for caring and teaching children during the lockdown periods, women have also been subject to restrictive measures which have affected everything from birth partners while labouring, the management of miscarriages and abortions, and delays to routine screening for a number of health conditions. Such restrictions have undoubtedly exaggerated the cultural bias that privileges mothers over fathers, often reinforcing the position of women within a designated domestic sphere, while men are often exempted from being part of the childcare solution. Debate continues to rage about whether these measures were fair, or indeed necessary. Like many other women who gave birth during the pandemic, I have experienced first-hand the emotional and physical toll of such conditions, compounded by the isolation of trying to balance motherhood with working remotely. Nothing can undo the hardships endured by women during this time, but the way forward from here does feel like a pivotal moment in the Welsh Government's plan to create a feminist government for Wales. Listening to and accepting the stories and experiences offered by the voices of so many women across Wales would be a powerful foundation for revolutionising the way in which we look at perinatal and parental physical and mental wellbeing within Wales.

As Wales emerges from the grip of a pandemic which has dominated our politics and daily lives for so long it is, therefore, time to turn our focus to how progress can be brought about. There is no reason why Wales should not be at the forefront of this change, leading the march and making real progress to improve the lives of women; as a nation we have all of the tools at our disposal to be leading that march and yet, we're not. Change may need to start at school level, but progress towards equality must also be made across all sectors of education in order to ensure that the principles of a fair and equal society for all are embedded within our culture and politics. As always, it feels vital to note that equality does not mean benefitting one group at the expense of another; instead, equality lies in creating a world in which everyone is treated fairly and given equal opportunities. It sounds simple enough, but as examples from nations such as Sweden have already shown, solutions are rarely that straightforward. Nonetheless, the creation of a feminist government has the potential to shape policy which can offer better outcomes for everyone. Yet if we are to achieve the vision set out by the Welsh Government, we need our arts and creative industries to remain strong and our education systems to raise future generations who are willing and able to enter politics. We need those politicians of the future to be ready to fight where there is injustice, to reflect the inequalities in the Wales we currently live in and to cling tightly to the imagination and vision of a fairer, more equitable society for all.

[1]'Leading the Fight Against the Pandemic: Does Gender 'Really' Matter?', available at: Leading the Fight Against the Pandemic: Does Gender 'Really' Matter? by Supriya Garikipati, Uma Kambhampati:SSRN

[2] 'What can we learn from Taiwan's response to the Covid-19 pandemic?', July 2021, available on the British Medical Journal Blog, at: What we can learn from Taiwan's response to the Covid-19 epidemic – The BMJ

[3] 'It's a distraction to focus on the success of individual women leaders during Covid', Clare Wenham and Asha Herten-Crabb, May 2021, Kings College London *Spotlight on Research* series, available at: It's a distraction to focus on the success of individual women leaders during Covid (kcl.ac.uk)

[4] 'Wales to put gender equality at the heart of Government – Welsh Ministers sign up to new approach to tackle gender inequality', Welsh Government Press Release, available at: Wales to put gender equality at the heart of Government – Welsh Ministers sign up to new approach to tackle gender inequality | GOV.WALES

[5] 'A Feminist Government (March 2019): A Fact Sheet', available at: Fact sheet: A feminist government ensures that decisions promote gender equality

[6] Cabinet reshuffle: Cheryl Gillan loses Wales Office – BBC News

[7] John Osmond offers an in-depth exploration of the impact, and fallout, arising from the use of all-women shortlists in Assembly elections in *Critical Mass: The Impact and Future of Female Representation in the National Assembly for Wales* (Cardiff: Institute of Welsh Affairs, 2010), pp. 8-10.

[8] 'On Balance: Diversifying Democracy in Local Government in Wales – Report of the Expert Group on Diversity in Local Government', p. 26. Available at: Report of the Expert Group on Diversity (gov.wales)

[9] This vision was outlined in a speech given by then First Minister, Carwyn Jones, in 2019 and then reaffirmed in the document 'Advancing Gender Equality in Wales Plan', available at: advancing-gender-equality-plan.pdf (gov.wales)

[10] Laura McAllister, 'The Basic Truth About Men, Women and Power in Wales', *Wales Online,* 17th March 2018, available at: The basic truth about men, women and power in Wales – Wales Online.

[11]Research by the European University Association, available at: Despite gains, women still highly outnumbered by men as university leaders (eua.eu)

[12]School Workforce Census Results 2019, available at: School Workforce Census results: as at November 2019 (Revised) | GOV.WALES

[13]Figures available at: Is Wales on track to become a 'world leader for gender equality'? (senedd.wales)

[14]'Government Agrees to Call Pregnant Women Mothers', *BBC News*, 25.02.2021, available at: Government agrees to call pregnant women mothers – BBC News

[15]'Bethan Sayed Steps Down from the Senedd After 13 Years as She Says Politics Isn't Family Friendly', *Wales Online*, 28th August 2020

SMYTH, SUFFRAGETTES AND WOMEN IN MUSIC TODAY: Odaline de la Martinez in Conversation

Steph Power

'Because I have conducted my own operas and love sheep-dogs; because I generally dress in tweeds, and sometimes, at winter afternoon concerts, have even conducted in them; because I was a militant suffragette and seized a chance of beating time to "The March of the Women" from the window of my cell in Holloway Prison with a tooth-brush; because I have written books, spoken speeches, broadcast, and don't always make sure that my hat is on straight; for these and other equally pertinent reasons, in a certain sense I am well known.'
Ethel Smyth (1858-1944)

From blatant sexual exploitation in videos and marketing, to a lack of women in top and/or creative positions, there are many contentious issues surrounding women in music today. High profile figures from Charlotte Church[1] to Kaija Saariaho[2] have given voice to serious concerns about the music industry at all levels and across genres, as many hard-won gains for women have either plateaued or, more worrying still, eroded in recent years. It was only in 1984 that Odaline de la Martinez made history as the first woman ever to conduct at the BBC Proms.[3] Since then, progress in representation for women conductors and composers at the Proms and elsewhere has been extremely slow[4], and it was not until 2013 – nearly 30 years later – that Marin Alsop[5] finally made the landmark step of conducting the iconic last night of the festival. So it seemed doubly shocking that Alsop's historic concert should happen to coincide with a storm of controversy which somehow – almost unthinkably – re-erupted around questions of whether women can and should conduct at all, thanks to some unguarded remarks by Vasily Petrenko[6] and others, such as Bruno Mantovani, Director of the Paris Conservatoire[7].

Beneath the subsequent bickering in the media regarding who said exactly what, how, why and in what context, the basic issue remains live in 2021: in classical music as elsewhere in music and in society at large, women – intersecting with people from minoritised ethnic and disabled communities, queer communities and the working class – have yet to achieve equal access, representation and status with white, cis middle-class men – or anywhere near that goal in many areas. It is just the tip of the iceberg that there are far fewer female than there are male conductors,[8] composers, arrangers, producers, broadcasters, critics and academics – a situation about which one can argue back and forth forever, but which will, ultimately, only improve with a transformation in cultural attitudes and behaviour towards women and non-conforming gender identities amongst men and women alike.

In the meanwhile, I wonder what the composer and militant suffragette Ethel Smyth would make of the progress thus far in equal rights and status for women were she alive today. For those controversies in the world(s) of music lent a certain irony to the commemoration in that year of Alsop's history-making in 2013 of a number of important centenaries around the women's suffrage movement, including the trampling to death of Emily Wilding by King George V's horse at the Epsom Derby, and the passing of the so-called 'Cat and Mouse' or Prisoners (Temporary Discharge for Ill Health) Act in 1913.[9]

De la Martinez is an expert on the music of Ethel Smyth, and has performed and recorded her extensively. In 1994, she conducted the BBC Proms premiere of Smyth's acknowledged greatest work, the opera *The Wreckers,* written between 1902-04 (and premiered in Leipzig, 1906), several years before Smyth eventually joined the Women's Social and Political Union (WSPU) in 1910. I spoke with de la Martinez about Smyth and about the current situation for women in classical music. But first, a brief look at Smyth herself and her background provides food for thought in terms of how deeply the iniquities are ingrained from not-so-distant social history.

*

In the Victorian England into which Smyth was born, it was unheard of for a woman to want to be taken seriously as a composer – let alone expect to be given equal consideration alongside prospective male colleagues. Women were just about acceptable as performers, teachers, and might perhaps compose parlour music for domestic use. But, for women of the aristocracy, music was generally seen as no more than a genteel, ladylike pastime; a situation which was replicated for women who, like Smyth, were born into the military upper classes – except that, here, there was usually a complete absence of understanding or sympathy for artistic pursuits beyond childhood fancy.

Imagine the reaction, then, of Major-General J.H. Smyth C.B. when, having encountered the music of Beethoven, one of his six daughters (he also had two sons) informed him that she wanted to become a composer – and to study composing at the Leipzig Conservatory, no less, where her governess had learned to play the piano sonatas that she found so inspiring.

When her father predictably forbade the idea and insisted

that she rather marry, Smyth embarked on a prolonged campaign of wilful rebellion which seems to have prefigured her entire life; adopting direct action tactics which included refusing to eat, refusing to go to church and locking herself in her room for hours. Eventually, in 1877, at the age of 19, she won through and was able to enrol at the Leipzig Conservatory as a pupil of Carl Reinecke. It was the beginning of a long and colourful musical career during which Smyth composed many substantial and accomplished works, including six operas, several large-scale orchestral pieces and a Mass in D alongside considerable other vocal and chamber music; a career during which she met Brahms, Grieg, Clara Schumann and Dvořák, was encouraged by Tchaikovsky, supported by some prominent artistic patrons and championed in England by the conductor Sir Thomas Beecham – but which nonetheless saw her continually having to battle for professional recognition.

Today, despite a number of highly successful performances during her lifetime and since her death – not to mention her 1922 elevation to Dame Commander of the Order of the British Empire in recognition of her services to music – Smyth remains shamefully neglected and undervalued. In de la Martinez' words,

'I don't know what it is – people don't give her, her due credit. But some of her works still have not been heard in London! There's a lot of brilliant music by Ethel Smyth and I thought we were opening the door with The Wreckers. But it opened and then shut, and people don't remember Smyth so much. It's a very sad case, it's heart-breaking really.'

Indeed, with Smyth, as with her later, fellow (so-called) 'woman composer' Elisabeth Lutyens, it is her boisterous, 'eccentric' behaviour rather than her music which continues to attract most attention.[10] In Lutyens' case, it is her alcoholism and notoriously acid tongue which seem to give added *frisson*, but with Smyth, it is her upper-crust country-bumpkinisms, 'mannish' appearance and many lesbian attachments – if only for the latter to be skated over with embarrassment or passing voyeuristic relish. Tellingly, Smyth's very commitment to women's suffrage is often painted as a direct result of her having fallen in love with Emmeline Pankhurst – which she may well have done, but which should not trivialise what became a commitment to the campaign so fervent that Smyth gave up composing for two years upon joining the WSPU. Moreover, she was willing to go to jail for women's suffrage, spending two months in Holloway Prison in 1912 after smashing the window of the Secretary of State for the Colonies, Lewis Harcourt.

Smyth's major contribution to the WSPU was nonetheless a musical one. In 1911 she wrote *The March of the Women* to words by Cecily Hamilton, which became the organisation's iconic anthem.[11]

Beecham famously described visiting Smyth in Holloway in his autobiography and, here, in an article for the Musical Times in 1958:

'On this particular occasion when I arrived, the warden of the prison, who was a very amiable fellow, was bubbling with laughter. He said, "Come into the quadrangle." There were the ladies, a dozen ladies, marching up and down, singing hard. He pointed up to a window where Ethel appeared; she was leaning out, conducting with a tooth- brush, also with immense vigour, and joining in the chorus of her own song.'

It is not hard to see how this tale – and it is often true of its re-telling, however affectionately meant – manages to ridicule both Smyth and the other suffragette prisoners, and to entirely gloss over the harsh, often brutal reality of life in jail for those determined to win votes for women. In de la Martinez' opinion,

I don't have any problem with the story of Smyth conducting with a toothbrush. I think that's all wonderful – they were singing her song, her choir piece. But I have a problem with the way that, during her lifetime, she was characterised as a really strange and unusual person, which with a man seems to be ok because it leads to the idea that they are geniuses – look at history and see how Beethoven has been talked about! But with women it's something to laugh at, it's something to ridicule with humour.

For those contemporaries who did give Smyth and her music serious consideration, there often emerged another problem; one captured perfectly by a critic's response to her Violin Sonata Op. 7 (1887), which was found to be 'deficient in the feminine charm that might have been expected of a woman composer.' In effect, Smyth was damned if she did and damned if she didn't, to paraphrase Eugene Gates (from the title of a paper on Smyth for the *Journal of Aesthetic Education,* 1997); if she wrote light, delicate music it was criticised for being 'weak' and 'feminine', but, on the other hand, her trade-mark assertive, muscular music was often held to be too 'masculine' and therefore 'unnatural' – which was how the violinist Joseph Joachim described her sonata.

Quite what the exact supposed difference is between music written by men and music written by women remains a mystery. But the idea that there *is* a difference became one of the most damaging and pernicious beliefs of 20th century music in gender terms, as the music of women composers from Smyth onwards was evaluated against some perceived masculine ideal. Such 'gendered aesthetics' can be found at the root of idiotic and offensive statements like 'women can't compose'; said by many, alas, but here, a direct quote from the then Artistic Director of the London Sinfonietta, Michael Vyner, in a late '80s radio interview which I myself heard, broadcast live.[12]

I quizzed de la Martinez about gendered aesthetics, and she admitted to having been initially swayed by those ideas herself, as many people were – including some feminists from the '80s on who argued that a more 'democratic', less 'hierarchical' ethos that women supposedly brought to the profession of composing extended to their actual music. I personally – as a queer composer and erstwhile performer – have always considered gendered aesthetics to be not just bizarre but objectionable; not least because the ideas ultimately appear to rely on stereotypes or over-simplified definitions of gender, often ignoring issues of transgender and, indeed, sexuality. For de la Martinez:

'It's ridiculous, I agree – I thought I could hear the difference and I can't. I've now been on too many competition juries where I don't know the names of the composers and I'm sure "that person is a woman" and then, after the people have been chosen, when you see who the names are, those people who I thought were women were not, they were men. So, from my point of view, you can't tell if a composer is a man or a woman. [Regarding Vyner's comment], it's terrible. But he was revered – so it's hard to believe with people. It also happened with Louise Badger – do you remember the woman who once ran the BBC Symphony Orchestra as general manager? – who said on the radio that women were not good conductors.' [13]

Obviously, de la Martinez is a composer as well as a conductor and at the time of interview was working on an opera trilogy about the beginnings of slavery, based on Aphra Behn's famous story *Oroonoko: or the Royal Slave* – but which, unlike the original (published in 1688), would be told from a woman's point of view. [14] I asked de la Martinez whether she agreed with Saariaho and others, that the awareness and status of women in music has plateaued or dropped off in recent years, or whether she felt improvements were still being made. Her response makes for sobering reading:

'Oh I don't think there's many improvements being made – I think it all has to do with novelty. When gay people started coming out, women conductors were coming out conducting – it's the same story. Did you ever see that fabled film **Antonio: Portrait of a Woman** ***about the Dutch conductor?*** [15] ***It's the same old story still. When women conductors are something of a novelty, they get hired, and no matter they're as good as men. The people hiring don't think about the women conductors, they think about the men. It's something that's been happening all along – I don't think it's gotten any better.***

'I think we fought some strong fights in the late '60s and '70s, we fought some strong fights in the '80s and so on. There's been some profit from it, but I think very little. In general the situation with the majority of women has not improved – no matter what you see in the media – and they're still earning a lot less than men. As far as women conductors are concerned, yes you can get on, but you don't get the same chances as men because the people hiring don't think of you. And a lot of women conductors won't say that because they're afraid.'

Returning to Ethel Smyth, de la Martinez had long been determined to stage her later, suffragette-inspired opera, *The Boatswain's Mate* (1913-14). I put it to her that the success of *The Wreckers* in the '90s – both in concert and subsequently on CD

– would surely indicate that such a project would generate a great deal of audience interest, particularly at a time when greater attention is being given to lesser-known or otherwise neglected composers of the early 20th century.

'I agree. I've been trying to find somebody to help me put on The Boatswain's Mate and I'd love to offer it to the Proms. There's one problem but it's easily remedied, and it's not in the music. The words are really 1914 – that period just after Smyth's years as a suffragette – so it just sounds old-fashioned nowadays. But it's really easy to take the spirit of what it means – it's just dialogue – and to rewrite it in modern language, the same way people translate Mozart's The Magic Flute because the old-fashioned German doesn't necessarily stand!

'Then The Boatswain's Mate would be a fabulous opera. It has a real feminist flavour but it's done with a smile. It isn't hitting you in the head but it gives you this flavour of a strong woman – very different from the strong woman of The Wreckers. And instead of the chromatic lines she used sometimes in The Wreckers, it's almost folky. It's very tonal, very approachable and is very beautiful music. Lilian Baylis[16] put it on at Sadlers Wells [in 1922] and it ran – it was popular. So it would be a hit now, I know it would.'

1914 saw the 70th anniversary of the death of Ethel Smyth and the centenary of her completion of *The Boatswain's Mate*. Of course, 1914 was also the centenary of the outbreak of World War I – at which point many suffragettes put their agitation on hold so as to join the war effort and concentrate on the immediate crisis gripping the nation. There would seem to have been no better occasion than to mount Smyth's opera – in the overture she uses the melody of *The March of the Women* – in honour of the many suffragettes who sacrificed so much to ensure that women eventually won the right to vote, paving the way to gender equality in law, if not yet in practice in society at large.

It was 2016 before de la Martinez was able to release her recording of *The Boatswain's Mate* for Retrospect Opera, with Nadine Benjamin, Edward Lee, Jeremy Huw Williams and Lontano. Today, the fight for equality goes on for women across the board, in music as in other aspects of life. For de la Martinez, that fight involves both pragmatism and a continued chipping away:

I don't know how much change there will be in my lifetime and that's why I think I decided a long time ago I would concentrate on the things I think I can do and try and make a difference and I think that's the only way. I don't think you can change the world but you might be able to change a tiny little bit of the world, and if you fight at it long enough you might actually be able to do it.

No doubt Ethel Smyth would have been determined to lend her wholehearted support.

---

[1] http://www.digitalmusicnews.com/permalink/2013/10/15/church

[2] http://www.artsjournal.com/slippeddisc/2013/11/the-composer-kaija-saariaho-on-sexism-in-classical-music.html

[3] Odaline de la Martinez was born in Cuba in 1949 and raised in the USA. She settled in the UK after winning a scholarship to study at the Royal Academy of Music and the University of Surrey, founding the ensemble Lontano in 1976. She has conducted, and her music been performed, by many ensembles and orchestras all over the world, and she has won many prestigious awards and accolades. A discography can be found here: http://www.lorelt.co.uk

[4] http://www.womeninmusic.org.uk/proms10.htm

[5] http://www.theguardian.com/music/2013/sep/06/marin-alsop-proms-classical-sexist

[6] http://www.newsinenglish.no/2013/08/30/new-conductor-strikes-sour-note/

[7] http://www.artsjournal.com/slippeddisc/2013/10/women-dont-want-to-conduct-because-its-incompatible-with-family-life.html

[8] Jessica Duchen has compiled an exhaustive list of women conductors, with links to biographies and websites on her blog http://jessicamusic.blogspot.co.uk/2013/09/fanfare-for-uncommon-woman-conductor.html

[9] This was a law which allowed for the discharge of suffragette hunger-strikers from prison when they became ill, only to re-imprison them as soon as they were sufficiently recovered, leading to further savage ill-treatment at the hands of the authorities through force-feeding etc.

[10] Rhiannon Mathias has noted that 'Smyth's musical accomplishments and involvement in the most acrimonious years of the campaign for women's suffrage did not, however, prepare the ground for the young women who reached student age in the first decades of the twentieth century' (*Lutyens, Maconchy, Williams and Twentieth-Century British Music* Ashgate, 2012).

[11] Ethel Smyth's The March of the Women composition set to suffragette stills, http://www.youtube.com/watch?v=LCtGkCg7trY

[12] Indeed, that comment, together with the sexism I myself suffered and witnessed as the then student chair of York University's ANeMonE ('A New Music Ensemble') led me to accept the job when the pressure group Women in Music invited me to briefly run the organisation after I graduated. The committee then included composers Nicola LeFanu and Errollyn Wallen, Enid Williams of the rock band Girlschool and Gemini's Ian Mitchell, together with support from de la Martinez, broadcaster Natalie Wheen, soprano Jane Manning and Icebreaker's James Poke among many others.

[13] 'Women can't conduct Brahms, and Mahler is men's music.' So said Helen Thompson in the 1970s, then manager of the New York Philharmonic.

[14] Part 2 was first performed in the USA in April 2013 and premiered in the UK at Martinez' biennial American Festival in London, October 2014.

[15] [Antonia Brico 1902 – 1989] http://en.wikipedia.org/wiki/Antonia_Brico

[16] http://www.theguardian.com/stage/2013/nov/19/fitting-memorial-lilian-baylis

Here are some links to further websites offering statistics and opinions regarding the status of women in (mainly classical) music today:

Some statistics released by Female Pressure for International Women's Day 2013:

http://createdigitalmusic.com/2013/03/time-to-act-sobering-stats-and-call-for-change-on-international-womens-day/

Ellen McSweeney's post for the Music Box, USA: https://nmbx.newmusicusa.org/the-power-list-why-women-arent-equals-in-new-music-leadership-and-innovation

Some Australian statistics (posted October 2013) from Women's Agenda: http://www.womensagenda.com.au/talking-about/top-stories/is-the-music-industry-sexist/201310173061

The UK Performing Right Society's 'Women Make Music' initiative 2012: http://www.prsformusicfoundation.com/Funding/Women-Make-Music/Background-to-Women-Make-Music

Concert pianist and Bangor University academic, Dr Xenia Pestova's 'Quick and Dirty Survey of Man/Woman Ratios in UK Academic Music Departments August 2013: http://xpressz.tumblr.com/post/57863437835/quick-and-dirty-survey-of-man-woman-ratios-in-uk

A June 2013 blog for the Huffington Post by Lara Baker, organiser of the AIM Independent Music Awards: http://www.huffingtonpost.co.uk/lara-baker/women-in-the-music-business_b_3472612.html

Helienne Lindvall's blog for the Guardian 2010: http://www.theguardian.com/music/musicblog/2010/may/24/women-behind-music

ANGUS MCBEAN: DIGNITY, BEAUTY & MAGIC

Adam Somerset

Photographs have two lives. In their content, their small scope of representation, they encapsulate a single moment. That duration may be as brief as a thousandth of a second. In their second life, in becoming an artefact, they are untethered to live across time. On occasion, a photographic image may be possessed of such force as to anchor itself to a specific time and place in the consciousness of memory.

It is the last Friday of May 2021, the place is the Aberystwyth School of Art. I have before my eyes, a photograph made by Angus McBean, the great theatre photographer. The conditions of infection control have eased but still remain. My nose and mouth are masked, but the image is there for the holding – without gloves. The hands of the artist who made the image a half-century ago once held the same physical artefact. The fingers of Angus McBean guided the pencil to make the signature that I now read. In this present moment, this granting of the first freedoms of movement, my own fingers are allowed to hold, with care, the image by its edges. It may be turned to different angles in the light. I am able to hold it at a full arm's length, to bring it close, to let the focus alter.

The price that Covid-19 has demanded that we collectively pay cannot yet be known; the pandemic, although apparently subdued, persists. But this portrait – of performer Marika Rivera

– is the first material image I have experienced after a time during which unmediated perception of art has been proscribed. By this time, the end of May 2021, fifteen months have passed in which galleries have been sealed, places of performance locked, public events cancelled. A part of our core humanness, the bulk of our existence as social beings, has been held in check. Above all, touch has been curtailed. Direct perception has been reduced to the familiar and the quotidian around us. Our attention to the world has been diverted, and restricted, to images brought via a screen. The screen is good for information; but it is deficient in feeling.

A physical image to gaze at after a period of sensory drought – and one that may be held – is special, but this image is possessed of a formal richness and a thematic complexity that ripple beneath its surface. If those qualities are preconditions for art, then the photography of Angus McBean is high art indeed. His biographer, champion and companion, Adrian Moorhouse, gave a talk at the National Library of Wales in 2016, in which he described McBean as, "the greatest photographer this country has produced", the country being Wales.

The first stage in appreciation of a photograph is to perceive the form in which it was made. Marika Rivera has made her transition from life to art not as a pixelated creation. The photograph of her that has emerged was birthed gradually in a chemical bath. That makes it different from an image made from the colour mix of a printer. McBean photographed Rivera many times, but this particular photograph, now housed in Aberystwyth, does not appear in reproduction in books about him. It has a single representation on the internet, which is poorly produced.

The original is A3 in size, with little resemblance to a reproduction on photographic paper. The medium is termed "vintage silver print". It has no gloss to bounce the light. The black that has been chemically formed in a gelatin-silver process is not a black made in the digital RGB process. The overall composition is made of daring contrasts of light and shadow, but it has no true black in the sense of an absolute absence of light. To look closely at the dark downward part of Rivera's dress is to see slivers of tone that are, in fact, folds in the velvet fabric.

The second stage in appreciation, comes with viewing the way in which McBean has captured his subject. He photographed every star of theatre and music over the decades of his professional career. Alongside the names of The Beatles or Vivien Leigh or Laurence Olivier, that of Marika Rivera is lesser known. The daughter of Diego Rivera was raised in Europe by her mother, Marie Vorobieff, and was first taught dance by Isadora Duncan at the age of three. She moved, via two marriages, from Paris to Dorset to Ealing in West London. She acted sporadically in films from 1961 to 1987 and died, aged ninety, in 2010.

One of her films *The Girl on a Motorcycle* has been programmed on a film channel repeatedly over the lockdown months. In a late scene, Marianne Faithfull steps off her motorbike and enters a restaurant in Germany. Marika Rivera plays a waitress and has the line: "Moment. Fruehstueck? Kaffee?" She makes a gesture whereby she sweeps her hair back for no obvious reason. The scene is fleeting, yet Rivera's presence is evanescent. Seventeen years earlier, in 1950, she had been photographed in her home. That is the photograph now between my fingers.

The composition that McBean created is one of high formal complexity. Rivera is posed behind a large candle in the foreground, which is placed a quarter of the distance from the lateral axis and rises half-way to the height of the picture. On its left side ripples of wax have melted and hardened. Rivera's head is positioned mid-way laterally and one-third down from the top. The focal centre of the image accords with the 'Golden Ratio' of classical aesthetics. A single candle has been placed to her left and five more candles run in an upward curved ascent to her right.

Her left hand holds her hair back, so that her profile catches McBean's light source. Her head is tilted in the manner of a old master's Madonna. Strands of hair catch the light. The note on the print locates the setting as Athelhampton Hall in 1950. Rivera was married at the time but in this image, she wears no rings. Her right hand holds the bulb of a water lily. The hand is positioned to follow a parabolic curve via the left hand to the top candle. A frame beneath the fabric of her velvet dress carries it outward to a point of equal distance between her waist and the top of her head. Braid stitching runs down the ruched sleeve and radiates out from the waist with seven more lines running around the hem.

The hand-written note on the reverse of the print reads: "*Dancing to the music of Ravel's Pavane for a Dead Infanta*". The words are a puzzle since Rivera, albeit a dancer, is manifestly not dancing. The words are less a description than a pointer. Ravel spoke about the title he had given his composition claiming it was: "an evocation of the pavane that might have been danced by such a little princess as painted by Velázquez."

The location of the image is Dorset, and the subject is Russian-Mexican, but it is a Spanish painter who is key to decoding this picture. The dress that Rivera wears is modelled on that worn by the five-year-old Margaret Theresa of Spain, the Infanta is at the centre of Velázquez' masterpiece *Las Meninas*. McBean's image can be fully apprehended as a rich and allusive homage to one of the most complex images in painting that treads the line between illusion and reality.

Doon Arbus in writing of her mother's work said: "a photograph should be allowed to speak for itself, without explanatory, contextual or biographical data." Yet that is not the way perception works. The static form of the image is insufficient. The observing eye yearns to know more. McBean sowed his images with scope for afterthought. He once explained: "I have never considered photography an art- how can anything that is just a mechanical process be an art? But *what goes into a photograph* may be an art."

The aesthetics of McBean present a challenge to critical writing on photography. The earliest photographs tended to be elaborate concoctions of design and very slow exposure. The concept that a photograph represented undiluted verisimilitude came more gradually. In the 1930s, documentary images from Spain's civil war were held to be true. In the 2010s, the same images were dismissed by partisan voices as fabrication. The period in which the photograph held its status as authoritative verity, the world rendered in a truthful image, was therefore brief.

Critical writing on photography found a determining voice in Susan Sontag. In her book *On Photography*, she wrote: "Photography implies that we know about the world if we accept it as the camera records it. But this is the opposite of understanding, which starts from not accepting the world as it is... the camera's rendering of reality must always hide more than it discloses."

Sontag extended her argument to the epistemological limitations of our photographic knowledge of the world: "[I]t can, finally, never be ethical or political knowledge. The knowledge gained through still photographs will always be some kind of sentimentalism, whether cynical or humanist...By furnishing this already crowded world with a duplicate one of images, photography makes us feel that the world is more available than it really is."

In *About Looking*, John Berger went a step further, observing that the world and the world-as-represented had in effect merged. Quoting Sontag, he wrote of "the objects that make up and thicken the environment we recognise as modern...Our very sense of situation is now articulated by the camera's interventions." In an age now where an image may become anything, where source and validity are open to question, the work of McBean has a refreshing clarity to it. It is emphatically not veridical, being bracingly and self-consciously manufactured.

Making art is a tripartite process, which involves eye and hand and heart. The heart alone is insufficient for a species that also needs to draw meaning-seeking from the senses. Meaning can derive from perceiving formal complexity, patterns-within-patterns, elaboration in preparation and depth of craft in execution. Art is the vector that links one human to another across time. These criteria are all met in the image of Marika Rivera in a hall in Dorset, maybe at dance (or maybe not), at some time in the mid twentieth century.

Angus McBean was, to use Johan Huizinga's phrase, an artist as *Homo Ludens* – the human who plays. And that makes him an artist of challenge for an age where art is often pressed to be instrumental, less a Kantian thing-unto-itself (ding-an-sich) but as a tool for ideological purpose. Art as play; art as craft; art as form and deep pattern; art as allusion. These are the factors that render McBean a significant place in the visual culture of Wales. Play lies at the core of his work. He took up early a habit of creating his own Christmas cards and, in 1936, designed one with a dualistic self-portrait – with a shadow of his head in profile dominating the background with a hand in silhouette mimicking the act of drawing, juxtaposed with another image of the artist leaning forward in the foreground, his mouth in the curve of a broad smile. The apposition of these images is richly metaphorical. The shadow and the smile speak of the dual aspects of being human, the private occluded self and the social being in public presentation. The smile that he gave to the word beguiles.

McBean died in 1990 at the age of 86. Quentin Crisp, whom he had once photographed, wrote a tribute to him, saying that he had dedicated his life to acting out a fragile illusion: "He played that life was happy; that all women were lovely – even Edith Evans; he played that love was everywhere. This philosophy made him delightful to be with, impossible to talk to and infinitely sad... He worked hard for his success, and when it came he enjoyed it chiefly because it brought him into contact with so many illustrious people... he was genuinely star-struck. I never heard him speak badly of anyone well known. In his eyes, celebrity made anyone adorable. In spite of his success he remained mysteriously modest."

Artists of depth always conserve that last inner territory of mystery. To understand McBean's aesthetics it is necessary to go back to the beginning. He was born in Newbridge, Monmouthshire in South Wales on June 8th 1904. Despite the surname the family had been Welsh for generations. His father, Clement Philip James McBean, was a mine surveyor and the family moved frequently around Wales. McBean attended Monmouth School and Newport Technical College where his fascination with photography began. His first camera was an autographic Kodak that cost £2 10s. He raised the money from the sale of a gold watch left him by his grandfather. A tripod and other equipment followed. The small Kodak was soon abandoned for a quarter-plate reflex. It was called the Popular Pressman and was expensive.

But he was also at work in another craft. His mother had been active in amateur dramatics and the son began to make masks in Bryn Mawr. At the Lyceum Theatre in Monmouth he was involved in making the sets, props and costumes. In London, where the family moved after the death of his father, he filled his room with masks. He received a commission to make a nose mask for the renowned actor Ernest Thesiger. His work was much admired and more commissions followed. For seven years he earned his living by working in the Liberty department store in the antiques department and learning about restoration. Off-duty he spent his time with photography, mask-making and watching plays in the West End.

In 1932 he left Liberty's after thwacking a customer with a bolt of cloth. He grew himself a beard that was long, square and slightly reddish. Meeting the trio of designers who collectively called themselves Motley he made pieces of medieval scenery for a play that starred John Gielgud. With no-one else available he made medieval shoes for the whole company. His work became noticed in the gossip columns. His masks of Greta Garbo and Lloyd George drew public attention.

Hugh Cecil, a leading portrait photographer in Bond Street, became aware of McBean's work. Cecil motored to McBean's studio in his Rolls Royce and declared the work "terrible but interesting." "I can easily teach you to be a photographer" he said. "What I am interested in is your ability to make a picture. Quite a different thing and one no-one can teach you." Cecil himself was engaged on a project to develop a new camera, so for almost a year McBean executed the portraits that went under the Cecil stamp. When the Prince of Wales arrived with a lady companion whom he wished to be photographed he scrutinised McBean. "The Prince kind of squinted at me", McBean recalled, "Mr Cecil, you've grown a beard. I don't remember you having a beard." McBean mumbled: "No, sir, I mean, yes,sir, I have grown a beard" and busied himself with putting his lights in position.

McBean was unpaid but he had evening use of the studio for his own work. As an apprentice he put aside his own style in order to imitate. Lenses and lighting were just the beginning at this stage of photograph-making. The 12 by 10 plate negative had a special coating with a matt-surfaced emulsion. The raw image could be embellished with the use of a pencil. It is the way of the gifted apprentice to outgrow the master. McBean was dissatisfied with the Cecil look and set up his own studio in Belgrave Road in Victoria. Photography was still taking second place in his life to the making of masks and models. Masks were in mode, not just for the stage but as a regular item for fashionable wall decoration. A Mae West doll earned him more publicity. In 1936 Ivor Novello requested masks for a production *The Happy Hypocrite.* His delight with the result led him to ask that McBean take the publicity photographs for the show. The photographs in a dramatic black and white proved to be a great success.

On the set of *The Happy Hypocrite* he met Vivien Leigh. It was an association that was to last decades. Photographs in all the glossy magazines followed. The names were illustrious: Charles Laughton, Edith Evans, Laurence Olivier, Diana Wynyard, Rex Harrison. 1937 was the year that was to define McBean's place in the canon of photography's greats. Eugene O'Neill's *Mourning Becomes Electra* had been a big hit and a glossy magazine commissioned a picture of its lead, Beatrix Lehmann. The first Surrealist exhibition had taken place and McBean had been impressed by the painter William Acton. The photograph that ensued was elaborate in its preparation. The actress is swathed in stiff taffeta and is juxtaposed by a huge hawser with hook. She is Electra on the quayside, but McBean's lighting has merged her into the rope and wood. The magazine was delighted with its image of star transformed into a kind of mechanical mermaid.

A series of actors and dancers followed to his studio and all were given an extravagant, surrealist treatment. The studio filled with props. But the motive of beauty was never far away. His surrealism was a means to add frisson and strangeness to photographs made to please.

In the McBean studio, the actual photography session was an end-point to days of pre-work. The artist L Roy Hobdell painted backdrops. Props were fashioned from plaster and wood. The use of sand became a regular, in part because an early work used some and the studio was left with a vast quantity as a result of an over-order. The ascent to the theatre world's photographer of choice was rapid and as quickly abbreviated by the advent of war. Theatrical tours flourished but the era of aerial bombing closed the theatres of London. The Belgrave Road studio was closed and McBean removed himself and a quantity of his glass negatives to the house of an uncle in Bath.

As a result of friendships in Bath, McBean was prosecuted under the proscriptive legislation against acts of male homosexuality. He spent two and a half years in prison for offences against the mores of his time. In prison in Lincolnshire he photographed fellow inmates and produced, directed and dressed play productions. He naturally feared for his future career, scandal and absence making a potent combination. But, the Second World War over, one call for his services followed another. Stratford wanted him for the American visitor, Claire Luce. His photographs were published in "the Tatler." McBean had survived potential ignominy.

A new studio was bought and recreated. The location in Endell Street was better with close proximity to the places of theatre and opera. He became the official recorder for Stratford and the fledgling National Theatre. He recorded productions of every Shakespeare play and made a unique collection in theatre's history. In London there were plays by Christopher Fry and Terence Rattigan, big new musicals from the USA in the form of *Carousel* and *Oklahoma*.

In contrast small scale review shows were in the hands of the talents of Joyce Grenfell, Hermione Baddeley and Hermione Gingold. In the studio McBean stretched his medium with effects of montage and multiple exposure. This second invention of surrealistically-inclined work produced arresting images year on year. The methods that he developed had a spin-off in the production of the uniquely idiosyncratic Christmas cards. His lustre was such that now up to eight hundred cards went out across the world. Employment at the studio reached ten with assistants, retouchers, lighters, dark-room workers and secretary all required.

One of his commercial commissions was for a beauty product. He chose a member of the chorus line from a revue he was photographing at the Cambridge Theatre. He paid his model £4 and her picture was to be seen in pharmacy windows for years to come. It was the eyes that had caught his attention. Those four pounds went to a young Audrey Hepburn.

McBean was the recorder without equal of London's theatre and Vivien Leigh was a perennial subject. From a *Twelfth Night* of 1955 she is in half-profile to the camera. A dress of sumptuousness and size flows in a full gorgeous sweep. The flow of the dress is mirrored in the arrangement of the curtain behind. In 1951 she is in full profile, her nose abutting Olivier's cheek. The production is *Julius Caesar*. She is Cleopatra in full costume, and he is Mark Anthony. These were stars at their theatrical apex.

In 1951 he photographed Richard Burton holding the crown just above his head as the young *Henry V*. It is a symbol for the life to come. The eyes are luminous and arresting. The pocked right cheek can be seen but only with a closeness of scrutiny.

McBean's image-making was motivated by beauty. "Luckily Miss Avala, my retoucher, could see to that", he recalled. As for Burton: "We got on so well together, because of his Welshness, which he never let anyone forget."

McBean was a master of velvety blacks, half-tones and chiaroscuro. Vivien Leigh again, in 1937, has her head tilted downward. A black hat casts a shadow that is so posed as to just touch the edge of the pupil of her right eye. It is mirrored by a line of dark that sculpts her left cheek. The photograph made its way to Hollywood and paved the way to the role of Scarlett O'Hara. McBean's mastery of the balance of black and white is consummate. A picture from 1950 comes from a production of "the Innocents." Flora Robson is in mid-distance and holds a lamp that throws its light upward on her face of deep disquiet. In the foreground the children, Miles and Flora, are seated. The girl's head is composed to be at the height of Miss Jessel's waist. The children are playing cards, the impossible white of their nightwear next to a lighted candle. In a single image it says everything about Henry James' masterpiece ghost story.

The 1960s came and so too new camera technology. McBean said: "As it became easier to take the pictures, I think my pictures became less interesting." In the new era a raft of new signatures were added to the visitors' book at the Endell Street studio. The recording company EMI sent his way the biggest names of the new music. Cliff Richard, the Shadows, Tommy Steele, Adam Faith, Johnny Kidd, John Leyton, Marty Wilde, Billy J Kramer, Freddy and his Dreamers were precursors to the most famous image of them all. Four young men looking out over a balcony. "A gangling group of four young men in mole-coloured velveteen performing suits of a terrible cut" was how McBean described meeting the chart-topping Beatles.

McBean was an artist who started young, was active for

decades and left a weight of work behind. The physical legacy amounted to eight and a half tons of glass negatives. No institution in 1970s Britain wanted them and Laurence Olivier suggested the USA. Harvard bought four and a half tons for $40,000. The studio was sold to an assistant. There was no room for the storage of antique images; four tons of glass negatives of all the regular studio sittings were destroyed.

Angus McBean was in hospital for his eighty-sixth birthday. He ate birthday cake with berries and ice cream and died that night of heart failure.

A person dies twice; so ran a saying in Pharaonic Egypt. The first is at the time of death itself. The second is when the last memory, the knowledge of direct acquaintance, itself comes to die. Angus McBean the man is still the subject of memory for a few who can recall his zest and his dedication. But after the life comes the legacy. The critical judgement of history is unpredictable. Critical approval was to wane immediately after his death. By the time of a retrospective at the National Portrait Gallery in 2006, McBean had become "a generous and somewhat fey portrait photographer, with a pronounced fondness for props and light-hearted gimmickry."

Two decades into the new century and the vast legacy that he left behind has an unanticipated prescience to it. Lord Snowden, a fellow photographer who in 1951 had applied to be McBean's assistant, later described his motivation: "He wanted to make people look their best...to look beautiful". McBean's photography suited the grey post-war Britain but it was also a slower time. A session to create the image rightly would entail a half-day of preparation in the studio. The photographer lit, directed and staged his subjects. "He created dignity, beauty and magic", Snowden added, "which seem to be so frequently missing today".

Dignity, beauty, magic; all are present to me in Aberystwyth in this moment of pandemic. Marika Rivera is held within my hands, released from the circumstance of life and limit to dance hauntingly between her candles for time with no end.

'IN THE CHARNEL HOUSE CORRIDORS': Robert Minhinnick in Iraq

John Lavin

'I defy anyone not to make art about visits to Amiriya and Babylon in Iraq. My discovery of both places has had a huge impact on how I think and feel. But I had to go there to write, as I have to experience the particularity of places...'

Robert Minhinnick, speaking to Eamon Burke (Wales Arts Review, 25/07/2018)

'Entering and leaving Iraq meant arduous journeys across implacable desert. The experience has had a major effect on my writing.'

Robert Minhinnick, writing ahead of two performances of 'An Opera in Baghdad' in 2013

'Every supper, you said, might be the last.
So maybe that's the way to live,
The way we should read our books'

from 'The Bombing of Baghdad as seen from an Electrical Goods Shop'

Robert Minhinnick's visit to Iraq in 1997, between the two Gulf Wars, proved to be a pivotal moment for him as an artist. From 'The Thief of Baghdad' in 2005s Welsh Book of the Year, *To Babel and Back*; to the searing, 'After the Stealth Bomber', in 2017s *Diary of the Last Man* (his most recent collection of poetry and one which marked Minhinnick's record third WBOTY); it is clear that his subsequent writing has been greatly informed by his experiences there. When I interviewed Minhinnick via email for *Wales Arts Review* during our *A Fiction Map of Wales* project in 2014, he reiterated the point and I couldn't help but feel that he was rightly asking for more from me in terms of my outlook and ambition, both as an editor and interviewer. I felt indeed that he was asking for a more outward looking and empathetic outlook from Welsh and indeed Western artists as a whole:

Iraq changed my life. ...Ever been in a sewage pumping station in Baghdad? When it's 100 degrees F? Humbling. Those men are heroes.

And of course, Robert Minhinnick *had* been in a sewage pumping station in the poverty ravaged Baghdad of 1997, where there was a constant fear that 'with no spare parts and no electricity, the sewage plant... [would not be able to] ...pump the effluent.' (This had happened earlier in the year when the temperature had been 130 F.) These 'ingenious men' are heroes because they keep the plant running in unbearable conditions, 'toil[ing] at the gears, concocting repairs to them from scrap metal' but nevertheless 'fearful of the limits of their skill.'

All of this is detailed in 'The Thief of Baghdad'; perhaps Minhinnick's greatest essay to date; a relatively short piece that is nevertheless packed with acute observation, hard won poetry and ever darker information that ultimately leaves a lasting mark on the soul. We are told that 'the average Iraqi child consumes three grams of protein per day' and that this figure is very likely an exaggeration. Nazaar, the author's cameraman and guide, tells him that in Iraq there are 'more children than cockroaches'. Minhinnick's gifts as a poet / essayist can be easily seen in the following passage, where he matter-of-factly details the hopelessness of a seven-year-old called Ali's prospects, before ending on a note of poetry, which, rather than being for effect is both needed and in keeping with the subject matter.

If he is unlucky, Ali will die. If he survives he might hawk tapers or cigarettes in traffic... Or herd goats in the rubbish field. And if he is very lucky, Ali will find work like the man who now passes, riding a cart of gas bottles. He will drive through warrens like this, tapping a spanner on the bottles, the poem of the gas man welcomed into the houses of the poor, his donkey waiting at the roadside, shackled with a stone.

By adding musicality and even a sense of positivity to this long sentence detailing the best possible future-world the boy is likely to see, Minhinnick does several things all at once. Firstly, he evokes the world of the current gas man, which leads us to thoughts of *his* childhood and journey to get to such a coveted position. Secondly, in doing this, he also brings to life a warren-like world of heat and poverty such as the average Western reader has never really considered. Thirdly, that 'poem of the gas man welcomed into the houses of the poor', conveys a sense of an additional, non-financial reason why this is a desirable job, which is to say that it is work which benefits the community. Minhinnick conveys a strong sense of community between ordinary Iraqi people in this essay, from the engineers at the sewage plant who are justly proud of their work, to the market traders at the *suq*, to Umm Ghada, the haunted guide to the Amiriya bunker (a subject we will discuss in detail shortly). Finally, as it is explicitly an injustice that the occupation of being a gas man in these forlorn warrens should constitute the upper limit of a seven-year-old's future possibilities, the musicality and positivity can't help but have an inverted feel, as though something is not right in the order of things; which, of course, it very evidently is not. Minhinnick conveys this by quickly silencing the 'poem of the gas man', with the full stop of 'shackled with a stone', which acts as a metaphor not only for Ali but for the situation of many of the children in Iraq. It is often Minhinnick's abilities as a poet which can make him such a compelling essayist. He has the ability to illuminate a piece of reportage with a combination of imagery and musicality that can make the point of the piece clearer and more poignant to the reader; enabling them, as it does, to also perceive the situation on a more instinctive and empathetic level.

That the final section of 'The Thief of Baghdad', has also been made into a film-poem by Minhinnick (in collaboration with Peter Morgan and Peter Thorpe) called *Amiriya/Black Hands*, confirms the often invisible line between prose and poetry that he walks in his essay writing. The piece is an unqualified success, fusing Minhinnick's original camera footage of his visit to the Amiriya Bunker in 1997, with a declamatory reading that has the structure and rhythm and power of poetry. This section details Minhinnick's unscheduled visit to the Amiriya bunker, which was targeted by a smart bomb during the first Gulf War. The poet is led by a female guide, Umm Ghada, and he 'begin[s] to decipher bouquets of plastic flowers, soccer shirts', as well as 'curious shapes' in the ceiling, which he thinks might be bats. Then he has a moment of revelation: he suddenly realises where he is.

> I have already been here. By courtesy of television. The BBC had broadcast a news conference in which US High Command had shown the Finnish blueprint of Amiriya [the building was made by a Finnish construction

> company], it's air shafts and other entry points. Military technology was so well developed that a smart bomb had been launched which had entered the building's ventilation system and so, we were informed, destroyed the target... I remember feeling a mixture of pride and wonder, jewels in the gut, as the bombing technique was explained. ... I don't recall asking what the significance of Amiriya was.

The significance is soon revealed to him as 'light pours through the smart bomb's entrance'. There are over four hundred photographs lining the walls, some of elderly people, mostly of teenagers, all of whom were sheltering in the bunker during the forty-two day bombing campaign carried out against Baghdad. And then:

> Other photographs show what was discovered when the fires went out. The heat had welded the doors to the door frames. There were no escape routes. So the children's bodies were fused together as blue clinker.
>
> And the bats? No, no ...they are not bats. They are *hands.*
>
> People were tearing at the concrete with their hands. ...They died on each others' shoulders. When the bodies were pulled clear, the hands stuck to the ceiling. Black hands. Black hands of the children of the mother of all wars.

The footage of Minhinnick's journey in the *Amiriya/Black Hands* film is from a handheld camera and therefore quite grainy, however, this fragile quality only serves to add to the sense of menace and tangible despair that permeate the film. Often it is better to simply let poetry speak for itself but in this case to see the barely conceivable horror of which Minhinnick speaks feels needed, even if it is hard to take. We see photographs of the charred, amorphous bodies and reflect on how unspeakably apposite Minhinnick's 'blue clinker' analogy is. We see for ourselves with something of the dawning horror that Minhinnick must have experienced himself that the odd shapes in the ceiling were once human hands. It is very hard to conceive of, let alone describe but Minhinnick takes it as his duty to guide us 'through the charnel house corridors' just as Umm Ghada, who lost eight family members in the bunker, leads the poet. The film closes on a photograph of a beautiful young boy that died in the bunker, and it is impossible not to imagine his suffering and agony and the suffering and agony of all those around him – and to then despair.

Amiriya/Black Hands is a film/poem about hell on earth and the purgatory that came after. It is without doubt one of the most devastating pieces of film this writer has ever seen. As such it is not difficult to imagine the impact that the visit must have had on Minhinnick. In 'An Opera of Baghdad' he remembers – or imagines? – finding a baby's tooth at Amiriya, where he had gone 'to hear the truth':

A milk tooth,
blue as a cinder. And it whispers:
coward, whose pain is it anyway?...

The poet knows he will probably never return to Iraq again; he knows that his empathy only extends so far. It is simply too arduous. But this tooth/experience will grow inside him and become a part of who he is in the future. The tooth continues to whisper:

You will carry me now
as a part of yourself...

Forever now
I will ache in the skull
of the man who stooped in the shelter
of Amiriya to pick the tooth
of a child like a rice grain
from the ash.

And so it has proved because Minhinnick's writing has undoubtably grown in breadth and stature since 1997; while the Amiriya bunker is a subject that he returns to again and again in his poetry; most recently in *Diary of the Last Man's* hallucinatory, 'After the Stealth Bomber: Umm Ghada at the Amiriya Bunker'; published a full twenty years after he visited Iraq. In this poem, Minhinnick turns his attention to the guide, Umm Ghada, who he imagines still keeping vigil at the bunker (however, when reading the poem for the T.S. Eliot prize ceremony he informed us that her whereabouts are currently unknown). He envisages her being nightly visited:

by the children, the old people,
but all a fog of flesh.
One body with four hundred souls

As in *Amiriya / Black Hands*, Minhinnick manages to convey a sense of the oppressive atmosphere of the bunker that bleeds off the page with the help of imagery that feels more likely to have been encountered in a nightmare than initially written down. 'After the Stealth Bomber' conveys the sense of an inverted world where 'Umm Ghada guards' the ghosts of her beloved ones, while forcing herself to relive the atrocity on a nightly basis. Perhaps she feels that she should have died instead and that in being denied death, she must remain to teach people about the atrocity. Certainly, the imagery with which Minhinnick describes Umm Ghada suggests that she has become at one with death:

> Yet no desert was ever so black
> as the sackcloth that Umm Ghada owns.
> Not the Syrian desert's
> Bedouin black, it's cairns
> Of cold stones.

'The Bombing of Baghdad as seen from an Electrical Goods Shop'; a beautiful poem coloured in equal parts by affection and desolation; brings us full circle in that it imagines how Nazaar, Minhinnick's guide and cameraman on his 1997 trip to Baghdad, might be living during the second invasion of Iraq in 2003:

> ...I suppose you're at home,
> ...Listening to the cruise missiles, the only
> Traffic out tonight on Palestine Street,
> While here in the window of Edwards Electrical
> Your city in the tracer's glow
> Becomes a negative of itself.

Minhinnick draws us back to Porthcawl and the jarring reality of himself watching the bombing of a city he knows and cares about on something as banal as a TV in a shop window. People can become inured, of course, against seeing war on TV; but Minhinnick has been to the Amiriya bunker and witnessed the aftermath of atrocity first-hand. And he has seen the terrible difference between TV reportage and the reality on the ground with his own eyes. Ultimately, he understands that empathy is the very least we can do.

> In a Guardian piece written shortly after 9/11, Ian McEwan, correctly suggested that:
> If the hijackers had been able to imagine themselves into the thoughts and feelings of the passengers, they would have been unable to proceed. It is hard to be cruel once you permit yourself to enter the mind of your victim. Imagining what it is like to be someone other than yourself is at the core of our humanity. It is the essence of compassion, and it is the beginning of morality. *(Ian McEwan, The Guardian, 15/09/01)*

In Minhinnick's writing he is seeking this same compassion from his audience; but he also wants us to feel empathy for the people we don't hear about on the news; for the so-called collateral damage of war; for 'the children of the mother of all wars.' Time and again in his work, he seeks to draw our attention to the interconnectedness of people and places:

> When I walk around the fairground [in Porthcawl] I'm walking along Babylon's Street of Processions. They're not so different. *('Building Driftwood Fires': An Interview with Robert Minhinnick by John Lavin. Wales Arts Review, 2014.)*

However, in his writing on Iraq he also seeks to show the harsh disconnect between our two realities. For Minhinnick, art ought to at least aspire to be an agent of change, rather than solely be an end in itself. Writers (and for that matter, their readers) shouldn't simply profit from their experience of the suffering of others through the prism of art. Like the tooth says: *'whose pain is it anyway?'* That Minhinnick's homeland is one of the countries aiming the tracer's glow on Baghdad is left unspoken but is, of course, never far from either the poet or the reader's mind.

WHY I STOPPED WRITING FOR WALES ARTS REVIEW

João Morais

The first time I really worried for my safety online was when the leader of the Spanish alt right tweeted, "OK, fuck this guy" about me to his 20,000 followers. I started receiving hundreds of abusive messages from angry Spanish people every day. To make matters worse, two of my four sisters were living in Spain at the time.

So what had I done to cause so much anger? Had I run over King Felipe VI's dog? Did I drop a full pint on one of Morata's metatarsals shortly before the World Cup? Was I caught noncing my way up the Costa Brava?

It was none of these. The truly heinous crime I had committed, that had resulted in randos trying their best to hound me off the internet, was to make fun of some chocolate.

It all started when I went to visit my sister Nia, who was teaching near Oviedo. We had gone to a supermercado to get some food and vino tinto for dinner, and I had stumbled across some small, sugar-coated chocolate buttons, similar to Smarties. They were anthropomorphised on the packet to have arms, legs, eyes, and big, bright red lips.

They were called *Conguitos*.

I had found myself staring at the Spanish equivalent of the Golliwog.

Not that you need to be to find this disturbing, but as a brown person myself, with one half of my family being from a small

African nation, I immediately felt a strong sense of objection to this anti-black imagery. I got my phone out and took a picture. Then I tweeted it with the caption, 'wtf there's this weird racist chocolate in Spain called 'Little Congans'.[1]

I didn't expect much of a response. I barely ever got a dozen likes on anything I tweeted (I place a higher value on my sanity these days, so I don't really use Twitter much now). But this tweet exploded. It started when a gaming account, busy retweeting everything they could find about Conguitos for some inexplicable reason, happened across mine and spread it to their less-than-receptive audience. Then Spanish cosplayers got retweeting it, before it hit the mainstream and went viral, garnering thousands upon thousands of retweets in a short space of time. I went to visit my mother for dinner on the second day. My phone didn't stop pinging with notifications. I had to half-seriously convince her at one point that I wasn't funding my PhD through selling drugs.

The situation was repeated on facebook where images of the tweet spread shortly after, fuelled not only by Spaniards, but also by the type of immigrant living there who proudly hasn't learned the language of their new home country (while no doubt calling themselves an "ex-pat" and voting against their own best interests to Leave). It's safe to say that, while I received a number of private messages from Spaniards who agreed with me (including lots from ethnic minorities working in retail who were forced into the indignity of putting Conguitos through the till), the vast, vast majority of Spanish-based Twitter users thought my tweet showed that I was something of an *imbécil*.

I hope you never have to experience seeing a grotesque avatar of yourself, which has no connection to the person you are, spreading in real time. I was told repeatedly that the age of a product was a valid excuse for it to dehumanise people. I was told that by saying a chocolate based on black people is bad, I was actually also implying that being black itself is bad. I was told that by criticising a bag of chocolates, I was also criticising the rich history and culture of where the racist chocolates came from. And because a bunch of British idiots I have never met behave hedonistically every summer in many popular Spanish coastal spots, I was told I was not allowed to hold an opinion about a chocolate that was marketed with racist 'native' stereotypes.

The American-style culture war had not quite reached the shores of the Iberian Coast at this point, but I feel like my involvement was one of the opening volleys. I was subsequently misrepresented in *El País*, *El Español* and other major Spanish publications about the whole hoo-hah. After thousands of retweets, quote tweets, and a countless number of replies (along with a couple of weeks of sleepless nights), I locked my account, so only the people following me could interact with me[2], as I should have done before the first journalist came sniffing around asking for a quote.

Even when the mob moved onto its next reason to be outraged, it took a while for my sleep pattern to return to normal, or for a ping on my phone to not spike an adrenaline surge in my system. But it was the impact on my sisters however, on opposite ends of the country, that affected me most. They endured months of 'conversations' with work colleagues and strangers, telling them why their brother was a pillock and there was nothing even remotely wrong with the small chocolates that were supposed to resemble black people. (Sorry about that, Nia. Hope you can forgive me, Robyn.)

*

At about this time I was also finishing off an article for Wales Arts Review about the Roald Dahl 100 Wales project. This year-long series of events, culminating in a giant peach being paraded down St Mary Street from Cardiff Castle, was initiated to celebrate 100 years since 'The World's Greatest Storyteller™' was born (in what was then) just outside the rapidly expanding city.

Among the exhibitions and events, the BBC put out a documentary on Dahl as part of its Great Welsh Writers series. Articles came out stating how 'growing up Welsh'[3] had moulded him. All in all, it was a very successful project, which I'm sure would have resulted in many pats on backs in the various QUANGOs that increasingly hold stead over public life.

But should we think of Dahl as Welsh, because he was born and spent the first seven years of his life here? Now, I'm a sufferer of 'well, actually' syndrome[4], and I disagree with the notion that we should think of Dahl as Welsh, or that we should attempt to claim some Welshness for him whatsoever. In my less than esteemed opinion, a crucial and often overlooked matter on this topic is perhaps what Dahl thought of himself. When asked about his family and upbringing on Radio 4's Desert Island Discs, Dahl said that he was 'Pure Norwegian, both mother and father, yes. Born and educated in England. I speak Norwegian and I have visited it nearly every year of my life, but I'm really very English'[5].

Dai Smith once famously said of Wales that it is a 'singular noun but a plural experience.' While we could take Smith's famous quote as a basis for much discussion about what Welshness actually is, I personally feel that if, like Dahl, you go on national radio and say that you are 'really very English', it probably means that you're Really Very English. To me, saying you're Really Very English makes you about as Welsh as fullback

Dusty Hare's three Really Very English penalties that ended Wales' five year winning streak against England in the 1980 Five Nations Rugby Championship. I imagine that Dahl would have agreed with Irish Catholic Daniel O'Connell MP, when he said in 1843 of his fellow countryman the Duke of Wellington (the Leader of the House of Lords at the time), that 'Being born in a stable does not make one a horse'.[6]

I made this point, among many others, in a 3000 word article for Wales Arts Review. However, the reason I have to tell you about this piece, rather than include its title and a handy link so you can read it for yourself, is because it was never published.

So what happened? Did Wales Arts Review refuse to publish it? Did someone censor me to protect their readership from my terrible opinions? Does someone within the publication really think they know what is best for people, and my words are decidedly not it?

Well, no. It was all my fault. And the reason was all in my head. My experience with the rabid defenders of racist chocolates taught me first hand something of how human nature works through the strange new prism of social media. I can't know for sure if Dahl and Conguitos fans have much in common, but if my experience with the latter was anything to go by, then I felt, at the time, pleased when 2016 finally ended and the Dahl piece became somewhat irrelevant.

*

There is also one other complicating factor that makes criticising anything to do with the arts in Wales pretty problematic for most of those attempting to do so. The pool of creatives in Wales is pretty small, and sooner or later it feels like everyone meets everyone. I once wrote a negative review of a national art competition's winning entry, then subsequently saw the artist at multiple social events for months afterwards, praying that our mutuals wouldn't introduce us. When it comes to the Dahl project, a lot of my friends had received grants to make work. A poet I really admire had asked me to collaborate. My natural inclination in all things is to take the piss, and my article was indeed undermining the work that my friends had put in. Not only did I not want to be potentially dragged over the coals again for stating an opinion, but I didn't want there to be any awkwardness if I bumped into any writer friends in the queue for the ice cream van at Roath Park Lake. So I let the piece go off the radar of the busy editor. (Sorry about that, Gary.)

Since then I've had any number of ideas for articles that I have suspected would piss off my peer group. But you would never have known, because I couldn't bring myself to write about them. But every time I've held my tongue I have contributed to our collective echo chamber. So I also can't offer you articles I could have written about issues like why does the head of Arts Council Wales hail the 'diversity' of Literature Wales' bursary scheme recipients, when 17 out of 21 are of the same gender? And in a year when a Welsh writer wins the Guardian Not the Booker Prize, what does it say about Welsh literature when that novel doesn't make the Wales Book of the Year Award, yet two of the three shortlisted fiction writers are from England? Also, are the Turner-nominated Gentle/Radical an activist organisation, or are they an arts organisation, just because they say they are? And is it hypocritical that the anonymous Wales Arts Anti Racist Union's commissioned report for the Arts Council demands accountability and scrutiny in the arts, yet the WAARU itself insists on the right to anonymity? (and why such hostility when you ask who they are?)[7]

Some people might wince at these questions. I will admit

that they do veer a little into Jac o' the North territory[8]. But I am not a culture war warrior. You won't see me debating wokery all over political YouTube like Lionel Shriver or writing books about free speech à la Andrew Doyle. The truth is I only have a handful of opinions on anything, and none of them are particularly spicy by today's standards. If I should be cancelled for anything, objectively it should be because I believe the greatest film ever put to celluloid is the director's cut of *Terminator 2: Judgment Day*. But such is the polarisation of our times that when I think out loud like this, and thus label myself the 'Just Here to Ask Questions' Guy, others will no doubt put me in the same pigeon-hole as the anti-vaxxers who insist that All Lives Matter. But exploring difficult questions which require complex answers shouldn't lead to social ostracisation. Getting it all out in the open, as far as I'm concerned, will only make the Welsh arts a more productive place.

*

I almost named this article, 'Why I No Longer Write'. But this would be a lie. Starting in March 2020, while everyone else was prolonging the national flour shortage crisis by getting into baking or changing their locations via VPN to Italy for free PornHub premium accounts, I did the other most cliché of lockdown activities and wrote the draft of a novella.

It was about the ghost of Jack the Ripper. I had done most of my research prior to the lockdown. I had started by reading the entire Ripper literary canon. Certain books, such as Hallie Rubenhold's *The Five* and Sugden's *The Complete History of Jack the Ripper*, I ended up reading several times. I went on dozens of Ripper Tours, and traipsed half of Spitalfields to work out the Ripper's probable escape routes. I hunted down copies of the original 1888 documents such as the 'From Hell' and Openshaw letters at the Royal London Hospital (which was purportedly sent to the esteemed doctor in a box with half a human kidney). I did almost as much research as I did for my PhD – enough to consider myself a Ripperologist, if I didn't think that term was as cringeworthy as fully grown adults who convey excitement with the word 'squee'.

But I couldn't keep the novella in the form I had written it in the initial draft. Much of the point of Rubenhold's previously mentioned biography collection is to tell the often overlooked history of the Ripper's five canonical victims. In it, she tells us about the eerie similarities of their lives – from early promise to alcoholism, then the breakdown of the family home, and finally, to the few choices women of the late nineteenth century in this position had – the workhouse, and inevitably the streets.

The Ripperologists worth their salt, such as the aforementioned Philip Sugden, are extremely sympathetic to the victims, and give good accounts of their lives, despite what you may have read from Rubenhold about Ripperology on social media. But if you walk around Brick Lane, you can't fail to see the naffness of the industry that Rubenhold counters. The Ripper, in the square mile directly east of The Gherkin, is a verifiable celebrity, and seems to bear more in common with Robin Hood for doing one over on the law than he does with the serial killers who purposely go after the most vulnerable members of society. There's a Jack the Clipper hairdressers on the corner of the street where Mary Jane Kelly was brutally mutilated, for God's sake. And a Jack the Chipper fish & chip shop. I'm surprised the grimey Nag's Head "Gentleman's Club" on Whitechapel Road isn't called Jack the Stripper.

And this brings me to my point: my novella, in its initial draft, focused far too much on the unidentified murderer himself, and not enough on the poor women he murdered. If I was to carry on down that route, I would be contributing to the problem that Rubenhold's book sought to challenge.

Some things simply don't need to be said. For example, try telling a friendly neighbour that Jimmy Savile actually raised a lot of money for children's spinal cord surgeries. Fictionalising an IRL murderer – while it is not uncommon – felt unnecessary. Fictionalising the victims of a crime also felt problematic. So I binned the whole thing, and started again. My father once told me that when he was a kid, and before the Hayes area of Cardiff city centre was redeveloped in the 60s, such was the urban legend around Mary Jane Kelly that grown-ups would often point out to him the site of her old family home. As such, Mary remains the only connection between Draft Zero and Draft One of this story.

It's important that I tell you all this for the point I am trying to make, but it is also important that I reserve the right to experiment in a draft which is designed to be seen by no one but myself. But even admitting this makes me nervous. The novella came second in a competition, so there is a good possibility of it being published. And the publishing industry (not to mention the readership itself) is not particularly kind in this day and age when it comes to stepping out of your lane.

Consider John Boyne, author of *My Brother's Name is Jessica*, who was hounded off social media for writing a book about a brother's reaction to his trans sister's transition (but didn't centre the trans character). Or consider Catrin Kean, the 2021 winner of the Wales Book of the Year for fiction with her novel *Salt*, who felt compelled to post pictures of her Barbadian grandfather after her win when it was suggested to her that the story was not hers to tell (it was based on his life). Also, such was the backlash to Kosoko Jackson, he had his book cancelled before it even came out, for the crime of being a privileged American and daring to make the antagonist of his debut novel an ethnic Muslim Albanian. The only notable example I can think of where the author didn't suffer is Andre Aciman for *Find Me*, which is about two men meeting after twenty years and rekindling a romance. Aciman is a straight, married man. But *Find Me* is a sequel to his 2007 phenomenon *Call Me By Your Name*, which was published before social media cancelling was a thing. Personally, I'm not so sure, on the basis of evidence, that he would fare so well if he was an unknown coming through right now.

Attempted cancellations over slightly contentious issues are everywhere nowadays. This is why I stopped writing for Wales Arts Review: it hardly seemed worth sticking my neck out any more. But I have a confession to make. I am also part of the problem.

*

Aberaeron holds an annual August Bank Holiday parade. One year, a bunch of locals decided to pay homage to their favourite childhood figures. It just so happens that these Ceredigion lads grew up in the 90s, but instead of choosing to dress up as the Teenage Mutant Hero Turtles for their float, or perhaps Triple HHH's D-Generation X wrestling stable, they decided to Feel The Rhythm and go as the Jamaican bobsled team from the film *Cool Runnings*. In order to do so – as all four lads are white – they darkened their skin, with three of them wearing dreadlock wigs like the character Sanka Coffie.

Now, I see nothing wrong with wanting to emulate your heroes. Did you dye your roots green when Billie Eilish did? More power to you. Got ink on your inner thigh like Janet

Jackson of Minnie Mouse giving Mickey a blow job? Not my leg, not my choice. But there is a widely accepted, negative contextual connotation when it comes to darkening your skin to appear black when you live in a white-majority country. *Look at me! Now I'm black! Isn't this funny?* You're saying to the world. *Black people aren't like the rest of us, so I am making fun of them,* you may as well be saying. *By pointing out that there is a difference for a cheap laugh, I am showing that I don't think we're equal. Being black is the same as a costume, like wearing a Viking helmet.*

The Cool Runnings float story came to us during Silly Season, when parliament is closed for the summer recess and news organisations have an abundance of column inches to fill. As such, it was a talking point for days. In a series of tweets, I explained how I thought that what the floaters did was offensive. It was generally positively received. But one person came back at me: I was seeing things in a 'rage', they said. And who, exactly, is actually offended by this? And what right did I have to be offended on another group's behalf? I am, after all, the wrong 'hue'.

I had to put my phone down for a second when I read that last word. Sure, if you don't know my family history, you might not know why implying I'm the wrong 'hue' might be offensive to me. I am often racialised as white, as is Ryan Giggs or the actor Stephen Graham, even though I am not. I saw red for a minute. I also felt quite vulnerable. I didn't expect someone to disagree with me so publicly and with such force.

So what did I do? Did I decide to get a grip, put my phone down and carry on with my day? Did I laugh at this series of ignorant tweets? Did I mute this antagonizer, and forget anything ever happened, because it was so inconsequential to my life that someone expressing a different point of view to me doesn't really matter?

I did none of the above. Instead, I quote tweeted their thread and performed the Twitter equivalent of Triple H doing a piledriver.

I started off by pointing out that you don't have to be of one specific BAME background to find blackface offensive. I asked if those unaffected get to decide what racism is (a point I'm not sure I agree with nowadays). I told them I found their description of me as the wrong 'hue' offensive, as half my family are black. I asked if they wanted my dad's number, so he could tell them how offensive it is. And while it's not my job to trawl the internet to show them everyone who finds it offensive, if they can't find anyone then they're not actually trying. But another person who found it offensive apart from me was the musician Kizzy Crawford, who has Bajan roots, who I quote tweeted as evidence.

A number of people agreed with me. I started to concur with Conan the Barbarian, when he said what was best in life was to crush your enemies, see them driven before you, and hear the lamentation of their women. After the individual's defensive reaction, I pointed out how they were in absolutely no position to take the high ground, and if this was how they asked for insight then I suggested they change their modus operandi.

Their replies became increasingly distraught with the more compassion and empathy my tweet thread received. At one point they dragged someone else into the conversation who had liked one of my tweets and pleaded not to be judged. But I was the victim now. The great thing about being a victim is that it brings results to those who demand them. The victim, on social media, is judge, jury and executioner. The victim, as it was in my case, can point out their 'truth'[9] and it will be accepted unquestioningly by anyone sympathetic. Despite being straight and male, I held the winning immutable characteristic in our game of woke rock paper scissors. The antagoniser subsequently stopped replying after a brief apology. I had won.

A couple of hours later, and with an important match on at the Cardiff City Stadium, I had forgotten all about this incident, and was tweeting how I had socks older than Wales v Austria match winner Ben Woodburn. I finally received a longer apology via private message. I chose to ignore how much it was eating up the individual, or how it might have affected their reputation.

I still don't agree with some of the language used towards me. But maybe I didn't have to be quite so mean. Maybe I didn't have to quote tweet that initial message, thereby drawing attention and ire to it. I knew what kind of reaction I would get from the Twittersphere by writing what I did. And for that, all I can say is sorry, Camille.

I regret my conduct that day on Twitter as much as I regret the numerous articles I never had the cojones to write. And most of all, I regret where it started, in letting that Dahl piece I wrote die. I wish I had the fortitude at the time to see if my argument had legs. I would probably have lost a few acquaintanceships from it. But then again, maybe I've done enough in this very essay you've almost finished that my next visit to the Roath Park Lake ice cream van is going to be a particularly awkward one. So maybe I'll ask if I can write again for Wales Arts Review. Because at least I've said what I believe to be the truth now, and I can't hide behind my paranoia any more.

[1] This is grammatically incorrect – 'little Congan' would technically be Congoleño, as many thousands of Spaniards pointed out to me. The diminutive suffix '-ito' conveys endearment or smallness in most cases, but I still think, like the academic Diana Palardy, that from the picture on the front of the packet and the noun onto which the ito was added, that the meaning is clear. See Palardy. Diana Q, "The Evolution of Conguitos: Changing the Face of Race in Spanish Advertising"

[2] I paid for a programme which deleted all my tweets en masse, and now auto-deletes any new ones I write after a few days. If you still use this dreaded social media hellhole then I recommend you consider doing the same.

[3] https://theconversation.com/roald-dahls-wonderful-wales-how-growing-up-welsh-moulded-the-anglo-norwegian-writer-63569

[4] 'Well, Actually' syndrome: a malady which requires the sufferer to correct minor points when nobody asked (and which ultimately have no bearing on the grand scheme of life). See also its precursor, 'To Be Fair' disorder.

[5] https://www.bbc.co.uk/programmes/p009mwxx (about four minutes in)

[6] A perhaps more up to date take on this can be heard from Wesley Snipes' character Sidney in the film White Men Can't Jump, when he says, 'You can put a cat in the oven, but that don't make it a biscuit.'

[7] https://twitter.com/privilegecafe_/status/1285197996452384768

[8] The self-styled 'cynical patriot' himself politically identifies as a centre right, small 'c' conservative, of which I'm not, and most of his writings are to do with his interpretation of 'in-migration' (what he sees as the continued colonisation of Wales by England). This is to point out that the passage here is not meant as a slur.

[9] "My truth", or variations thereof, is a curious buzz phrase as of late for the Very Online, which denotes that the truth is subjective, a position which is, objectively, not true.

AUTHOR BIOS

Gwyneth Lewis

Gwyneth Lewis was Wales' National Poet from 2005-6, the first writer to be given the Welsh laureateship. She wrote the six-foot-high words on the front of Cardiff's Wales Millennium Centre, rumoured to be the largest poem in the world. Gwyneth has published nine books of poetry in Welsh and English. In 2010 she was given a Society of Authors Cholmondeley Award recognising a body of work and achievement of distinction. Besides poetry, Gwyneth is an award-winning writer of non-fiction and screenplays: Gwyneth's first non-fiction book, Sunbathing in the Rain: A Cheerful Book about Depression (2002) was shortlisted for the Mind Book of the Year, and her first television screenplay, Y Streic a Fi ('The Strike and Me'), commissioned by S4C, won the 2015 BAFTA Wales for Best Drama. Gwyneth is also a writer of fiction: The Meat Tree, a space-age re-imagining of the tale of Blodeuwedd, is part of Seren's New Stories from the Mabinogion series. Her light-hearted novella, Advantages of the Older Man, explores the strange case of a Swansea woman who is apparently possessed by the ghost of Dylan Thomas. Gwyneth is a librettist and dramatist and has written two chamber operas for children and an oratorio, all commissioned and performed by Welsh National Opera. She is a fellow of the Royal Society of Literature, a member of the Welsh Academi and a NESTA Fellow.

Kaite O'Reilly

Kaite O'Reilly is a multi-award winning poet, playwright and dramaturg, who writes for radio, screen and live performance. Prizes include the Peggy Ramsay Award, Manchester Theatre Award, Theatre-Wales Award and the Ted Hughes Award for new works in Poetry for Persians (National Theatre Wales). She is a two time finalist in the International James Tait Black Prize for Innovation in Drama (2012, 2019) and The Susan Smith Blackburn Prize. She was honoured in the 2017/18 International Eliot Hayes Award for Outstanding Achievement in Dramaturgy. She works internationally, her work translated into fifteen languages worldwide, and is part of the visiting faculty at ITI: Intercultural Theatre Institute, in Singapore. She was the resident dramaturg/playwright of The Llanarth Group for many years, collaborating with the director, performer and actor-trainer Phillip Zarrilli. Kaite's plays Atypical Plays for Atypical Actors and The 'd' Monologues are published by Oberon/Methuen/Bloomsbury. Her first feature film, The Almond and the Seahorse with Mad as Birds films, will be released in 2022, featuring Rebel Wilson and Charlotte Gainsbourg.

Siân Melangell Dafydd

Siân Melangell Dafydd is an author, poet and translator. Her first published novel, Y Trydydd Peth (The Third Thing; Gomer, 2009) won her the coveted National Eisteddfod Literature Medal in 2009 and she was the last co-editor of the iconic literary magazine, Taliesin. She writes in both Welsh and English and often collaborates with authors and poets internationally to translate literature between minority languages. She works as a lecturer in Creative Writing at the American University of Paris, France and at Bangor University, Wales.

Elan Grug Muse

Grug Muse, born in 1993, is a poet and essayist from Gwynedd, North Wales. Her most recent poetry collection, Merch y Llyn, was published in 2021 by Cyhoeddiadau'r Stamp. In 2020, she was awarded a writer's bursary from Literature Wales to work on her first non-fiction book and was a Ulysses Shelter Resident in the same year. Her recent essays in Welsh and English can be found in O'r Pedwar Gwynt, Planet, and Wales Arts Review, and anthologised in Welsh (Plural) (2022, Repeater) and Just So You Know (2020, Parthian).

Horatio Clare

Horatio Clare's books include Running for the Hills, A Single Swallow, Down to the Sea in Ships, The Light in the Dark and Heavy Light. An author, journalist, broadcaster and lecturer currently based in Yorkshire, his home is the Cwmdu valley, where he grew up.

Liz Hyder

Liz Hyder has been making up stories ever since she can remember. She was a member of the National Youth Theatre and has a BA in Drama from the University of Bristol. Bearmouth, her debut book for young adults, won the Branford Boase Award, the Waterstones Children's Book Award for Older Readers, and was named Children's Book of the Year in The Times. Her debut novel for adults, The Gifts, publishes in early 2022. She grew up in London and now lives in South Shropshire.

Craig Austin

Craig Austin (@thecraigaustin) is a London-based writer and a product of a concrete South Wales new town. He is an Associate Editor of Wales Arts Review and a board member of Literature Wales. His writing has featured in Wales Arts Review, The Modernist magazine, The Lonely Crowd, and 'New Towns – An Anthology of Place Writing'. He is currently writing his first novel, a bitter-sweet love letter to late-80s Cwmbran.

David Llewellyn

David Llewellyn is the author of four novels, most recently A Simple Scale, and audio dramas including Cicero, The Picture of Dorian Gray, and Doctor Who: The Gates of Hell. His essays and reviews have appeared in Wales Arts Review, Planet and the Times Literary Supplement. He is also the short film programmer for the Iris Prize LGBT+ Film Festival, and lives in Cardiff with his partner, Dan.

Jonathan Edwards

Jonathan Edwards's first collection of poems, My Family and Other Superheroes (Seren, 2014), received the Costa Poetry Award and the Wales Book of the Year People's Choice Award. It was shortlisted for the Fenton Aldeburgh First Collection Prize. His second collection, Gen (Seren, 2018), also received the Wales Book of the Year People's Choice Award, and in 2019 his poem about Newport Bridge was shortlisted for the

Forward Prize for Best Single Poem. He lives in Crosskeys, South Wales.

Prof. Charlotte Williams

Charlotte Williams OBE is an academic, writer and activist. She is Honorary Professor in the School of History, Philosophy and Social Sciences, Bangor University and holds Honorary appointments at Glyndwr University and University of South Wales. Charlotte has researched and published extensively on issues of migration, race / ethnicity, and multiculturalism using academic, literary and popular media. She is co-editor of the groundbreaking text 'A Tolerant Nation? Revisiting Ethnic Diversity in Wales' (UWP 2003 and 2015). Charlotte's contributions to postcolonial studies include her memoir, Sugar and Slate (2002) which was awarded Welsh Book of the Year in 2003; co-editor of Denis Williams: A Life in Works, New and Collected Essays (Rodopi 2010) and regular contributions to Internationalist Journals including Planet, Wales Review Online, Wasafiri. In 2005 she was Chair of the judging panel for Welsh Book of the Year and again on the 2021 judging panel. In 2020 she was appointed as Chair of the Ministerial Working Group: 'Communities, Contributions and Cynefin: Black Asian Minority Ethnicities in the new curriculum' which reported in March 2021. Charlotte was awarded an OBE in the Queen's New Year's Honours List (2007) for services to ethnic minorities and equalities in Wales.

Cerith Mathias

Cerith Mathias is a journalist, producer, and festival director. She is a Contributing Editor of Wales Arts Review and writes on arts and culture for publications in the UK and US, with a particular interest in literature from the Deep South. She's a founding director of Cardiff Book Festival and Pontypridd Children's Book Festival and co-owner of Storyville Books, the only independent bookshop in the South Wales Valleys. A journalist and producer with BBC Wales for almost 20 years, Cerith was at the helm of political, current affairs and large-scale live TV programmes. She is a member of Monumental Welsh Women, the group behind the Hidden Heroines campaign which resulted in the unveiling of The Betty Campbell Monument in Cardiff city centre.

Rhian E. Jones

Rhian E. Jones grew up in South Wales and now lives and works in London, where she writes on history, politics, popular culture. and their intersections. After studying at London and Oxford, she worked in retail while working to establish herself as a journalist, historian and writer of fiction and non-fiction. She has written for various publications including The Guardian, Salon, Los Angeles Review of Books, New Welsh Review and the Morning Star. Her first book Clampdown: Pop-Cultural Wars on Class and Gender (Zero Books, 2013), a critique of British popular culture and politics from the 1990s onwards, was included in the Guardian's Best Music Books of 2013. She writes the blog 'Velvet Coalmine' at www.rhianejones.com.

Caragh Medlicott

Caragh Medlicott is a freelance writer and Senior Editor of Wales Arts Review. She is the author of several published short stories and has been shortlisted for awards including Narrative's 30 Below competition in 2021 and the Lunate 500 competition in

2020. A graduate of Cardiff University with a first-class degree in English Literature and MA in Creative Writing, she has also worked in PR, writing and coordinating pieces in publications including GQ, Forbes and Metro UK.

Dr Emma Schofield

Dr Emma Schofield is a South Wales-based writer, academic and essayist. A Senior Editor for Wales Arts Review, Emma has also appeared as a regular contributor on radio programmes including Radio 4's Front Row and the *Review* Show on BBC Radio Wales, having taken part in the BBC's New Generation Thinkers scheme in 2016. Emma's PhD thesis explored the connection between literature and devolution in Wales and she has written widely on the representation of women in culture and politics in Wales.

Steph Power

Steph is a freelance composer and writer living in mid Wales. Published by The Independent and Wales Arts Review from 2013 to 2018. Steph is Chair of Tŷ Cerdd, Music Centre Wales, and her music has been performed and broadcast at festivals and venues across Wales and beyond. She is a contributing author to The Cambridge Companion to Women in Music Since 1900 (CUP, 2021) and The Music of Simon Holt (Boydell, 2017).

John Lavin

John Lavin has a doctorate from the University of Wales, Trinity Saint David, as well as an MA in Creative Writing from Cardiff University. He is the founder and editor of The Lonely Crowd literary magazine and also the former Fiction Editor of Wales Arts Review. Lavin edited their short story anthology, A Fiction Map of Wales, as well as their acclaimed online series, Story: Retold. His criticism has appeared in The Irish Times, Wales Arts Review and many other places.

Adam Somerset

Adam Somerset has lived in Ceredigion for 31 years. He has written reviews and articles on theatre, politics, history, art, photography and politics for Wales Arts Review, Theatre-Wales, the Cambrian News, Cyfrwng, New Welsh Reader, the Institute of Welsh Affairs, Planet Magazine and Nation Cymru. His essay "A Life with the Cold War" was a prize-winner in the 2017 New Welsh Review Competition for Memoir. His essay collection "Between the Boundaries" was published by Parthian Books in 2019.

João Morais

João Morais was runner-up in the 2021 New Welsh Writing Awards. His short story collection, Things That Make the Heart Beat Faster, is out now with Parthian.